CW00496840

EXILE AND THE KINGDOM

Hilary Davies

Exile and the Kingdom

ENITHARMON PRESS

First published in 2016
by Enitharmon Press
10 Bury Place
London WC1A 2JL

www.enitharmon.co.uk

Distributed in the UK by
Central Books
99 Wallis Road
London E9 5LN

Distributed in the USA and Canada
by Independent Publishers Group
814 North Franklin Street
Chicago, IL 60610
USA
www.ipgbooks.com

Text © Hilary Davies 2016

ISBN: 978-1-910392-17-1

Enitharmon Press gratefully acknowledges the financial support of
Arts Council England, through Grants for the Arts.

British Library Cataloguing-in-Publication Data.
A catalogue record for this book is available
from the British Library.

Designed in Albertina by Libanus Press
and printed in England by
Short Run Press

In memoriam Sebastian Barker
1945–2014

'For poetry is what it is,
   This paradise on earth,
The Land of Gold, in which our lives
   Become what they are worth'

SEBASTIAN BARKER, *The Land of Gold*

CONTENTS

ACROSS COUNTRY

ACROSS COUNTRY

I

How it all begins: this is what gets forgotten,
Unwilled and inarticulate, the dark start in the morning,
Being carried by gods out into the starry night.
We are silent to ourselves: no familiar landscapes,
No lintel, inglenook to shape or stable space.
Just the road and its rhythms.
The reindeer saddle and the motor car,
The sighing desert and the plateau wind
Etch the first surfaces of particularity
And settle in our souls.

       I tasted the cold scent of before dawn
And awoke. The streets were hollow and strange.
My father and mother threaded upriver
Past milestones shadowy in the neon lamplight,
Catford, Dulwich, Tulse Hill and Wandsworth
To the great wall of the way west at Kew.
The city tipped and hinged,
And we crossed over the frontier into a translated land.

***

Land of water, land of stone
The hard Lord-treaders work their faith in bone

Land of tabernacles, land of holy wells
Land where coracles sail to holy cells

Land of baptism, land of rain
Bethlehem, Bethesda, Gethsemane raised again

Land of entrance, where the God draws in
To set himself, the fording place out of sin

Land of rivers, the Christ-cross prayer
Land where I first put my foot upon the holy stair.

II

O to be young and the white cliffs of Dover!
New as a chrisomer to the bright March blue
And the boat's wake gashing its path through the rolled-back sea.
As the juggernauts tumbled off the car-decks
I took up the map and began to navigate.

Let me praise now the départementale
How it turns from the traffic and the scream
Into the long, slow loop of highway,
This fugue of difference, this rosary of place
Strung with the glory of cornfield and belltower,
Granite, limestone, vineyard and cloister
On and on in the swoop of creation
And the evening come under the doved turret wall.

Sundown in the bars and hostelries; eyes glitter.
A little river trails its shimmer past the bread and wine.
Slender as aspen, slow as peacocks,
The lovers enter upon their matchless stage
To step that antique dance for the first time.
Each the unique, the unsurpassable sweetness
Lifts into grace, to the dappled courtyard,
To nightfall by the weeping willow,
To life's covenant in the first kiss.

III

Crossroads are sudden and everywhere:
Deep rutted and creased by the wheels of many minds passing,
The deerpath barely visible through the tangled chase.
How to distinguish the horizons of vision from our own folly's chasm?
A book in a bookshop can wring the spell.
I held it there a year, a decade,
Sucked on the arguments of polity and governance,
Sedulous in the maze of fallacy and self-belief.
Very sweet are the seductions of the lamplit room
Whose geometries, unchecked, autarkic,
Unhouse humanity; and luscious the meretricious fruit
Of the ideology tree. A man may squander
His whole birthright in those dark woods.

The lords of existence
Are neither economist nor philosopher
The Lord of existence
Shows himself not in systems
The Lord of existence
Is the sound behind everything
When everything is still.

IV

God's oven, that summer.
The land was turned to straw
And the trees tinder.
The white road led through the white wheat.
Men fell in love with silence in the consuming heat.

When does the door open?
How does the ear prepare
For what it does not even know
It cannot hear?

Some little slip, some little tear
Ajar things as they are,
Or seem to be.
Like tiny acorns breaking up the ground,
Their filaments as delicate as spiders' webs,
Root with power to raise a colossus.
So I crossed into church after church that summer,
Thinking of erudition, but beside me trod Love.
O my unrecognised familiar, subtle of subtles,
 Showing with open palm the forms
To piece together to learn the inlay of faith.

Liguge's the place where understanding
First ran over the stones like water evermore,
Where the renounced of the world in their radiating chapels
Hoisted eleison, and my spirit trembled at the door.

V

The bride stepped from her carriage
On her wedding day
What an upright man, what an honest man,
She heard her purpose say

The bride stepped from her carriage;
The bright December sun
Showed her her bridegroom smiling,
Showed the day had come

For an honest man, for an upright man,
That lost love was over;
She held tight to her father's arm
And stepped to the lychgate's cover.

She turned away from the cypress
And the shadow standing there
She turned her head to the altar,
This is my will, she swore.

'No, no, you will never lie
Quiet on that pillow
Your bedmate will be perfidy
And an honest man's sorrow'

Hate has eaten my bridegroom's heart
And remorse is become my fury
Now I must go the road of affliction
Searching for mercy.

VI

Guilt builds a grim tunnel in the soul,
Its starting point irretrievable, its end unattainable
For we lay the stones before us as we creep.
Guilt penetrates like sweating walls;
We smell and taste it in our food and drink,
Our very bones warp to its straitjacket.

      What metamorphoses . . .
This face mine, and not mine,
Not anything I ever thought I'd be
And these companions whom I accept
From ever more unseemly provenances
Until I am sick at myself.
The only way out now is on your belly
Under the weight of heaven.

It's this of course that terrifies:
The self-surrender. No more believing
That you're in control. Only trust matters;
Waiting, not willing. But this's as tremendous
As the great tremenda.

Once, in a fishing boat toward Skellig
I felt the continental swell
As sea put out to ocean,
And the roll reared up.
No measure but the dark blue breathing of the opening deep,
Where personhood dissolves beyond mere terror
Into the pure truth of mortality,
Into the absolute inefficacy of anything but faith.

VII

Only perdurance delivers.
Not one night of weeping, nor the taverns of despair,
Nor even the grandiose claims of conscience
Suffice in the end.
Mercy lies in continuance,
The acts repeated so often
We are astonished as we turn to rest
At the plains and forests and rivers over which we have come.
For years the seekers who walk with us
Have been burnt by the same sun.
Thanks be to the faces who have shown what love is, and does:
They are the mirrors beyond compare,
The accidents offered as our chance for freedom,
Our hope for deliverance, our signposts out of hell.

You came to me as in a waking dream
And I knew instantly I had to go the hard way with you
To learn how to love better.
For all true locatives are in the heart's country
Yet that road's the most mysterious to run.
Our path binds twenty years together;
My pace is so conformed to yours we are as one.
We know what miracle each day is to be done.

Ultreia! Over the blue hills at morning
With staff and burden and drum
Out of hope's slaughterhouse, history,
We pilgrims forever come.

SONGS FROM THE LEA VALLEY

AS I TOOK MY WAY FROM ISLINGTON TO STAMFORD HILL

At Angel we always got lost.
The fork did it, one way meandering northward
Up to the blustery grasslands of Hampstead
But my father was forever trying to escape,
Escape out of London, to the delectable water meadows
Of Cambridge, Ely's sweet pastoral.
How was it this seasoned geographer,
This faster-than-all-the-others RAF navigator,
Ensnared himself so? A confusion,
A blear came on his mind there
At the grind, the peeling billboards,
Close tenacity and tenement buildings,
Layer upon layer of faith and struggle
Darkening down into the mud.

As we inched up Kingsland
O all the tongues of the world crowded in on us
And I opened my ears. What savannahs,
What monkey-hung temples, turquoise gardens
Shimmered out of those sentences,
What accents of dread and feud and tears?

Suddenly over the hill we crested
– The tall plane trees pointed to the clouds –
And all down the valley rolled on the west wind
Prayer's cadences out of a thousand mouths.
And the girl in the back of the car
Felt the jolt of the future,
The strange to loved, unvoiced to neighbours' tones
Grown; how one day she will stand at her gate here
And the caravanserai of grace will be home.

MORNING COMES TO THE CITY

Morning comes to the city:
Heavy with dew on the autumn air
The gardens lift their wings and crackle a little;
Sheds drip and the fox slides to his lair.
My neighbour's boiler does the first toot of the day
And the washing lines' webs stream.
Sideways and inwards all our lives jumble
Into this tiny compass of making ends meet,
Making do, taking care, taking root,
Loving and struggling, and always the world revolving
No bigger than a man's thumb held against the moonlight,
A whorl-blue top hung in everlasting night.

ON STAMFORD HILL

My neighbour sits in his garden:
Orotund as butter he intones his Torah,
His ten children sturdy as apple trees
To show how strong are his loins.
This man has been, once, to Snowdonia
Where, looking down the wind-drenched mountain,
He thought he saw Mount Carmel sloping through olive groves
To the purple sea. Look, even now
He bends again to dance the dance of his maker's glory,
To lift the chant of his arrowed praises
And send it like geese over these English terraced houses flying.

SHABBAT

Shabbat: without sound the rift-deep sea and salt the prayer
Over the collapsing lean-to and the feast of booths.
The moon is desert big, hooking open
These kitchen roofs to a show of palms
Remembered among the elderberries.
Hear them, O Lord, their supplications rising
Out of marsh mist, flashing off the Isle of Dogs
As far as Vitebsk, Vilnius, and the village fiddler
Plucking light feet in a trim of laughter,
Bowing faith's quick fantastic.

IN THE FIRE-FROST MORNING

In the fire-frost morning the geese drive south
Trailing hosannas over the estuaries
And the beasts on the clockhouse stir.
From Tottenham Hale to Hackney Downs
The trumpets of day sound
And the gulls swarm up like heralds
Over the sleepers. 'Awake! Awake!'
Throw open your skylights, thrust your heads to see:
Horseshoe thicket is afire with dawn
And the waters on Spring Hill teem.
Doors, dance. Fill the houses with praises.
God's promise blazes in the reedbeds,
Bursting over the winter willows and sallows
All the way down to waiting Walthamstow.

SEVEN SISTERS

On Stamford Hill two towers stand:
Swifts and swallows mew them round.
The road racks over holy sands
Where seven sisters sleep underground.

The queen's last cross at the four winds hangs
– Lady, have mercy on the scuttling crowds –
Over the years close forgiving hands,
The ferryman still ferries to the Rose and Crown.

Out of the bulrush swans rise
Walking on water in the loud sun's van;
Unnoticed under the buzz of our lives
Beggars and saints sweep over the land.

MAY

May on the Lee in the water meadows:
Hawthorn bursting, blasting
And, in the branchy sun, swans swaddling their nests;
May to the lovers in the bulrush beds
Whose kiss is still as skylarks in the summer blue;
And May to dogs and toddlers at the river's edge
Living life-heaven. This place is home
Where one day we came walking
Away from remorse and heart-grief
And found the may in her glory
Showering forgiveness and Horseferry Bridge
Leading over the water to a ransomed land.

SCARLET ROSE
stillborn 18.08.2008

Out in the marsh lies Scarlet Rose
Where the black Lea through its mudbanks
Past Old Ford and Three Mills and the Roman road flows.
Do you hear their feet flying? The tramp of men
Dying for empire again and again
Ever since we first cut down the alders with stone.

Out in the marsh lies Scarlet Rose:
The deer run on Epping hill and the beeches ring
With groves of blackbirds and the dun of hooves;
Look at the wild kites and model airplanes chasing
Their tails in the clouds! Look at the shroud
Of the dead queen in her hunting lodge
And the staircases of power.

Out in the marsh lies Scarlet Rose,
Who smiled in the darkness and never saw
Day or night. Cities, stand still.
Tyrants and governments, drop beneath the tides.
The Lea flows past their graveyard to the sea.

Out in the marsh where the salt wind blows,
Out in the marsh lies Scarlet Rose.

IN ABNEY PARK

The angels are praying in Abney Park

Up and down Church Street hammers the city:
Buses and lorries, the motorbike's scream,
Fire-engines, sirens, car radios, convertibles,
Strutting and wailing their terrors and dreams.

The angels are praying in Abney Park

Here in the city trade is empire:
Sweet fruits in the market, the broad coster cries,
Jerky chicken, linguine, halva, cinnamon, kosher,
The blood of the five seas salts our lullabies.

The angels are praying in Abney Park

Mark our fortunes! Past me the stream
Of the living, the coming, laughs, stops, flows,
I am mayfly, thistlefleck, among the nations
Sifting and surging on the Old High Road.

The angels are praying in Abney Park

Here we lie: under the green and the urban nettle
Where a brook flew by
And the sun and snow have settled
Season by season we listen to the world's great cry

The angels are praying in Abney Park

IN THE VALLEY OF THE LOT

AH, THAT I COULD FOLD MY ARMS AROUND TIME

Ah, that I could fold my arms around time,
And so enchant her,
She would not take you.

NIGHT'S CLOAK

Come away. Come away.
Do to me with your broad hands
All the things that I would have you do.
I wish you delight from my breast
Arcing through your fingers.
I wish you succour from my thighs
As they learn to bear you. May our mouths
Feed on each other as on bread and apples.
Sweet, salt love, come away.
Night's cloak is cold and everlasting.

AUBADE

This is the early season, and the sun
Comes more for his business than for us:
Long before we turn to light
The pierce of birdsong stabs us awake
So that we listen separately an age before we break
Truly from each other's arms, considering
How the day will carry us amongst the crowd,
Still for this moment sleeping,
And will not rise as long as we draw out
For ever our embrace; not desirous,
Unless of tenderness that vanishes
With the light's long fingers warming us.

O let all those who shall discover after
And think, like us, the world never rose but on them,
Leave in this grass, this morning, their cool silver imprint,
Bind their limbs together to barricade the sun.

LOVE SONG

Now I must turn from you, although my soul
Speaks noisily its delight the livelong day.
We must go in the world: take taxis, trains,
Responsibilities; be adult; learn how to gainsay
The leap, the beat, the quickening heart.
Others press round us, urge us to betray
With smiles and ministrations that curious spark
Which like bright sun breaking through the grey
Of winter snaps from the flint. And we stand still, amazed
To be the unsuspecting stone from which life springs.
Only think of this: the hour's no power to bring
That'll unmake history, undo my seeing of your beloved face.

THE ELDER

Twenty years now since under this elder
We first embraced. Do you remember
Her bright arms flying, the fleeting, flashing
Light, and the clouds scudding? How wild
And uproarious was our happiness!

Twenty years now since under this lintel
We passed, and the house stood around us.
Do you remember the child in the elder
And her golden hair? The doves
In the leaves and the berries' blood?
How we raised the tent of our love under the eaves!

Twenty years and each night, my companion,
You watch the moon move through the branches.
It silvers your hair. O my heart's beam and protector,
Beneath the elder vaulting our heaven:
May she hold us forever far from the stars' cold lattices.

ON LYMPNE HILL

On Lympne Hill the birds dart endless summer.
At our joy's edge, the beeches roll their crowns
Down over ditches and marshes to the rainbow shore.
Shingle waves blue with bugloss;
Blood poppies, and the lemon hawk's flower feather
Burst caresses into our faces; light-fire,
Sea-fire, wind-fire spark between heart and furnace
And the train scudding past cattle and steeples
Trumpets the day.

       Look to the lighthouse,
To the salt-fired gardens and the tended marriages,
Hook us upon the vine of love's glory
Twined round the matchless horizon.
You turn towards me, burning and happy,
That boy running the clouds over and over
Pell-mell into the hollows, this man
In his years reaching with all his might
Far out on life's cantilever to touch his soul's blue.

EASTER SUNDAY, TENBY

My love, upon the headland
Breathes the sea's great sigh
Light haven and lifeboat
Under the chapel's eye

The mermaids ring with praises
The holy island's rim
And dogs are racing on the beach
Their timeless, joyous hymn

The boat longs in the harbour
The fish hope in the deep
The sea has ringed us round with love
And rocks us as we sleep

My love, upon the headland
Sits a churchyard; still
And glowing in the April sun
Blaze all Christ's daffodils.

IN THE PUMPING STATION

I stood in the pumping house by the great machine.
Men moved around her. Black, red, white, gold, green
She moved in her prism of steam. The rafters and children waited.
Summer light fell on the rainbowed floor.
And through the window I saw you sitting in the rose garden
Still as the flowers you watched.

       The clouds rose higher and higher
Filling the steel vaults and the roof of heaven,
Tower upon tower and columns of hope building
Till all was white and desirous and ready.

Then the lever fell. The faintest tremble
Like a sublime monster waking from sleep
Before the oil like silk drew up the pistons from some well
Deep within. On what wheel of white and gold and green
We flowered in the pumping house as the axle span.

Even so you watched as one by one
The rose links opened and parted
And I saw you borne away on them,
Floating out from time's dynamo in the pumping station
Floating away above the roaring world
Out over the marsh and the estuary and down to the sea
On the ark everlasting.

NEW YEAR AT ABERAERON

I met my friend as we walked by the shore,
Arm in arm with his lover,
Her white-gold hair flying and tracking the wind.
All four we trod at the turning year
On the shingle-shod ground. In my ear
Was the whip and roar of the shearing sea.
We crossed over the bridge of the harbour
With the sun at our back.
      Ah, my husband,
Let me cup your face with my fingers
By the bright houses and the shouting children
Out on the land's ledge, hung on time's edge
Where Scorpio with her white arms
Flies up into the twilight,
Where the world's great arc wheels
And the souls of the darkening boats
Hanker for the sea.

COVADONGA

Through tides of rain we drove the mountain road.
Rivers thrashed trees downstream beside us.
Far below, the ocean sucked and dug.

At Río Seco the menfolk in the café
Signed themselves above the thick red waters.
Upon the road no-one among the mists and dripping beeches
No soul upon the road to Covadonga.

Covadonga! Water like thunder.
The little healing pool
Gone under God's surge.
The blast bulges outwards,
A new world birthing
All we fear may come,
And us beneath it.

Such little hopes,
Such sticks of momentariness
Caught in the ferns
An eyelash from the drop.
Everything we thought would hold us
Gives like cornerstones,
Like citadels, before the flood.
Onto this one thin ledge
We creep up under the overhang
To where our Lady of the Waterfalls
Keeps her courts of prayer.

Here is the all and only sanctuary
Our tiny bric-à-brac of suffering –
A piece of gauze, a notecard, a candle
Slung above the stupendous water.

Queen of our tragedy, bend your still face
Over the perpetual thunder;
Be with us when we go
Down over the anvil into the deep
And our soul's sounding.

CROSSING THE LINKS AT ST ANDREWS

Evening's ripple tipped at the horizon:
That clear, bright light of a northern place in summer,
Promising so much, so much – a glance,
The salt sea-scent of love along the promenade,
Voices embracing down the granite-blue streets.

Ah! I thought, it is time. Time for me to walk
Out here alone and conjure our future
Tranquil together as the tide comes in.
I walked to the beacon: the hills to the north
Were golden with what we would do.
On what exploration will we go in our hearts!

But out beyond the reach of the town
The wind got up its armies
And blew the seagulls past me like butterflies.
This was not my child's soul
Roaring to the roaring air ebullience
Nor, suddenly, were you with me.
The salt pricked tears and the mountains
Withdrew like a mirage into the dusk.

I said to myself, no matter, it is just the sunset
Over the perfect lawns making you melancholy;
Soon he will be by your side again
And all shall be well.
I crossed the links in the slanting light
When a couple I knew came towards me.
As they passed, I caught how she lifted her face,
Pearled with love, to his gaze
So strong I turned in their wake to watch them.
O lovers! In the soft rose light
Carry your orb of promise
Into that glittering chamber!

Each step they took I held in my mind's hand,
Their shadows growing fainter and smaller upon the cloudless links,
Till they vanished completely into the immense sky.

Then abrupt on that sea path I noticed the air grown cold;
Like a swift ghost against the wall I knew
That here was an end to dreaming,
That you had done with discovery of what lay ahead of us,
All that we had been was rolling in on the shingle
And the road away from this headland
Led for me only out along its darkening foreshore
Where your love's face scattered into farewell against the coming stars.

WHEN WE TURNED WEST OUT OF HIRSCHTAL

When we turned west out of Hirschtal
– The stream spreading through the trees
And the bare trunks just springing –
I remember turning the wheel, the feel of the chunky leather
Slipping in and out of my hands, and checking the way by the roadworks
In the forest, and turning the car towards home.
Away from the sweetness of what we had always done:
Discovery, splendour, the intimacies, glory, always by rivers.
So the road unravelled before us, as it had always done.
We drove. All in my heart encompassed
And not even the knowing of it,
So joyous, as it had always been.
Oh, live with me ever these memories
Of Hirschtal, of the birds' melodies
Louder than the flight of the world through time,
How the moon leapt out of the mist
And the deer jumped over the gardens.
All this we trailed like a comet behind us
As I turned the wheel west towards death.

BY THE DARK LAKE

The geese rise in the night.
They cry beneath the moon.
Out on the water a sound like snakes
Slides nearer, and black life
Breaks under the pontoon.
Dear God, we came here for quietude,
Hope in silence,
But the dark gives no gift, no prayer.

Look at the moon in her copper serenity,
Loosing the veils of immortality,
Yet my soul is not in her carriage:
It is trapped in the reedbeds,
Far from her promises,
And the gleam of the lamprey is close.

We are never prepared for this –
Never prepared for the dark lake,
For the boat with its sharp wake
Skimming across the water towards us,
For the immovable sorrow at the land's edge
Where the waves flicker,
Where at the two worlds' crossroads
Two mighty shadows meet.

UNDER THE LINTEL WE STOOD TOGETHER

Under the lintel we stood together
Looking towards a winter garden
Sleeping to spring. I placed my arms around you
And my head on your heart. But already
You were the vine, I the column
And the spirit moved fast against your breast.
I braced my strength upright to lift you
Like a blackbird threading the world
On its song hung in the twilight branches
And then gone.

So strong you held me and so many years
So few ago at the door of life.
How you pushed wide the windows of my soul
In that moment when you stepped to meet me
And bent your head in a kiss.
What alpha and omega touched us in our bodies' embrace.
So it is true the wings of heaven
Offer their shade to lovers if we only discern it,
The gold falling like rain on the grass
Of our lives grown together, love's blossom
Soaring its canopy mighty as cathedrals.

At the lintel peaks sunrise.
East settles over your face:
Outwards the wakening garden beckons
And your frame's compass flickers fast
Towards the mystery:
Love binds bone to soul –
How can this diamond be shattered quite?
Let drop one tear to show it is not so.
Hold me one moment more
Before the stone rolls round the heavens
Towards the earthquake hour
When you and life let go.

I TOUCHED YOUR MOUTH

I touched your mouth.
The last kiss.
I pressed your breast
To give you breath.
One last time before the door
And the white companion.

NOTHING PREPARES US FOR THE DESCENT OF THIS STAIR

Nothing prepares us for the descent of this stair,
Your hand on the banister, flailing:
Roar, desperation, silence,
Sunder's brute arrival.
Your loved face turned to stone
Even as the thought reared over us
Like a cowl. Out of some other cosmos
Understanding sent its javelin
And I heard rise from my own mouth
The howl of the hounds of the underworld.
How can an instant stop up your gaze to me,
Love vanish like a negative from your sight?
Where are the barges at the water's edge,
The warriors with uplifted swords, the sables?

Only your stare as the veil slipped between us
And my fingers scrabbled at the closing door,
The echo whispering from the passageways
Down which you sank away from me
Into the dark tide which brings no tomorrow:
Sorrow, sorrow, sorrow, sorrow.

GRIEF

No-one told me how like fear grief falls,
Nor that a serpent crawls within your bowels
At midnight, eats and eats all that's loved, familiar,
Whispers to all things: no.
Grief takes the dearest intimacies you had
And hangs them in a row marked never more –
The walk upon the evening battlements,
A wine glass lilting by the sea,
Your head bowed low beneath the elder tree –
So grief draws up memories from her bottomless store
Of pain. Sit quietly, and the knife blade comes;
Atop a bus the ghastly puppeteer
Snaps without warning at our soul's strings,
Jacks in the circuit of our tenderest brain
To wolf howl in the forest night.

Grief is reliving by a thousand cuts:
Each bend we swung across the fields of France
And every counted pearl appearing
Strung on the scented dusk of Aetos.
Grief is orphan, where once there was companion,
The turning to, the gesture, the shared, created world
Staked like a dull rag upon a picket,
A cage of longing hung beside a road.
Grief knows. She is the death in life,
Closer than our own bone.
She is the gangplank walk above the jutting cosmos,
Our fall down through the spheres, alone.

IN HIS ROOM

The sun is up. The spire is on the rooves.
O gong relentless, earth in her turning sings
To her fire lover. Heaven is a burnt blue
Pouring into the elder tree.

What shouts from the builders as the beam went in:
The house opened upwards to take its frame
Where once you flung a dove pair
Out of their grave into light.

Our home hung on this apex year by year –
The pillow clouding warmth around the hours
I waited for your foot creak on the stair,
The motes where time was married to eternity.

Words cannot tell how the bolt fell;
And like a guillotined head our life rolled away.

The sun is up. The window glares.
Earth, relentless, turns to her fire lover
Who tracks his circuits
Round an indifferent room:
Forward or back mean nothing
Since not in this life nor anywhere
Will they ever lead home to you.

HOW LITTLE WE KNOW OF PARADISE

How little we know of paradise –
Is this true? Have you never felt
In the blood the pull of the blue
Where the chalk chutes down?
Nor the deer spirit leap
Through the wind waves in the grasses?
These are the tall paradises of childhood.

How quickly we leave them for the strong
And glowing dark of the bed,
The paradise that transforms us.
Against this, the philosophers' stones
Are gravel slurried indifferently down the stream.
We walk in the orchard of ourselves
Being our loved one's garden.

This is trinity: more complex
Than ever we guessed in the growing of it
When we were simply exploring together
All the minute specificities
Which make this triangulation one, unique.

Pluck them like apples, each one a cosmos –
The lighthouse waving us away to Ireland;
Sardines and lemons in salt-chopped Pylos harbour;
The different rooms on silent afternoons
When we lay wrapped in each other's spirit:
No sweeter integer ever possible alone.

Death: if only we could think it wanton,
Like a child jabbing her fingers into the hearts' mesh
And leaving one half formless, hanging.
But it isn't so. Energy merely departs.

The apple tree of union
Robbed, the succulence dried like mud
Along the roadside. The pointlessness
Of all that was. This simple thought destroys.

– To think we thought it myth,
Our exchange at the gates of paradise –
Memory for the lived life of perfection.
There are not words to say
What this dull plain is like:
No water, ever; the stones like scurf
In a wind that frets with an unending cold
The stumps of happiness.
What moan breathes from the canyons,
What monstrous understanding
Paradise gives as she withdraws.

WALK HERE WITH ME

Walk here with me. We do not know how long.
The braided waters cross the marsh beside Bomb Crater Pond.
Bullrushes sing by the causeway,
In the leafing copses. And through the air we hear
The tumble of the swallows, their high-cloud mewing.
The sun was all around us. O my darling
How in the harvest of our days we were
And on the swans' backs the pearls of life
Streamed.

　　　Now the water of your breath
Breaks in a rainbow over each moment
We walked together where the willows and alders
Stretch their arms heavenward
And the cormorants circle
Over the rowers – o so full of life! –
Beating into the future.
But here, see, my heart is hung on the hawthorn
For you with your stoop stride never
Never never will walk by my side
Along the sweet Lea river nor lift your head
To hear the geese cry keening, ever again.

SESENHEIM

Ah, Sesenheim, the orchards blossoming beneath the clock tower,
Bower upon bower of white and the barns dreaming
In the soft afternoon hour. Our words moved
Under the eaves like pilgrims with their staves
Between the trees.
       'Let's halt,' you said.
The unsteadied world inched a notch
Though I willed us on. By the last meander
A bench beckoned.

Here in the cool lays of the green-dark stream
Swans unfurl their crowns,
The heron strikes. This is the secret way
The river rose when lovers wheeled upon the willowbank
And the sun stood still.

Ah, what I would not give
To hold her there in the heavens now
And see your dear face by the water's glory,
And pay no heed to the barge above our heads
Bearing its dark freight towards the sea.

WE WERE IN THE STREET

We were in the street.
Thigh to thigh we burned.
All summer I waited for your return
From over the sea and when I leapt
Across the threshold into your arms
The scent of your body was cinnamon
And your lips wine.

I was faint, faint
With the sweetness.
I shall be faint with this sweetness
All the rest of my life;
Though now you lie not with me
But another lover under the chestnut tree.

LORD, DESCEND

Lord, descend.
Come in the heat and light
Of afternoon.

Fill my head with bees
And not the buzz of grief,
And not the buzz of grief.

LET ME COME UNDER YOUR ARM TONIGHT

Let me come under your arm tonight,
Dove of my heart. In the dark
Look out of the skylight at the stars.
The pillow takes the press of your head
Like my life your presence,
The mark of my going out and my coming in.
Our life is held in these fingers;
You are the stay of everything my soul longed to do.

How can the bowstring of my being snap
When all this was ours?
Planets, did you hear the crack
At your bitter poles? Where,
Though I run across the wide world's
Empty oceans, will I catch your voice?

Only in this room when I lie on our bed
Can rest from these wild thoughts come – grace's gift
Greater than flood or vanished continents:
Love of you matchless ever and darling in the palm of my hand.

TELL ME, MY DARLING, OF THE LIFE WE HAD

Tell me, my darling, of the life we had,
Of what was unique in cosmos and in time,
Never before nor again in this place,
Nor with this face, these hands, these eyes.

Remember your strength as you lifted me skywards
In St James's Park? Did you guess how my world's poles
Rocked away from their axis, what brightness,
Sudden as the sun's arc, caught my soul?

In the moor scent of the Welsh hills we wandered
By a whirlpool under the pattering-leaved rain;
Our love was crimson and golden and copper
Laid down like time in the rock's living grain.

Who now shall hear with me the shriek of the red kite
Over the valley floor? Or the Alpheos dark in its reeds?
Can you taste the souvlaki and wine
Still, and the chasms of the Peloponnese?

Who will hold in the eternal mirror
The shape of the woods going down to Lalinde
Or the talk that day by the shimmering river
How man must face the caverns of his mind?

Space and time hold us prisoner, or so it seems –
Those walls stretch insolent to eternity –
How shall I ever touch you again except in dreams,
Flung from your orbit into infinity?

Yet on this one brief mote hung here crosses the whole:
Our lives are crystals on creation's web;
Only now and now and through this light burns a world
Where what we are shines meaning from the dead.

THE CORPUS CHRISTI CLOCK

We stopped by the clock at the corner of time.
At the turn of the year, at the coldest tide
In the town on the dead fen
This dead animal moved.
Carats of flagrancy and pride
In its levering head, tracking
Pinprick, pinprick, pinprick.
See the mandibles of famine
Snacking on the mechanism of dread.

All for a measure, to measure
The trains and the oceans,
The billow of commerce
In those blank-blink eyes.
Out of our own desire the beetle comes
To lay the seed in our brain.
This thus is time:
The chaindrop of calculation
And the shut box.

Corpus Christi!
The roll of the earth turns the frost to blood
And in the air hangs the still tree
Waiting the moment in eternity
For the husk to burst.
From this fruit all singularities flow.
A place which has no speech for time,
No place from past, beyond, but is the now
Of footfall printing birth
Upon the snow of our existence
Tilted into the long low ray of grace.
The camber of this life shone
On your face this winter afternoon
To let arrive the transfigured thing:

One single span of our loved lives outflanks all reckoning
At the empty corner by the sullen locust
Hustled abruptly up into God's whirlwind
And out into immensurable night.

GOSCAR ROCK

Wrack! Wrack! By Goscar Rock
No turning back, the tide's run out,
The continents shift their deserts far down
Beneath the sea

The town clings like a sea star
A little crust of man
Earth cracks along her ledges
We lie beneath the lee

You lie beneath the lee, my love
You lie beneath the sands
Of that time we mistook
As given into our hands

The moon leans on the window
The fishermen light the dark
Down the beach of time where we gather
To vault into the deep

Ah, time! We have no home here
Burst like the shoals' fire!
Leap from moments' ladder
We flash upon the shore

A spark, a birth, a galaxy
Where time's horizon's lost
Eternity's eye dazzles open
On the razor of Goscar Rock

IN THE VALLEY OF THE LOT

We came across the crayey Lot –
What seas have lain here through the centuries –
The cliffs are made of life
Up whose sheer walls we steer.
The fall beads fear, the song of far below
And time's drop. We drove along the edge of space,
Blue, blue and white, your face light as a pearl
Around its seed of dust. You saw, where I did not,
Your road darkening to a dazzle
Stripped out and strung like a chord
Towards its perfect note.

So the path led: the jolting track,
The long-forgotten well,
The lichen knitting life and stone,
Our journey's door as dream
Now opening green upon the arbour.
O little oak trees in the forest,
The garden of the earth was ours!

And you sat in it, content. I felt
The incandescence settle, start to thrum
Like a halo in the wood which rode
The shadows on its ring of fire.
You stared silent into that soul glare,
Time's oil crushed from moss and lavender,
The myrrh of longing and memory and coming home.

What leaves rustled in your mind then,
What herald bugled in the balsam air?
As your frame merged with night
I heard them thronging through the undergrowth,
Lamb and ewe hustle, ghostly,
Brush with their warm breath the limestone wall.

They moved like a still wind of spirits
Whispering to their shepherd of eternity.
At the door you listened in the waiting forest
Till the moon fell and the sheep bells
Called from beyond the hinge of darkness,
Over the threshold between thicket and infinite
Where world and soul forge one.

* *crayey* = *chalky*

RHINE FUGUE

for Hilli and Albert Menden

for our friendship on the banks of the Rhine

*Der eigentliche Kern der Freundschaft: ein Glaube,
ein Hoffen, ein gemeinsames Werk!*
ANNETTE VON DRÖSTE-HULSHOFF

RHINE FUGUE

I

Night Train to Cologne

The first journey alone, heady, disquieting:
The tick of the rails carries me away from comfort
To Flanders. The poplars, the locks, the barges,
The dead's enclosures. I am far now
From mother's and father's arms;
The language changes. Trees are other
In this other tongue, the doors of the strange
Swing wide. Into the gloaming
Arrows the train through Ardennes wood.

Black. All that's reflected back
Is my own face upon a darkening river
Along which arbitrary cities flare and dim.
Man's machines close in. The engine slicks
Across a mesh of silver sleepers; steep walls of living,
Hung with cloths and clothes, stop out the sky.
Beneath the girders we glide towards those small-shop destinies,
Drowsing.

       Midnight. A curve. A glint of water.
The locomotive shifts its eye,
Tracking between towerblocks a glimpsed star.
Out of the river bank she rises; raises
Spines of gold, gantries of fire.
I never saw such a cradle burning,
Heaven's perpendicular, jewel aflame.

The train homes on between the sleeping houses
And right upon the dark base of the tower
Sets its point. The spires rear over us.
It seems we creak with scarcely a sound or motion

Softly, inwards, inwards –
How time hangs like a silent bell
Between the carriages! – and all the travellers
As if fallen under some sweet spell
Lean their heads upon each other's shoulders
And follow with their gaze the beacon by the water,
The light path resting on the answering water.

Walberberg

Dark. I am very far now from father's and mother's arms.
We wind to the timber frames of Walberberg;
My place is set past midnight in the plate glass window:
Meat and cheeses I am invited to eat.
How solicitous are these custodians,
How their syllables hide my trespass!
I come bringing with me disturbance, asymmetry,
The shadows of ambush shifting
At the edge of memory, the smell of a foreign night.
Behind the softened consonants and gestures
Stretch the vast, untried plains of incommunicability
Where we must meet. I see beads of effort
Pearl on my host's forehead.
His room is thick with words battling
To reach this silent visitant,
The kingdom of his hospitality spread all before me
And yet from my outsider's exhaustedness
Spring only tears.

    My guardians draw me to the terrace;
The night gulps cold, and I stand still and stare
Where out beyond the terrible alchemical chimneys
Glare red bloom and blue steam over neon-lit Wesseling
At whose feet across its desert flood plain snakes the Rhine.

Easter Sunday Journey

At Walberberg the river's invisible.
Nothing is what I expected it to be.
The garages sleek, the cellars fat,
The tribe assembling for flan, coffee, cream,
The witch's tower waving on the hill.
Observance changes. How the tang of the bell
Pierces my heart with this strange chord
On which hangs my first cross swaying
High above the hedgerows, that first confusion.
What new, odd alloys in the mind refract.
Among the green man's tongues the children search for hares.
The daughter of the home's flung headlong for adultery,
The witch's cries glass out my soul.

* * *

Easter's tithes are gathered. We set
Our compass towards the star followers
And butchered virgins of Cologne.
Down the driveway moves the car, confident
Into the shearing rain. The land is veiled in water.
We flick onto the autobahn: the driving's fast,
Faster – the thought shoots like a tracer –
Faster than we would at home, and in the outside lane.
The windscreen wipers' metronome beats wild.
Out of the mists rear the retorts of Wesseling,
Phosphorescent and signalling in the cauldron air.
My host is buoyant – 'Bald sind wir da' –
He's eager for the awe he knows is coming,
Anticipates the wonder on my astonished face.

Shock. Brake. Tail lights point and blaze.
From behind, a crud sends us spinning
Down our own rapids. The motor screams.
And in this dream I turn and turn
Through a slow orbit of fortune, cause and consequence,
The forward skitter of the years and second understanding.
The moments tick toward eternity.
I reach out my hand and see the wise men
Braced for hope beyond the windscreen,
My companions' mouths stilled to the O of last things
As by the rising waters of the Rhine death let me go.

II

Blücher encamps at the Rhine

Winter. Into the forest.
The light slants through the trees.
This must be swift work
And the wood must be swift too,
Wood that will bear and bend
And take the water and not break.
Our clearing's quick, axe, adze, plane,
Two hours at most to shape each rib and backbone.
The charcoal burners fled us first:
Now they creep from the undergrowth
To hoist the hammock-kettles up into the branches
And stoke them full with larch and pitch-pine.
We've made them captains of the still coals burning;
Their sorcerers' camp-shadows rear against the night.
That's when they show us how to bake hedgehogs,
Try those place-names round our awkward tongue –
Weisel, Bornich, Bacharach, and the most prized,
Kaub's toll-castle, reefed in floe-ice
Like a ringed princess.
                    The ground is freezing.
Canvas hangs in boards beside the pots of tar
Whose reek fills our lungs and thinking
From smear and daub, again, again,
The double, triple layering to make the pontoons
Strong as web steel, so wagons, horses, gun-mounts,
The traverse footfall of ten thousand men,
Can ride the chasm of the snow-blue water,
So we can pass like sleet on the steppe wind,
Fiery as crystals sheeting through the fir trees,
Glistening and gone across the blood-plain of the night.

New Year's Day 1814: Blücher Crosses the Rhine

'We had it from Deinet's daughter,
Jutta, the one who married over the river,
A man from Perscheid, God help her.
They were moving oxen in the farmyard
When the toddler slipped, and cracked her head on the ice.
So she had her in her arms and was comforting her
With a stick of sugar. Suddenly, the mist lifted;
The sky was blue as a plover's egg.
"Look up there at the moon-ghost",
She said to the child. In that moment
She heard it, like a thousand altar bells,
Which she thought very odd, since Christmas was over
And she was not in church.
      "What's that noise coming up from Steeg?"
She asked her husband; and saw, within the pale of his eye,
As he gazed over her shoulder,
Row on row of black-coats bobbing,
A blur of red and gold and silver,
Caught the tang of horses and the musk of men.
Couldn't understand a word of their shouting,
Even the German was difficult, and the strangest thing –
How the riders of the little ponies trotting
Indifferently amongst the march and clatter
Sat hunched right up over their withers,
Half men, half beast.
      Hour upon hour the mass moved;
She went in, saw to the geese,
Who were peevish and fevered by all the upset,
Scrubbed pans, butter-churns, cut bread,
Fed the baby, checked the little one for bruises,
Swept up in the kitchen – and still,
When the light went down
And she was wiping her hands by the window –
Still the armies came, as if they would come for ever

Until she and the oxen and the tree
Printing its sundown shadow on the chapel wall
Lean their crosses in the lee of an east wind,
Until stakes and lances and defences
Are dust whisp sifting over the brow of the hill.'

III

At Ottmarsheim

At Ottmarsheim the Grand Canal d'Alsace
Splices like an axe through bone.
Factories rise yellow from a dusty plain
Where only eucalyptus grow.

At Ottmarsheim the marketplace is blank;
A café awning rattles in the breeze;
Cats lie dozing in the shrivelled fountains;
Eyeless houses stop the air we breathe.

At Ottmarsheim the valley stretches wide;
Behind the sawmills' flues
A heron stalks his muddy, trickling empire;
Gravel feeders crack and choke and boom.

At Ottmarsheim a little door stands open.
Awkward, thirsty, we tread the cool ground.
This space has no end and no beginning,
Infinity's small round.

Sudden the singer raising to his maker
Notes laddering the blue
And praises ringed the sounding air around us
At Ottmarsheim where the soul's wingbeat beats true.

At Oppenheim

On the rose terraces at Oppenheim we stood
And gazed over the river; June sun, high summer.
Vineyards ran their green rods up and down the hill.
Two swans circled in an antique skirmish,
Willow fronds tickled the whizzing bicyclists.
These lattices grow around a stranger's temple;
Under his gable we are received, chairs set,
Linen spread, and from the cellar beneath his home
He has brought the wine. We raise our glasses;
Like lovers' fingers the tendrils in the crystal
Coil their sweet shoots about our heads.

      Four or five or many,
We sit at his table as the afternoon flowers
Across the garden, and laughter, and music somewhere.
Here is made a dance as of clear waters braiding,
The slopes of joy descending in these eyes, these gestures,
A light which for this moment we shall never empty
In our glass of wine.

Green ran the grasses by the riverbank
And evening dropped like a drape from heaven
To touch with her hem the golden Rhine.

In the Rhine Wood

A man sang in the wood
Whose bird cries filled my days
Their sip and sweep and swallow,
Their bunter and chatter,
Their high, longing curl over the trees' tips.

A man sang in the wood
And the whole forest leant forward.
The valley floor boomed back his melody
And the walls of the combe closed round.

A man sang in the wood.
I never saw him, imagined his legs thrown forward in the sun.
So he passed along the river, and sang
As the motes and the butterflies
Rose and sank in the waterlight
And the blackbirds a thousandfold answered him

IV

Worms: In the Jewish Quarter

'I dreamt I was in the city again:
Halfway in the street, between the immaculate gables
And the scrubbed cobbles. I looked up,
Wondering at the perfect plaster and the lack of damp.
There was discreet lettering on the shop fronts,
Orderly furniture in the windows.
Odourless air. I advanced a step.
My foot cracked in the silence but no-one answered it.
Not one door opened, nor child's pinafore caught on the wind
Flashed at a corner. The stars, the moons,
The geese and the green trees were all gone
From the lintels, the names shorn away.
What cold hand touched my heart!
Jittering, I followed the alleyway down
Round the familiar bend to the well, the centre.
I hung over the dark rim to search the way in:
The cistern was dry, like an eye blinded.
So I leant under the lime tree and dreamed.

And as I dreamed, they came.
Crowding down to the water and chattering,
Passing the babies from sister to sister,
All the daily things slipping from their lips,
Like the lap of a stream running,
Moving, bobbing and returning
As if it would never end.
I saw them all, as I dreamed.
Little Lili Reichmann, Abigail Moses, Ruth Levine
With her fierce glances, stout Rachel Oppenheim
Always blithe. Round the well they clustered
Their loves, hopes, merriment, drawn on a skein
Above their heads and spinning in the sunlight
Like the crown of heaven.

Just so had I seen their faces illuminated,
One night, amongst the press of the crowd,
Their eyes aflame as the door swung open
And the men surged, exultant,
From the transformed house with the new Torah
High on their shoulders in the blaze of His canopy.
Pluck the zither, beat the tabor, the street was full of dancing,
Gather the throng towards the ark, the centre;
Ruth, Lili, Abigail and Rachel, raise Him a sanctuary
That He may dwell among you.
I saw the flares like stars through stormclouds
Dip and flicker down towards the synagogue
And one by one by one by one the voices flickered also,
Winking and vanishing until all was silence,
The door closed upon them and they were folded home.'

The Jewish Cemetery, Worms

The season between New Year and atonement
Is when our women count the book of life.
The boxes for this are made of cedar
And laid up in niches cut in the very wall.
Inside the whole year lie the white measuring bands
Till Rosh Hashanah comes.
Then we put on solemn clothes and go in a group for protection
Out past the chains hooked open onto the world's marketplace –
The stares, the smells, the nudges,
The tainted meat and strange-familiar voices,
A hail from our friend, the carpenter,
The fishwives laughing and offering fresh roach from the Rhine –
Down the imperial highway to our dead.

This gate leads home
For here we trace the ladder of our suffering and belonging;
Among the green graves, by the bubbling fountain
We wander and endure.
Here prayer is trod; memorial is learning;
Each pebble marks the pilgrimage of souls.
See Alexander Wimpfen, the cynosure of loyalty,
Bearing humiliation, hindrance, the sneers of office
And master's desecration, eleven years
Saving for a corpse's ransom
To bring his teacher back into God's ground.

Walk the boundary, follow the witness
Around the circumference of what we hold dear:
All those who vanished between homeland and traintrack
Counting eternity to the rails' tick-tack.
All their minds' territories, all their souls' store
Are wound in the taper of memory
We make from these ribbons and light in the synagogue
During the days of awe.

In this garden I saw
The book of the abandoned temple lie
Open; the names of the unburied
Were written from floor to ceiling, door to door;
River mist rose like fire through ruined windows
And the disfigured walls led in all directions to the sky.
Belief is terrible in these enclosures:
Judge a moment what the truly iniquitous might feel
If they could really re-enter their own horror.
And not to enter is worse
For out of that silence breathes only the hollow of the abyss.
To such refusal what response can a man's soul give?

Silence is God's. We measure the tapes of the deeds of the living
And bring them to him; we measure the deeds
Of those who have shown kindness, over and over,
Even the smallest. They have no number
And that also is terrible. God's mercy burns
In his high places and his peace is an army with banners
Facing the dark. Sound the shofar underneath the cypresses;
The headstones lean towards its calling note
Beyond all consolation that can ever on this earth be uttered,
Beyond all sin this or any other Jordan
Can carry away like blood.

V

Printing William Tyndale's New Testament, Peter Schoeffer's
Workshop, Worms, 1526

Come here and see the frameset of the word:
All night in the printshop we enter its alchemies.
Where does it come from? There is nothing apparent
That would make man's silence break.
Yet breath breathes out of the mind
And starts to move. Like water, it runs
As if to no law, but watch more astutely
And you will see it ekes mountains
Down into dust. What fools would we be
In our children's eyes if we tried to catch
This quicksilver under the pump with our fingers
Though armies march to its rhythms?
Speech is a decanting of souls
Into the commonwealth of potential and witness
That is life. With the word consolation,
A dozen sisters crowd into the room,
Full of gifts: compassion, lightness, sweetness,
Bringing fortitude or peace –
How germane these are, yet none the same.

Words are blood, passed down the centuries;
They spill, are spilt, and some, from being tiny
Or despised, shape all our destinies:
What was a thorn once before it was a crown?
Here flow rivers where words hesitate
And gather behind pressure
Till the flood is right and the freight's let go.

This man brings it, towards evening
When shadows cloak, and we are grinding the inks.
He's known, and watched, for the company he keeps –

Men who preach at street corners, deniers
Or repeaters of sacraments –
He goes into the ghetto and learns from the Jews.
And out of it all comes this:
In the retort of language to language
He turns what can only be guessed at
Into a new and startling alloy
Whose structure shifts the world.

Our business is this:
Using our alchemy to get his message out.
From mind to printed page's a universe,
Messy, complex, interlocking.
The eye must never cast wrong
Or the thought's thrown out.
Pressure brings it to birth
In the noise and stink of the print room,
The tick of the sorts in the fourme, oils and liquors
To fix the impress, the whole purpose
Of this distillation of thinking,
Grapes or olives sweating their sap.
So the press comes down as our body leans to it
And the words are strained in their thousands
Ready for draught.

But how shall they spread across the frontiers?
These words are not for kings nor ecclesiarchs,
But for the rock that's every man's and woman's soul.
Safety's paradox is daylight: wagons brought before the door,
Awaiting flour or oil or wine to seal the cargo
And the softest lamb's wool weave layered in
To safeguard the words. What terror
Winching these bales out over the driving Rhine stream,
What prayer as she buoys the ships up and out

Like crystals on her rolling spine!
Elect for London. For the Stapelyard
Where our merchants deal among the cranemasts,
Where the traders in outlaw slip with their parcels
Down Dowgate, All Hallows, Amen Corner
As the curfew bites. Tonight,
Over all these patchwork islands,
In hedgerow and churchyard,
The tinder is laid to the stake.

VI

Bonngasse 20, 16 December 1770

This is the moment in the dirty city –
Saint Remigius, ring out your bells! –
Frost across the rooftops and the hard floes
Cracking the riverbanks, the sweet wizened apples of winter.
Light flows down the ladder into this room,
The spirit's descant at dawn.
Heaven breaks apart to let enter the dance
Of the beloved world and the angel.

But what are the rhythms of our trackway drawn
Towards the horizon? How green the blooms
Of youth! The plateaux of the seven fells
Set off steep dreams, not pity.
Not knowing, we savage the forests of hope
With a hacksaw: for we shall be victors!
How we lay waste, how small the chance
We hear his footfall, see his sandal.

Cry sustenance, cry succour:
All gone behind us. Towards this space time grows.
Square to the angel on the ground of doom
Because it comes always to this: the call
Which breaks like scattering glass across our tenancy
And no way back. This is for ever. Life's knell.
The wheeling spheres have stopped their icy dance
To watch us wrestle with God's angel.

What is the fight? Death. Our password? – Must it be?
I know the reply. But is that the answer?
The struggle to spark form
Before we have nothing left to tell
Is desperate. Have we nowhere to go

But float into the dark? My adversary's stance
Says this is not the question. Touch him to find the truth
Of what faith is: hope's veiled candle.

Frailer than the grasses of the field we flicker,
Our grapple no stronger than a mouse in the storm.
For hour into hour the journey to the womb
Of transfiguration grows darker. The little knowledge sells
Drops by the wayside like a ghostly currency
Lost. Not sight – listen! – our sinews, plucked, compose
Chords to break apart heaven and carry her dance
On the fragile soul's song rising amidst stark fugues of angels.

VII

Godesia

Today the boat *Godesia* is alight with flowers.
Today is feast: her guests have come to town.
Along the quayside bob their flickering coats and dresses,
Their greetings striped in many-coloured sounds.

Tiny *Godesia*! Her prow casts into the running flood;
Fragile as a waterboatman she rides
The stream's gold hair.
The breeze is sweet, the riverbank green,
Between the cliffs of memory she glides.

      At Unkel the ferryman
Criss-crosses our path with his purse of farthings.
How he's grown weary of landing his armies on the other side;
Far happier he swaggers in the marketplaces,
Speaking in tongues, and at night dreams
Amber-eyed Marie from over the river
Brings a crown to his bed.

Memory. Like a report of trumpets in the canyon,
Resistant beneath our conversations,
We catch the boom.
Sirens lie in the slate reefs, *Godesia*,
And in the cry of the sudden swimmers
Windmilling helplessly by
On history's current.

What games are played here by the waters?
The barges go down, go down, without a pilot
To know the lairs: the tribal whirlpools
And the arsenals, boiling;
Gold greed and the swirl of insult,
A twisted message arrowed from the balconies,
Silos sliding,

Two by two
Four by four
Nation by nation
Ghost by ghost,
Into the dragon's hillside.

O the melancholy of broken-backed bridges!
For razed cities never gave garlands.

So praise healers who heal in seclusion
And the builders of harmony
Whose vision's tender as spider's steel
Suddenly illumined by dew.
What kind of strength does it take
To cultivate roses in a time of war?
What kind of pilgrimage, to wait?
To kneel against the darkness in a blacked-out room?
To tend, invisibly, the roots of peace?

Godesia, star of the river,
Your passage confounds conquerors.
Redeem us by your cargo.
The vineyards bend towards you in the setting sun.
Our children race the deck, shouting with happiness,
The chairs face every which way as love meets his friends.

Dock now under the evening trees.
The journey's over.
At the crossroad between Peter's rock
And Hotel Dreesen stands a chapel.
There is really only room
For one man
Or one woman
To pray there.
But the candles are always
Multitudinous
Like hope.

EXILE AND THE KINGDOM

EXILE AND THE KINGDOM

I

NOCTURNS

Lord, let me come again into your presence.
The times are difficult, and night after night
Beneath the door curls the thin smoke of hypocrisy.
Sleep brings no respite but a throng of fretted images:
The rostra talking to the multitudes,
War's insect engines on a desert wall,
The bulldozed coffins.

In the forest, bird croak, rodent shriek
Echo as in vast industrial halls
Encasing us, and looking at the firmament
Induces only terror. Ah, am I so shrunk down,
Lord? To this place all have warned me of,
Doubt's unlit well, the slothful creeping through her galleries
To find them all the same, and sapping will
Ever to question them again, ever to believe
They are not true? How did we come here?
That first thought: is it worth it?
What difference does the beetle, struggling with his dungball,
Make, when the world's willed to dissolution and the solar fire?
Or, humanly, our scuttling worries running before
The tide of our own dead? Then there's the heartache
At the core of things: attachment, the blank certainty
Of letting go, the arbitrary wing of accident,
Wrong gene or partner, a lifetime bled into the dusty ground
Of non-fulfilment, the waste that issues from indifference,
And posthumous mindset conferred by fame.
Unhindered, these postulates gather
And by their very stupefying number,
Like slogans chanted in the marketplace,
Prevail.

The step is obvious:
Why should we not accept ourselves as measure
Since this at least is comprehensible?
Work hard, gain expertise and exercise it,
Receive acclaim and sit atop our own particular tree
Gathering all activity to us
For the days go in and the days go out
The cars and the buses and the trains round about
All our doings, and there's a myriad reasons not to stop,
The daily bread and the weekly shop
The necessary career and the newspaper reading,
Mortgages, bills and pensions savings;
The world is cruel but our house is warm,
If we just keep busy, we will come to no harm.

Until that night which throws us on our knees
And we lean out, retching, over the abyss.
Lord, do not leave me in this dreadful place.

* * *

What shall teach us? How shall we learn?
Sometimes still, as in a dream, you come to me,
Favourite, mercurial uncle, bouncing that admired loquacity
Back and forth all afternoon with my father,
Exulting in visits to Bayreuth, Bergonzi at the Met.
And the largesse of your library, dispensed without afterthought –
'You like it? Then have it!' – embossed Hans Andersens,
First editions, Utrillo, Bonnard, Ceri Richards watching from the walls.
I'm older now than you were when you died.
When did I first discern a straining, an agitation –
Remember the Steinway sent back peevishly after just one assay? –
A kind of madness in the talk, as if the talk were action,

Or a sanctuary from sirens calling from the deep.
Then silence, black dog, the curtains closed at noon
And we, uncomprehending, turned back at your door.
So down the years the pattern, a threnody of envy,
Of being passed over, colleagues' perfidy,
Of all you had not achieved.
Finally, dark things said between brother and brother,
Your wife's head against a wall.
No children. No consummated marriage.
Too strong the claw raking you back to the hissing fireside
Where son and mother reciprocally egged,
Altercated, tore at the fabric of each other's soul.
Each month you swore you'd never again give her
The chance and each month once more
You'd drive the valleys' claustrophobic road
To meet her. All this I saw,
And how for you it ended – my favoured, exotic uncle,
Who wrote books on Satie and Poulenc and the leitmotif in Wagner –
After thirty years still the icy shock of Severn water
The horizon unstable, slipping,
Your watch laid carefully by the bedside.

How it looms now, your prodigious codicil:
In your papers no will but a diary
Where in ash you wrote your heart's longing
For a soul woman, wifely counsellor, sweetest of bedmates,
And so begins the first understanding:
That the impossibility of loving begets despair,
And despair kills.

II

MATINS

Endure with the one who, from his night sweats,
Wakes in the livid hour before dawn and is afraid.
This is our hinge time: where from the past foregather
Our mentors in affliction, those whom we betrayed.
This was the mother of it, a carelessness we did not even notice,
So much repeated we wore it like a skin.
Insouciance, the callow pride
That tosses off as nothing its foolish actions,
That self-preservation which makes us slink behind the wainscotting
Or push the trophies of preferment between us and our friends.
Malice too: the rivals that we bad-mouthed,
Anger in committee, back-room machination,
And the sliest, embedded in the laziness of the quotidian,
Those innumerable little capitulations to self-love.
Now tread the mighty deceivers to be reckoned with,
Glittering and chattering their fandango of promises:
The world routes make immortal;
I am fulfilment; this is ecstasy.
Behind their drabbish voices spreads a wake
Of things unspeakable, of lives pierced by no sorrow,
Just airless, monolithic, neon rooms, sealed off against contrition,
Where the self's so full of its own story
It never minds the slumber of the heart.

The owl ends his hunt and in the dawn the barns awake.
Cock crows and through it breaks our climacteric:
Sweat turns to blood and we stand naked in the courtyard,
No keys, no money, nowhere to run,
Our very identity abandoned somewhere
In a misspent night, and the truth
About what we've done, and done a hundred times,
Descends upon us like a waterfall.

It is a perfect sickness: mind, body, soul
So penetrated with duplicity we could not even see
The canker in our face. But here in the suntide
Nothing will cover the gangrene of irreparability:
The knowledge that, through us, another person
Must eat the bitter pottage of sin.

III

LAUDS

How different the first time – still naive in these matters,
So long a road of transgression unbeknownst still to go.
Very young, in that acute stage of grieving
Which is filled up with anguish at the revelation
Personal sin is real.

     And the hard city not caring,
A hostile jangle; out of turn, the dappled quays
With their enlaced lovers; out of turn,
The times you walked these boulevards in gladness.
The buildings flashed their prison staves
As I ran through Châtelet and Montparnasse and Clichy
Like a starving dog looking for eyes that would see my distress.
But I was alone and dumb in the city and no-one reached out.
By the river I stopped. The boundaries of my capacity were met.
Turn around and go in.

     One step into the gloom.
O Lord come to our aid. O make haste to help us.
A businessman, a baby dandled in her father's arm,
Young men stooped upon the little benches,
Hands cupped round heads like stones beneath the rain.
Lean against this pillar and listen.
The vault draws in and points towards the spot.
Outside the mighty city and its traffic dim
And time begins dilating like a butterfly's wings
On words encountered in another country
Whose stamp, from passing through innumerable minds,
Had been effaced.

Love never ends. The soul shivers at it.
Love endures. Love does not grow angry.
Love hopes. I lie down on the floor.
Even if I have all gifts without love I am nothing,
Words sputtered like kindling in the wind.
The building crackles. Recognition. Terror.
One single, constant, unadulterated note
The greatest of these is love.
In the church of the martyrs St Gervais and Protais
I have come through the impossible door of asking.

Grace falls like rain on a late summer afternoon.

IV

TERCE

What is strength in the parch of noonday,
When the sun, like a copper core,
Stops in the heavens? The spirit lies upon its cellbed
In an exhausted sleep, fitful with memory,
Meaning's fading arc. Here on this dull road
In the breakback field and hum of office,
How to retain that sudden downrush
Of the numinous that was supposed to change us?
This is the travail of the contemplative
Who like a climber on the rockface
Has put his hands and feet a thousand times
Into the crevices to get the test and operation
Of it, to fit his fingers to the ledge
And sense the difference between unsound and true.
The preparation of the mind through vigil
Brings its own knowledge: the athlete's arcing
Of the ball, a jockey's pacing,
The engraver's resolute hand, a dancer's sweated grace.
So practice accrues a constant witness,
Like water rising in a silent well.

Once I saw this: early Christmas morning,
A country church, exhausted –
The community's great celebrations done –
And just two strangers in the congregation,
But to them through the vestry door slowly approached
The priest. And slowly, very slowly, began the blessing,
Not easy, each word forced as from hard compressing pain
And light invoked as though a bitter heirloom,
Incumbent, cheerless, what travesty
Of hallelujah and the holy flame.
But as we watched, the church fell still

And stiller to the only sound,
His long, gasping, harrowed dredge for air.
Lord, have mercy. Christ, have mercy.
He kneels: the rack of the world is in his body.
Take this. Eat. Drink. We are the city-not-forsaken;
His hands tremble at the raising of the cross.
Not for our righteousness, except his own compassion,
A lifetime's husbandry, so that within the blaze of pain
He can endure. Early Christmas morning,
A cold wind beneath the door.
The congregation shivers. The peace of the Lord;
And also with you. Over the mountains we drove in silence,
And the priest in his agony travelled with us.

V

SEXT

Universal? Have I always loved my brother,
Made no distinction? Never despised my neighbour
For his ignorance, nor wanted to exclude?
Not turned away from a face because it did not interest,
Or there wasn't time, or let something more important occlude
The chance of friendship? The years make humbler, cautious;
The waiters are philosophers, the dustmen visionaries
And he who exalts himself will never understand
He treads a pointless road. Learn then from the pilgrims
You encountered: the colleague whose whole life was service,
The murderer's mother shouting in the soup dole queue,
The widow praising God for the years her husband gave her,
The stinking outcast in the stairwell you once gave water to.
That hostel at Sainte Eulalie – a long, hot afternoon
And lunch's clutter, dreaming in the sun –
Cracked awake by hoof clack on the cobbles,
The breath and sweat of mare and rider
In a sweet embrace, and care, by the cooling river
For their undertaking, the carriage of the soul
Through rock and gorge and forest
Towards the heaven-flung censer and the meadows of Montjoie.

NONES

The philosopher said, 'Even if I saw a miracle,
I would not believe', and kings have shut them out
With key and padlock. No need. Miracles never
Will dance their way, for miracles are a conversation
And do not proffer themselves to those who cannot hear.
It makes me smile to think how much the philosopher
Loved the story of the blind man restored to sight
Who thought objects were two-dimensional
Until he learnt to see. What miracles
In the hedgerows do we pass by, unsaluted?
Or those we credit to chance:
The boy I met in a hotel by a river,
Love of whose country long outlasted him
And fused my soul with France;
The hired stone cottage in the hills whose owner
Stepped with his making eye straight
Into the house of friendship in my heart.
But made miracles exist in another sphere,
Not instantaneous; they are the fruit
Of faith and tenacity; a lifework's web of endeavour
Revealed when the light shines through.
So you came towards me on the college lawn
After estrangement; the willow dappled back and forth
The years across your face, and we walked together
In the remembered garden, criss-crossing love
And love's misprision, what we had done wrong
Or failed to do; power's conceit and friend's rejection,
The gift of family and nullity of hate,
Until night fell, you asked, I gave,
I asked, you gave, forgiveness.

VII

VESPERS

Hosanna's the hardest, not the easiest, thing:
It makes the sweat to drop in an old man's beard
So much does he know of darkness and death's road. ·
Benediction is that act of cleansing
Which stops us going as our own gaolers
Down into the dungeons that we built.

Sing, sing with cymbals and in the sanctuaries
Send the heart out onto the high combes
And round the evening tables to uncover
What it should honour, for the heart is hungry
To garner illumination into the barns of praise.
What is a midge in the eye of the Lord –
All that is bought, owed, earned, inherited,
The grabs and saws of growth, the stridor of the corporalities,
And soaring palaces stretching their fingers to the edge of doom –
None hang from heaven, none display
God walking in his universe as I saw today:

The guests are gathered in the church at Salle,
The light falls on the floor;
The choir sings out the Magnificat;
The bride stands at the door.

The bride stands at the door and waits;
Her handmaids dress her hair.
The bride stands at the door and waits;
Her father brings her here.

And then across the fields a wind
Comes and catches the rose;
Her veil flies up like flame;
Above her head a fiery tongue it throws.

The guests are gathered in the church at Salle
The light falls on the floor;
For all eternity the rose
Stands at heaven's door.

[Note: 'Salle' in Norfolk is pronounced 'Saul' locally]

VIII

COMPLINE
Chapel of Our Lady and St Non, St David's, Wales

Dusk. A windy garth. The dead are in their rows.
Firelights warm the houses. Ravens pace the moor
Where seafoam blows and the young race, amazed,
Towards the tonnage of the sea. One star.
The oldlands bend towards it and the town huddles
In the oldlands' arm its infant bones.
Lord, let your servant at the soul's very edge and promontory
Walk where the chapel of the fathoms grows
And saints lean from her windows against the night.
This place is succour where a life coheres:
Innocence and loss, hope, wisdom, regret and thanksgiving
Placed out of the wretched street and ragged kitchen
Upon the stupendous altar
Against whose rock life eternal lifts and booms.
Eleison. Ave. Magnificat.
Past, present, future are your servants,
And faith the handmaiden that knows.
Dark closes in. The rooks draw home to bed.
God grant us a quiet night and a perfect end.

ACKNOWLEDGEMENTS

Grateful acknowledgements are made to the Royal Literary Fund, a Fellowship from whom allowed part of this collection to be written. Thanks also go to the editors of the following journals or anthologies where some of these poems first appeared: *Acumen, Agenda, The Jewish Chronicle, Scintilla, Scintilla* special Anne Cluysenaar edition *At Time's Edge, Temenos Academy Review, This Life on Earth, The Poet's Quest for God* (UK), *Gesher* (Australia).

The art work on the cover is a sculpture by Paul Bothwell Kincaid, entitled *Crucifixion, a processional cross* (2008), an assemblage of found objects of bones and roots sourced from a Greek hillside (Rhodes), 2003–4. The artist has generously allowed its reproduction here.

CW00496094

LINE

LONDON

GREEN

LONDON COUNTRY

LINE

LONDON

GREEN LINE

LONDON COUNTRY

LINE

LONDON

GREEN LINE

LONDON COUNTRY

LINE

LONDON

GREEN LINE

LONDON COUNTRY

LINE

LONDON

LONDON
COUNTRY

ISBN 185414 251 8

First edition published 1984

Second edition 2001

Published by Capital Transport Publishing
38 Long Elmes, Harrow Weald, Middlesex

Designed by Tim Demuth

Printed by CS Graphics, Singapore

© Laurie Akehurst

Acknowledgements for the First Edition

Bernard Davis, commercial manager for LCBS during a large part of the period covered by this book, provided the information dealing with the organisation of the company. Nicholas King's detailed knowledge of the company's vehicles enabled him to give us a comprehensive survey of the many events to occur in the fleet. Peter Graves submitted material dealing with the bus routes and Albert McCall much of the information on the Green Line network. The route maps were drawn by Mike Harris.

The authors also acknowledge the assistance of Stephen Fennell, Brian Speller, Guy Brigden and James Whiting in various aspects of the preparation and, of course, the many photographers whose work is used throughout this book. Grateful thanks are also due to the London Country employees who gave valuable and willing assistance during the compilation of the first edition.

LONDON COUNTRY

Laurie Akehurst and David Stewart

Capital Transport

PREFACE TO THE SECOND EDITION

WHEN THE first edition of this book was published in 1984 London Country Bus Services Ltd was still very much in existence but, with the spilt of the company on 7th September 1986 into six much smaller concerns, including four operating companies, the complete story of the history of London Country proper may now be told. The Company owed its creation and demise to the whims of politicians. It was created on 1st January 1970, as a subsidiary of the state owned National Bus Company, from the former Country Buses and Coaches empire of London Transport Board when that body passed to the control of the Greater London Council. The demise of London Country came in 1986 when the policy of the Government of the day was to privatise the road passenger transport industry. The National Bus Company was broken up with a view that its subsidiary companies would eventually be privatised. London Country was felt by the politicians, in a competitive environment with the proposed deregulation of bus services, to be too large to be treated as a single entity – thus the split into four separate operating companies, all of which were privatised by 1988. The years from 1970 to 1986 saw tremendous change, in the light of a greatly falling demand for bus travel, with the traditional operating methods and route pattern inherited from London Transport in 1970 being transformed into a much leaner operation with a largely modern fleet and a greatly changed operating area. The transformation was, as might be expected, not brought about without many difficulties and it is to the great credit of both management and staff that the position of the Company in 1986 was a vast improvement on 1970.

In preparation of the second edition of this book I am indebted to the many photographers who have been so very helpful in contributing their material. Special thanks must go to John Bull, Ken Glazier and David Ruddom for their valuable assistance in the preparation of this book. Acknowledgement must also be made to the London Omnibus Traction Society Annual Review publications covering the years 1973 to 1986 and to editions of the London Bus Magazine.

Watford, August 2001
Laurie Akehurst

CONTENTS

LONDON COUNTRY TAKES OVER

ON 1ST JANUARY 1970 a major new bus operator was born when London Country Bus Services Limited, a specially formed subsidiary of the National Bus Company, took over the green bus and Green Line coach services of London Transport.

This simple statement conceals the most far-reaching and fundamental change that had occurred in the organisation of London's transport since 1933. The seeds of the change can be found in the London Government Act 1963, which led to the setting up of the Greater London Council on 1st April 1965. The GLC was given a number of major powers, including overall responsibility for transport in its area. In due course it persuaded Central Government that it should control London Transport, and the Transport (London) Act 1969 was passed to effect this. A provision for the relinquishment of the greater part of LT's operations outside the GLC area was included and under this the operation of the Country Area buses and Green Line coaches was transferred to London Country. The name London Country Bus Services Ltd was registered in October 1968 and the vesting date of 1st January 1970 coincided with the overall control of London Transport moving from Central Government to the Greater London Council.

Above left **Scenes such as RF 229 standing at Great Bookham terminus represented the old order, together with the LT tubular steel shelter, and vintage bus stop post with early deep flag. But change was in the air – the traditional RF would be superseded by more modern buses and the stop flag would be replaced by the Department of Transport style sign. The long-standing 432 was also destined to be swept away, to be replaced by an extension of route 416 on 31st August 1980, one of many route alterations which would be made to the network in a climate of falling traffic levels and the provision of, or in some cases lack of, local authority financial support.** John Bull

Left **In addition to the vehicles themselves the new company had to change the signs on its garages and other buildings and this could not be achieved overnight. This spring 1970 view shows RT 3127, which is covering an RML working on the busy route 480, taking on passengers outside Gravesend enquiry office, the latter clearly showing the corporate identification of its previous owners. Route 480 was probably London Country's busiest, linking Gravesend to Dartford and Erith, with the first buses starting just prior to 5am and eight buses per hour being provided at certain times. The intensive service still allowed time for this conductor to exchange a few words with his driver in this shot.** Barry LeJeune

BULLETIN

A Newsletter for all the Men and Women of Country Buses and Coaches

Private : for the information of staff only

No. 13

NOVEMBER 1969

COUNTDOWN — FIVE WEEKS TO GO
A NEW ERA FOR COUNTRY BUSES

Management Team Appointed: More about January Changes

JANUARY 1, 1970 will not be just the start of a new year. For Country Buses and Coaches it will be the start of a new era—with a new name and a new parent body.

After 36 years as part of London Transport, one of the world's largest passenger transport undertakings, Country Buses and Coaches will become a self-contained unit. The London Transport fleet name will disappear from the sides of buses, to be replaced by "London Country"—the fleet title for the new company, London Country Bus Services Limited. But "Green Line" will still appear on the side of coaches—keeping alive one of the world's most famous coaching names.

Parent body of the new company will be the National Bus Company, which has 67 subsidiary companies operating throughout England and Wales, with 22,000 vehicles and over 80,000 staff.

SELF CONTAINED

So London Country Bus Services will be part of a very large transport family. But the aim will be to keep the company "local" and wholly self-contained.

Heading the management team which will lead London Country Bus Services into the seventies will be a Member of the Executive Board of the NBC, Mr. C. R. Buckley, who becomes Managing Director of LCBS.

General Manager will be Mr. G. Fernyhough, whose connections with Country Buses and Coaches go back to 1935, when he was appointed an assistant district superintendent. He became operating manager in 1954.

Mr. H. F. C. Adcock, Traffic Manager of Country Buses and Coaches since March, will hold a similar appointment with the new company,

Mr. C. R. Buckley, Managing Director of London Country Bus Services Ltd.

and Mr. L. A. Stimpson will continue to be in charge of Country Bus and Coach Engineering, as Chief Engineer. A newcomer to LCBS, but not to public transport, will be the Secretary, Mr. D. W. Passmore, until recently Secretary of Devon General.

For the longest serving members of the staff the name of the new parent body under which LCBS will push ahead into the future probably stirs memories of more than 30 years ago. For the "National Bus Company" then operated services in the northern area of the present Country Bus territory,
Continued overleaf

A Personal Message from the Managing Director

AS Managing Director of London Country Bus Services Ltd., I have much pleasure in joining with you in forming the new team to run the Country Bus and Green Line services.

This issue gives details of some of the changes that will come about from January 1, and uniformed staff may like to keep a copy while on duty so that they can answer enquiries from passengers.

PRESENT RATE

It is not thought that there will be many radical changes in the undertaking in the immediate future. As you know, you will retain your present rate of pay and conditions of service, including sick pay, pension rights, travel pass, etc., as stated in an extract from Staff News given to you recently.

I am confident that we will all continue to serve the travelling public with the quiet efficiency which has for so long been associated with Country Buses and Green Line.

I wish you good luck and contentment in your work during your service with London Country Bus Services.

MANAGING DIRECTOR

traffic function covered the two distinct segments of Buses and Underground and further divided the buses between the Central and Country areas. Consequently, many of the administrative and engineering functions would have been duplicated if each branch of the business had possessed its own separate support disciplines. To overcome this, many facilities were provided by creating central, or common user, departments providing functions such as Accounts, Budgeting, Catering, Legal, Estates, Publicity, Public Relations, Commercial and Fares, Staff Recruitment and Welfare, Pensions, Payrolls and Passes and Permits. On the engineering side, the Railways and Buses were almost entirely separated, but the bus facilities of Chiswick and Aldenham Works, Purchasing and Stores were common to both the Central and Country areas.

...sly mean ...e area— ...ntenance

...rned, the ...be: what ...fares and ...the new ...omething ...in detail. ...t up the ...9, makes ...C and its ...mercially ...ovide an ...on the

...ly linked ...nagement ...conomies, ...increases ...assengers. ...be auto- ...nand and ...between ...and those ...but lose

...ve many ...BC sub- ...ies. Now ...to be a ..., it may ...services

Mr. G. Fernyhough, General Manager of the new company.

with these other bus operators and with British Rail.

There has already been a major swing to one-man operation within green bus territory and in the future driver-only buses will appear in many new areas. In 1970, 138 new single-deck buses will be delivered. Provisional plans for 1971 include 90 new coaches for the Green Line fleet and 90 high-capacity double-deck buses designed for one-man operation.

The change that occurred to the Country buses on that date appeared to the public to be a minor one, if indeed they perceived a change at all. While buses carried the new fleet name reasonably quickly Gibson and T.E.L ticket machines were never modified thus London Transport titled tickets continued to be issued for several years. The Green Line fleet name continued without alteration thus only the legal lettering gave any indication of new ownership. The reasons for this were largely contained in the organisation and structure of London Transport.

Traditionally, most bus company management had been divided into three disciplines – Traffic (or operating), Engineering and Secretarial/Accounting. London Transport adopted a different approach because its

already been advised of the effect of the changeover. The build-up of the...

...well be possible to improve services and through facilities in conjunction

Men at the top in LCBS

● Here are some details of the careers of the men who will be playing leading roles in the LCBS company.

MR. BUCKLEY, who is 55, was educated at Birkenhead Park High Grammar School and joined Crosville Motor Services at Birkenhead in 1929.

He was appointed Divisional Manager, Crewe, in 1942, and three years later Divisional Manager, Merseyside. He became Deputy Traffic Manager in 1957.

In the following year he was appointed Traffic Manager of the Bristol Group of Companies, and returned to Crosville in 1965 as Director and General Manager. He was appointed a Member of the Executive Board of the National Bus Company last month.

Mr. Buckley has held office in both the Merseyside Section and Chester Group of the Institute of Transport. He is a Director of the Wales Tourist Board.

Mr. Fernyhough is as well known in country area garages as he is at operating HQ. He joined the old LGOC in 1930 and five years later was assistant

district superintendent with Country Buses. In 1946 he was an assistant divisional superintendent with Central Buses then, in 1951, went back to Country Buses as divisional superintendent (north), becoming operating chief of the country services three years later. He is 59.

Another well known figure is Mr. Adcock whose transport career began in 1924 and who has been associated with Country Buses since 1938. Now aged 61, Mr. Adcock became divisional superintendent (south) in 1949, and has been traffic manager since last March.

Mr. Stimpson, aged 43, who joined Country Buses six months ago as divisional engineer, has had a wealth of experience in bus and coach engineering during 29 years with London Transport. He was formerly an assistant divisional engineer with Central Buses.

Mr. Passmore, Secretary to LCBS, is a Fellow of the Association of Certified and Corporate Accountants. He has been secretary and accountant of Devon General since 1961.

FINDING OUT

Some new arrangements will apply from January 1 to passengers with travel enquiries. Written enquiries concerning Country Bus and Green Line services should be sent to the Traffic Manager at Bell Street, Reigate. Telephone or personal caller enquiries will be dealt with by LCBS garages, local Country Bus and Green Line enquiry offices, the London Coastal Coaches enquiry office at Victoria Coach Station (01 - 730 0202), the enquiry office at the Green Line Coach Station, Eccleston Bridge, Victoria (01 - 834 6563). Green Line enquiries will also be dealt with at LT enquiry offices in Central London, and through the London Transport telephone enquiry service—01 - 222 1234.

LOST PROPERTY

Passengers' enquiries about lost property should be made to the nearest LCBS garage—in person or in writing —after January 1, instead of to the lost property office in Baker Street.

7

Private—NOT for publication

LONDON COUNTRY BUS SERVICES
TRAFFIC CIRCULAR   No. 1

In operation on and after Friday, 9th January, 1970, unless otherwise stated.

Message from the General Manager

The London Transport Board will cease to exist on 1st January, 1970, and every member of the Country Bus and Coach staff will be transferred to London Country Bus Services, which commences operations on that day.

I wish you all the very best of luck and happiness with our new Company in 1970.

31st December, 1969

1

made. For months before the actual split a small joint team of London Transport and National Bus senior managers examined each facet of the operations and recommended a structure for the new company, designed to be able to function as a largely autonomous unit from its first day. However, it was clear that many things could not be set up in the time available and would have to continue to be provided by London Transport in the short term. The new company reported in mid-1970 that of some 40 identified functions, it had taken over 32. This had been achieved by the creation of two new departments under the Secretary and Chief Engineer together with the provision of new sections in the Traffic Manager's Department. The new company had employed a number of additional administrative staff. In some cases London Transport continued to provide support services for several years particularly concerning vehicle overhauls, destination blind manufacture and ticket machine maintenance.

London Country's garages were mainly elderly premises with limited maintenance facilities, mostly equipped only to deal with the standardised RF, RT and Routemaster buses which formed the bulk of the fleet. They relied heavily on the huge London Transport stores and overhaul systems which virtually totally rebuilt each bus every four to five years. The rear-engined single deckers and more sophisticated designs were a recent innovation and problems had already started to appear before the split. It was stated at the time that it would take five years to modernise garage maintenance facilities by the provision of pit extensions, heated dock enclosures, better lighting and improved craftsmen's shops.

Without central workshops or a stores system and with no means of setting one up in the time available, it was obviously going

This entirely logical but complex intermix made the split of 1st January 1970 a far from simple exercise. The solutions offered were to prove not ideal in some cases and the first few years of London Country's existence saw a series of further organisational changes designed to correct deficiencies and adapt to new circumstances.

It must be remembered that a bus company cannot stop running to allow a full-scale re-assessment of its operations to be

The Merlins were London Country's newest buses as typified by Amersham's MB 108 seen outside its home garage in April 1970. The London Transport fleet name has been neatly painted out on the yellow band while, surprisingly, the bullseye has been retained albeit with the fleet name painted out. The MA allocation was for just two Merlins for its share of the 305/A and 455 and as none of these routes passed the garage this bus has worked back to Amersham, probably from Gerrards Cross, on route 353. The building in the background with blue doors is the original Amersham & District premises which, by this time was in use as a private car garage.
Colin Brown

8

to be impossible to do without London Transport's help for some time. With hindsight the level of co-operation received was remarkable, but there was an inevitable problem of priorities within London Transport when spare parts and workshop resources became scarce. An agreement was made between the two companies to provide mutual assistance. In event of breakdowns on the road passengers could be transferred to the next available bus of either LCBS or LT. The engineers continued to offer assistance as required and spare Green Line coaches continued to be available at either Victoria or Riverside LT garages. All staff were allowed to use either London Country or London Transport canteen facilities. It was also London Country's urgent need to update the fleet and reduce the reliance on London Transport. It was estimated that it would take between five and ten years to achieve the goal of 100 per cent one-man operation.

Apart from the first 138 AEC Swift buses delivered in 1970/1, which had been ordered in 1969, all new vehicles were to be of designs already used elsewhere in Britain, but not by London Transport. The need for new vehicles quickly to both up-date the fleet and expand one-man operation also led to the acquisition of too many different types. As well as new AEC Reliances and Leyland Atlanteans, second hand AEC Swifts were transferred from South Wales and orders for Atlanteans, Daimler Fleetlines and more Swifts were diverted from Midland Red, Western Welsh and South Wales respectively. The advent of the Leyland National led to another type, including some pre-production examples, and the special needs of Superbus at Stevenage meant a small number of Metro-Scania single deckers.

Even in a well-organised company this number of new types over about three years would have stretched engineering resources. In London Country, trying to set up a new stores system and without proper Central Works facilities, the result was bound to be trouble. Add the consequences of the difficulties experienced during the mid-1970s in obtaining adequate spare parts from manufacturers and you have all the ingredients of a crisis.

Services operated by London Country suffered some periods of appalling unreliability and vehicle allocation schedules became extremely flexible to say the least. Many buses had been cannibalised for spares and vehicles were being hired for long periods from more fortunate operators. This was a situation that made the provision of a vehicle works of their own an essential for London Country, and at long last such an establishment was opened in January 1976 at a site in Tinsley Lane on the Industrial Estate at Crawley.

On the operating side things were rather better, although not without problems. The driver, conductor, supervisory and manage-

LONDON COUNTRY BUS SERVICES LTD
BELL STREET · REIGATE · SURREY   REIGATE 42411

Press information   No.6/70

LONDON COUNTRY ADOPTS NEW SYMBOL : FAMILIAR 'BULLSEYE' DISAPPEARS
IN THE COUNTRY

Since 1st January this year the green country buses and Green Line coaches formerly part of London Transport have now become part of the National Bus Company. The N.B.C. operates buses and coaches throughout the rest of England and Wales.

A new Company 'London Country Bus Services Ltd.,' has been formed and slowly but surely the familiar 'London Transport' slogan on the side of the Lincoln green buses is being changed to 'London Country'. At the same time the famous London Transport bullseye symbol is disappearing from the green buses and coaches. Its place will be taken by London Country's own new symbol :-

Designed in conjunction with the National Bus Company, the new motif represents the green ring around London in which London Country operate, and naturally suggests the wheel and movement. The angled bars give a feeling of perspective, suggesting operation in depth with a hint of 'transport amidst green fields'.

The symbol will be used not only on the vehicles; all company publicity, garages, enquiry offices etc., will be easily recognisable by its display.

The London Transport bullseye will, of course, continue to be used by London Transport on its buses and underground trains.

OFFICE OF THE TRAFFIC MANAGER
25th March 1970   REIGATE   6/70
D33/BJD

ment structure was capable of continuing to function largely without London Transport support. Independent training services were quickly established and the Head Office central facilities such as licensing, shelters and stops, staff records and some planning already existed. Some other functions including fares, tickets, public relations and publicity were established late in 1969, mainly taking specialist staff from the equivalent common service departments of London Transport. However, even here some items took time to organise. As an example the publicity was produced by London Country at Reigate, but continued to be posted at stops and shelters by London Transport staff for some months. A longer lasting association occurred with ticket machines, some of which continued to be serviced by London Transport's ticket machine works at Effra Road for over ten years, albeit on a contract basis.

London Country set about painting some RTs in a pleasing Lincoln Green livery with a Canary Yellow band instead of the former LT cream band. The company's newly devised logo was applied in the same yellow to the offside rear panel. RT 4495 stops at Watford Junction where the new LCBS logo can just be seen forming the lower part of the joint British Rail, Underground and London Country totem sign. Colin Brown

One vital aspect of both operations and engineering is the attitudes of the staff and their Trades Unions. Upon its inception London Country continued to honour all existing agreements currently in operation under LT. Staff conditions of service and rates of pay also continued unaltered and staff transferred into the new company retained their London Transport travel concessions, but new staff were given travel facilities on LCBS only. It is pleasant to record that the general level of understanding and co-operation was excellent over the period of the company's existence. Stoppages were limited to a few local disputes, but progress in improving working practices and removing out-dated restrictions was marked. Indeed, much of the success achieved in introducing new and improved services after

the 1980 Transport Act can be put down to the enthusiasm of drivers in gaining new passengers in the face of competition on coach services.

An extremely well produced in-house quarterly journal, *London Country Matters* in glossy A4 format, first appeared in June 1970. This publication provided topical articles, announcements from the management, details of and alterations to the fleet, staff appointments and retirements, historical articles and social news from the garages. After the 11th issue appeared at Christmas 1972 it was discontinued, with profuse apologies from the editors, to be replaced by a corporate NBC style publication of considerably reduced content. By this time the parent company was starting to inflict the corporate image with a vengeance!

However, returning to 1970, in the new Secretarial and Accounts Department at London Country, almost everything had to start from scratch. Just about the only separate section in London Transport which could be isolated easily was Traffic Audit which was responsible for the checking and analysis of all drivers' and conductors' waybills, vehicle log sheets and related revenue and mileage information. As previously stated support functions had to be established and new staff employed to administer them. Consequently the office accommodation at Reigate was too small to accommodate the additional staff and an early decision was taken to extend the premises. The original 1930s structure had a dead-end – awaiting possible extension and a new building was designed to complement and blend with the old. As an interim measure office space was rented in Redhill. This housed all the new staff of the secretarial function who gradually took over tasks performed by London Transport without loss of continuity.

The office extension began late in 1970 and was completed and occupied in March 1972. This brought the entire Head Office operation on to a single site for the first time, although some offices remained in use in the old East Surrey building on the corner of Bell Street and Lesbourne Road. The remainder of the buildings originally used by East Surrey in Bell Street were on a long lease to another company rendering them unavailable.

One of the areas of progress in the administration function was in the use of computer technology. The opening of the office extension saw the installation of a computer capable of carrying out many of the payrolls and audit functions. This was developed and updated over the years, although the direct management control passed from London Country to a new company (NBC Computer Services Ltd) created to manage all NBC computer facilities. More recently, microcomputers and other sophisticated computer-based technology enabled administrative savings to be made and efficiency to be improved.

Two members of the London Country Board of Directors were Mr Cyril Buckley, Managing Director, a man with wide experience in senior management positions within the BTC group, and Mr Geoffrey Fernyhough, General Manager, who had been

Operating Manager of the Country Buses and Coaches Department of London Transport prior to the split. The Chairman of the new company was Mr T.W.H. Gailey, C.B.E. who was also a member and chief executive of the NBC, his deputy was Mr J.T.E. Robinson who had been chairman of the working party set up to manage the take over of London Country. The remaining two members of the Board were Mr G.D. Neely and Mr G. McKay. All had a vast experience of the bus industry. Other senior managers were the Traffic Manager Mr Harry Adcock who, upon retirement in 1971, was superseded by Mr John Talbot from West Yorkshire, whilst the Chief Engineer was Mr

Len Stimpson, from London Transport. The Company Secretary, Mr Dennis Passmore came from BET Group company Devon General. Thus the team combined expertise from several sources. After Mr Fernyhough retired late in 1972 the post of General Manager was abolished. Mr Derek Fytche took over as Managing Director when Mr Buckley retired in 1976, and on promotion to Regional Director of the NBC in 1981, he was succeeded by Mr Colin Clubb. Such was the size and importance of London Country that the post of Managing Director was a very senior NBC position and Messrs Fytche and Clubb came with extensive experience in other Group Companies.

In October 1972 MB 91 was painted into the NBC corporate bus livery and RP 44 was chosen to appear in the NBC dual-purpose livery. Other buses soon followed suit as depicted *above right* **by MB 111 on the Dorking local route 449 and** *right* **RP 12 seen in Romford in March 1973 while working on cross-country route 724.** Capital Transport

As was previously explained, under London Transport the operational and engineering functions were managed quite separately and London Country inherited the following organisations.

The engineering function was divided into four districts:

South East:

Northfleet	Dartford
Swanley	Dunton Green
Chelsham	Godstone
East Grinstead	Reigate

South West:

Crawley	Dorking
Leatherhead	Guildford
Addlestone	Staines
Windsor	

North West:

Garston	Hemel Hempstead
Tring	Amersham
High Wycombe	

North East:

Romford	Grays
Harlow	Hertford
Stevenage	St Albans
Hatfield	Luton

The operating department was split into six districts:

South:

Reigate	Dorking	Godstone
East Grinstead	Crawley	
Leatherhead	Chelsham	

South East:

Northfleet	Grays	Dartford
Swanley	Dunton Green	

South West:

Windsor	Staines	Guildford
Addlestone	High Wycombe	

North West:

Garston	Hemel Hempstead	
Tring	Luton	Amersham
St Albans		

North East:

Hertford	Hatfield	Stevenage
Harlow	Romford	

Central: Based at Western House, Oxford Circus this district was responsible for the operation and control of Green Line services.

It will be observed that the allocation of garages to districts between the two

Attempts at a new image on Green Line had to be helped along by all that was available – bus-seated Leyland Nationals. They were not popular with coach passengers because of their spartan interiors. But, none-the-less, over a period of seven years London Country acquired no fewer than 543 of them in various guises, mostly employed on bus work. In fact London Country had the largest fleet in Britain, and possibly in the world. LNC 59 sits on Reigate garage forecourt in June 1974. The London Country polo has been replaced by the NBC corporate red and blue » within the polo silhouette. *Colin Brown*

departments varied which could cause problems in liaison. At some garages, mostly the smaller ones, a friendly atmosphere prevailed amongst all staff but at other garages the traditional LT *us and them* culture continued to apply between the two departments.

The operating organisation changed considerably over the years to reflect a reduction in staff numbers and eventually of the garages. Significant changes were the abolition of the South Area from 30th December 1973 and the subsequent abolition of the Central Area. To achieve a more co-

Support the Flowers in the City Campaign

The modern coaching image came in 1973 in the form of five luxury coaches with Plaxton bodywork in the all-white National livery which incorporated the London Country fleetname. In 1976 they were numbered (without class prefix) 1–5, but a year later they gained the P class letter. Un-numbered **SPK 204M** is seen on private hire work at Ludgate Circus passing under the railway bridge which was subsequently removed as part of the Thameslink scheme. Mike Harris

ordinated approach where Area Manager and Area Engineer shared offices and worked together with the aim of providing the best possible service to the customer a major change took place in 1978. In April the existing grades Charge Depot Inspector and Engineer In Charge were superseded by a Garage Traffic Superintendent and a Garage Engineering Superintendent respectively.

From 1st October the four districts were upgraded to the following areas:

South East:

Northfleet	Dartford
Swanley	Dunton Green
Chelsham	Grays

South West:

Reigate	Crawley
East Grinstead	Godstone
Dorking	Leatherhead
Guildford	Addlestone

North West:

Garston	Hemel Hempstead
Amersham	Staines
Windsor	

North East:

St Albans	Harlow
Hertford	Stevenage
Hatfield	

At headquarters a Field Operations Manager and a Field Operations Engineer were responsible for major matters of policy while each area was controlled by an Area Manager and Area Engineer who were responsible for all operations in their own area.

It took some very determined action in the late 1970s to achieve the turn-round in the fortunes of London Country, leading to the greatly improved performance following the vehicle and staff shortages of the mid-1970s. From being the *poor relation* in NBC, London Country became a consistent performer among the forerunners in operations and contributed a small pre-taxation profit from 1977 onwards.

A poster placing the changes at London Country Bus Services into a wider context.

The National Bus Company was formed when 54 bus companies all over Britain joined together

Chapter 2

AN AGEING FLEET IS INHERITED

Garston's RF 687 when photographed at Watford Junction in early London Country days was fairly typical of the fleet. The London Transport fleet name has been painted out but the bullseye on the front has yet to be tackled. RFs worked on the 385 group of routes on a Sunday instead of the RTs, which were used during the week – one of the last operating economies introduced by London Transport in 1969.
Colin Brown

T O THE average enthusiast, the Country Area fleet of London Transport at the end of the 1960s was a comfortable and familiar entity in an otherwise fast-changing scene. The RT type and RF type continued to dominate the fleet. More modern vehicles were represented in the form of just over 200 Routemaster types and some 14 RC coaches. Some of London Transport's new generation of buses in the form of 109 Merlins and a few rear-engined double deckers were allocated to the Country Area.

Those who delved more deeply observed that there was no place for complacency. Overhauls on Country stock in the past few years had been very much in decline, and indeed the last red RTs were now passing through Aldenham overhaul. The familiar spiral of rising costs and inflation was beginning to twist more tightly than ever, and Bus Grant had begun to influence operators in their selection of vehicles and in their policies of fleet replacement. Some noticed that more than 73 percent of the Country Area fleet dated from the 1950s and

even the late 1940s, while some 56 per cent of the entire fleet consisted of rear-entrance double deckers quite unsuited for one-man operation. The National Bus Company had a policy of a 12-year life for its fleet thus 925 vehicles inherited from London Transport exceeded this criterion. It must be remembered, however, that London Transport's system of overhauling meant that a completely reconditioned vehicle returned from Aldenham Works.

The engineering management of London Country found itself the inheritor of 1,267 vehicles from London Transport. By far the largest component in this total was the RT class with 484 representatives, and although many of the bonnet numbers in this series were relatively high, dating from the first half of the 1950s, some of the bodies were more than 20 years old. Sixteen of these RTs were in store at the time of transfer and were never to operate for LCBS. The next most numerous class was the RF, totalling 413 machines. The ordinary buses and unrefurbished Green Line vehicles demoted to bus work all dated from the early 1950s and

totalled 238 vehicles. Another 175 vehicles had been refurbished and modernised in the past five years in an attempt by London Transport to upgrade the Green Line image and were rather grandly regarded as coaches. Due to the rapid decline in the Green Line system in the late 1960s some 25 of these had already been demoted to bus usage and given yellow relief bands instead of the pastel green relief carried by the Green Line vehicles.

There were 209 Routemasters, most of them from the end of the production series; these consisted of 97 RMLs of 1965/6 vintage (there had been 100, but three of them had

Right **Inevitably the image of the new company was initially one of an elderly fleet – passengers probably did not realise that it was never the less more reliable than many of the new buses that were to come. Seventy per cent of the fleet was made up of the RT and RF classes, the newest already 16 years old. RT 620 was one of twenty eight RTs to appear in Green Line livery in 1960 to undertake relief duties across the network and was one of twenty to remain in this livery until November 1969, when they were given London Transport fleet names and were fitted with adverts. Seen at West Croydon Bus Station in May 1970 this bus now carries the second new fleet name – the short-lived London Country gold version – to be applied within six months. The light green relief band is still carried, together with London Transport advertisements for Green Rover tickets.** Colin Brown

Centre right **Swanley's RT 4099 stands at Chelsfield Five Bells terminus on 13th June 1970 while working on the busy cross country route 477. On Saturdays and Sundays Chelsfield received a regular service through to Dartford, but on Mondays to Fridays saw only irregular shuttles to Orpington Station. A new side advertisement for Green Rover tickets which contains the new London Country logo has been fixed but the rear panels still feature the LT bullseye. There were a number of different blind displays to cover short workings on the 477, but the conductor has correctly set the side and rear panels to show the appropriate points for the through run. In 1967 London Transport had started to introduce just whole route numbers on the rear blinds of RTs and RMLs on a progressive basis as service revisions necessitated new blinds but, by 1970, some garages were yet to be so equipped. Swanley's RTs finally received them in 1971.** John Bull

Below left **One hundred RMLs were introduced into the LT Country Area in 1965/6 on to some of the busier RT routes which, in some cases, enabled the number of buses required to be reduced through headway reductions. In addition to trunk routes they also worked on busy town services as, at the time of their introduction, high capacity single-deckers with automated fare collection methods were in the future. Three of the RMLs returned to LT in exchange for three XAs required in consequence of the Blue Arrow introduction. RML 2421 is seen at Watford in 1971.** Capital Transport

Below right **The long established practice of using a Green Line coach which would not be required until after 9am to perform bus work during the morning peak period continued under London Country. RMC 1456 is captured in April 1970 at Windsor garage performing a journey to Datchet on the normally RF worked route 445 before finding its way on to the 718 for the somewhat longer run.** Colin Brown

Above **MB 88, seen at East Grinstead, was one of a batch of 33 conventional one-man-operated buses introduced by LT to the Country Area from 1968 on some of the busier RF routes and on some of the less well used RT routes. They were spread somewhat thinly across the network and route 434 (Edenbridge – Horsham) was only partially converted from RF. The first 150 Merlins had low driving positions which may be determined by the position of the driver's signalling window and the height of the steering column.** Mike Harris

Above right **Route 430 was the first Autofare standee route to be introduced in the Country Area on 23rd November 1968. While the concept of high capacity standee single-deck operation may have been acceptable to central London commuters it was completely unacceptable to the shoppers, mothers with children and the elderly who formed a large proportion of passengers using Country Area MBS routes. Problems with the ticket issuing equipment were resolved in February 1971 when the buses were worked as conventional omo following decimalisation of the currency. But the minimal seating, high steps,**

problems and driver disputes over the use of the centre exit doors caused the buses to be extremely unpopular with the travelling public, who saw them as grossly inferior to the conventional buses that they had displaced. Passengers dubbed them 'cattletrucks' – a sobriquet that they justly deserved. The 36ft length made the buses unwieldy for traversing the many narrow roads through the housing estates that they served. High driving position MBS 420 was one of 75 of these buses that were inflicted on various town routes across the network. Steve Fennell

been moved back to the Central Area by London Transport in November 1969 in exchange for Leyland Atlanteans). The Green Line Routemaster fleet comprised of 43 RCLs dating from 1965 and sixty-eight RMCs dating from 1962, some of which had been demoted to bus work in 1969. The remaining vehicle was the venerable RMC 4, the only one of the four Routemaster prototypes still in service, which had Leyland units and an Eastern Coach Works body.

Recent modernisation was represented by 109 Merlin vehicles based on the AEC Swift chassis. One of these, XMB 15, had been one of the prototype vehicles delivered in 1966, the fortunes of which had already been remarkably volatile; it led a quiet existence on the fringe of the Country Area at Tring working route 387. Thirty-three of the Merlins formed the MB class, an orthodox attempt to form a standard vehicle for rural routes with the passengers seated, and 75 vehicles were classified MBS for town routes

in which a maximum loading was achieved by requiring most of the passengers to stand.

With all of these vehicles the evidence was of the renowned London Transport aims to achieve a high degree of standardisation. The RT and the Routemasters were probably the epitome of fleet standardisation on a worldwide basis, whilst the Merlins were certainly envisaged as being the future generation of standard vehicles at the time they were ordered, though events were to prove otherwise for London Transport. The sad fact, as far as London Country's new man-

agement was bound to be concerned, was that the standardisation was generally accompanied by high age and by unsuitability for the requirements of the 1970s.

The rest of the London Transport bequest was made up of five small classes. Most senior of these were the RLH vehicles, seventeen lowbridge double deckers used on routes in the Walton – Staines – Woking – Guildford corridor, dating from the early 1950s and claiming some affinity with the RT class, mechanically at least. Their life expectancy was already known to be highly

The only scheduled GS worked route was the 336A which linked Loudwater Estate with Rickmansworth. GS 17 is captured laying over at Rickmansworth Station. The bus was outstationed at Loudwater and worked exclusively by Driver Harry Cross who lived locally. Under arrangements established in London Transport days, Driver Cross paid in his takings to Rickmansworth Station booking office and visited Garston Garage on a Friday for his bus to be re-fuelled or substituted and, more importantly, to draw his wages. When Harry retired in 1971 he was presented with a cheque from grateful passengers. Until withdrawal of the route in March 1972, the bus was no longer outstationed. Barry LeJeune

limited, and they were to pass out of the fleet with little ceremony. Next, and probably most quaint, were the GS single deckers, the so-called Guy Special based on the Guy Otter chassis with Eastern Coach Works 26-seat bodies for use on sparsely-trafficked rural routes or those with physical restrictions. Dating from 1953 (there had been others built in 1954, but these did not pass to London Country), there were ten survivors from the original 84; five others remained with London Transport as staff transport vehicles for a little while. Of these ten, seven never ran in public service for London Country, the only requirement for their use being the Loudwater Village outstation near Rickmansworth on route 336A; GS 64 had been in store since May 1967.

The RC class comprised fourteen AEC Reliance vehicles with Willowbrook dual purpose bodies introduced in 1965 for trials in respect of future Green Line stock; but due to various problems these vehicles had mostly been placed into store and only two were in use as late running stand-by coaches for the 727 service. Finally, eight Daimler Fleetlines formed the XF class and three Leyland Atlanteans were transferred from London Transport's XA class. The Fleetlines and Atlanteans had both been new in 1965 (although the Atlanteans had not been licensed until 1966) for experimental purposes to assess London Transport's future requirements of double-deck fleet. The eight Fleetlines had generally been based at East Grinstead for the 424 route, although there had been times when they had been exchanged with the Central Area. They appeared to have come better out of the comparative trials with the Atlanteans, as Fleetlines were to be ordered to a total of 2,646 vehicles by London Transport in the following years, whilst the Atlanteans were

discarded at a relatively early juncture. Towards the end of 1969, three of the Fleetlines had been repainted into a special livery for the new *Blue Arrow* service in the expanding town of Stevenage, and were replaced at East Grinstead by three XAs from LT who received three RMLs in exchange.

Additionally, 12 service vehicles were taken over from London Transport, the longest-lived being four tree-loppers that lasted until summer 1979. The Ford marque was largely continued in the fleet, with nearly all purchases in subsequent years being from that manufacturer.

The RC coaches went on to the busy cross-country route 727 in early London Country days. RC 10, still retaining signs of its former ownership, is seen at Watford Junction forecourt. At this time the stop was under the station entrance canopy and the coaches were obliged to compete for space with taxis and private cars but later a dedicated slip road made life a little easier for the coach drivers. Colin Brown

At last legislation permitted one-man-operation of double-deck buses on ordinary stage services. London Country's first such operation was to use the existing crew-worked XA and XF buses on route 424 for omo, from 27th June 1970. XA 48 is seen in Bancroft Road, Reigate shortly after the conversion and is doing good business. Barry LeJeune

RT 4789 stands at the Tilbury Riverside terminus of route 370, where connections could be made by the ferry to Gravesend. The two centre side panels have been completely repainted and the new gold fleetname applied, together with the company's legal lettering. The 370 was a frequently running trunk route linking Tilbury with Grays and Romford, but the conductor has not set the side blind correctly, allowing rather more of the 369 route display to be visible. Barry LeJeune

Not all that was green became London Country property. Twenty-one green RTs and five GSs remained owned by London Transport after the handover; these were used as staff buses to and from the LT works at Chiswick and Aldenham, although most of them were outstationed at London Country garages. There were also a few red vehicles used in this way, which presented an interesting sight when parked in LCBS garages at weekends. Conversely, London Country inherited the practice of keeping two vehicles in central area garages as spares to cover Green Line breakdowns or emergencies, and so an RMC remained outstationed at Riverside garage and an RF at Victoria garage. Later in 1970 specific vehicle identities for these were dropped, and any suitable vehicle from, respectively, Guildford and Hemel Hempstead became used.

Finally, traffic requirements towards the end of 1969 had shown need for more RFs in the erstwhile Country Area than were available, and so five red RFs were operated in the Country Area at a variety of garages. These passed on hire to London Country at 1st January 1970 and remained in use for some while until replacements were to hand: RFs 325, 341, 374 and 388 were used until 20th February 1971 and RF 393 until 24th November 1970.

The livery of the green vehicles taken over by London Country was perpetuated although the block-lettered fleetname LONDON COUNTRY soon appeared on many vehicles. More as a gesture to the new regime, RT 4742 at Garston garage gained the new fleetname on 1st January 1970 itself, and sported the new title in gold lettering. However it soon became apparent that the decision had been taken to adopt a bright yellow relief in place of the cream or pale green inherited from London Transport, so far as the bus fleet was concerned. The yellow colour soon spread to the fleetname and yellow transfers supplanted the gold. Fleet numbers were not exempt and yellow numbers soon appeared, in a new style of typeface. Fleet identity was further enhanced from mid-1970 by the use of the new company symbol, the ring-and-bars motif, said to symbolise the green fields encircling London, but soon rather unkindly dubbed the *Flying Polo-mint* or the *Flying Bat*. It was, however, decided that vehicles destined for early withdrawal would continue to wear the cream relief. By the end of the first year of the new ownership many vehicles had received London Country *dress*, giving rise to various combinations of LT Country livery with the new order. Nevertheless, it was some time before all traces of, say, the cream-band relief, disappeared altogether.

As will be described later, it took quite some time to transform the fleet from the London Transport standard with a vast amount of crew operation into a *National* standard with 100 per cent one-person operation. Dates for the last passenger operation of the ex-LT classes may be of interest at this juncture. First to go was the RLH, in July 1970, followed by GS (March 1972), XA (January 1973), RC (January 1977), RT (June 1978), RCL (January 1979), RF (October 1979), MB and RML (February 1980), RMC (March 1980), MBS (November 1980) and, finally, the XF at the end of December 1981. Even one or two classes new to London Country since formation were to fall by the wayside, but by the end of 1981 the Company had removed all influence of its London Transport vehicle ancestry with the exception of two historical vehicles (RMC 4 and RF 202) kept for special purposes.

If it seems unkind to suggest that the Broadway powers had allowed the Country fleet to be in a run-down condition at the time of handover to the National Bus Company, the record is mitigated to a degree by the fact that 138 vehicles were on order for the Country Area at the time of handover and these orders passed to London Country. They were for the 33ft 5ins version of the AEC Swift, which had been adopted by London Transport as a more manoeuvrable bus for London requirements than the 36ft variety. Deliveries of the type had recently commenced to London Transport as the SM and SMS classes (respectively to a generally-seated or generally-standing layout) and the Country vehicles had been pencilled in as numbers 101 to 148 with Park Royal bodywork and 449 to 538 with Metro-Cammell bodywork. These were intended to allow the withdrawal of the RLH class and the earnest start of RT withdrawals. Exactly how matters would have progressed from this point onwards had Broadway remained in charge of the Country fleet is one of those pleasant points which will always be a subject for debate. Following Trade Union acceptance of the Phelps-Brown Report in 1964 London Transport produced a projection of its fleet in 1974. In the Country area the main change was that all RTs would have been replaced by FRMs (Front Entrance Routemasters), but in the event only the prototype was to be built. London Country had its own immediate answer to surprise the pundits when an order was placed for 90 Leyland Atlantean double deckers with Park Royal bodywork, and for 90 AEC Reliance

Green Line vehicles, also with Park Royal bodywork. The irony that the red fleet had chosen the Daimler Fleetline and the green fleet the Leyland Atlantean, the exact reverse of the XA/XF comparison trials, was one of the first piquancies to sink in.

The seriousness with which the need to update the London Country fleet was felt is realised when it is considered that these orders called for 318 vehicles to be delivered in just over a year. (In the event other factors were to intervene and delivery would take rather longer.) Counting the five red RFs on loan to London Country, these orders would, on a one-for-one basis, enable the replacement of exactly one quarter of the fleet. As if to stress the point, a number of public mentions were made of the need to update the fleet.

But Rome was not built in a day, and London Country could not be built in a year. Amongst the problems faced by the company was that there was no Central Works at which vehicles could be overhauled or given major maintenance; nor, at the time, was there any overhaul programme to keep the older members of the fleet in serviceable

condition until replacements arrived. For several years, London Country had to rely on London Transport facilities for the overhaul of vehicles, and during the first few years a great deal of work was farmed out to contractors and to other NBC subsidiaries. This problem was to be gravely accentuated by a nationwide shortage of spare parts and replacements in 1973/74 which, worse, happened to afflict particularly the types of vehicle then operated by London Country.

The immediate programme envisaged the replacement of RLH and RT vehicles, with the added attraction that the intake of vehicles would be suitable for one-man operation, the sacred cow of the NBC at this time. In itself, this aim meant that the elderly RF class, suitable for one-man use (if not to entirely modern standards), would have to remain in service for a few more years; and so an overhaul programme for RFs was immediately put in hand. Most of the Green Line RF fleet was to receive a full Aldenham overhaul over the next two years, these vehicles being selected because they were already in relatively good condition as a result of being refurbished in the later

1960s. They would then last until the second half of the decade, whilst it should be possible to withdraw the unmodified examples somewhat earlier.

Even by mid-1970 it was clear that the vehicle replacement programme was not likely to be enacted as rapidly as had been hoped, and that more life would be needed from the veterans of the fleet. Accordingly a programme started in July 1970 for a number of RTs to receive attention at Aldenham. Officially classified as a repaint, this process nonetheless involved relatively substantial attention to the bodywork of

The first of the class to be re-painted was RT 613 in August 1970 in the pleasing Lincoln green and Canary yellow livery with yellow fleetname and number. Some of the RTs in this livery ran without adverts and very attractive they looked! RT 4755 stands in the Wood Street yard at Kingston in summer 1971 displaying the new livery and contrasting with the equally clean London Transport and British Rail liveries behind. The London Country 'Flying Polo' logo was to prove to be short-lived when the parent company, the National Bus Company, began to flex its corporate muscle. Colin Brown

many vehicles, tantamount to light overhaul. Both in the case of the RF and RT vehicles visiting Aldenham, however, body exchange at overhaul under the London Transport *works float* system was not permissible, as the enabling legislation covered only vehicles owned by London Transport themselves, and so vehicles retained the same combination of chassis and body. Officially the components were not separated, although it has been established that this did occur in a number of instances. Even this programme was not sufficient, and following another forward projection of requirements it was decided that full overhauls of selected RTs would be necessary, the programme being upgraded suitably from January 1971.

At the start of 1971 the RCL class became due for overhaul, and these were all dealt with, implying the retention of the Routemasters until late in the decade at least. Since the Reliances ordered for the Green Line fleet were clearly intended to replace the RMCs and RCLs and to enable one-man operation, the further corollary was that the displaced coaches would be used to assist the withdrawal of the RTs. This forecast proved to be accurate although the new coaches took rather longer to arrive than expected.

Meanwhile, deliveries of the Swifts ordered by London Transport for the former Country Area commenced in May 1970, though as the vehicles had been ordered by LT they were all to be delivered to Aldenham and checked over by London Transport prior to being passed to London Country. This was a process which was to delay the commissioning of several vehicles later in the series. Although originally intended to be classified SMS, London Country took an early decision that the vehicles would be operated as the SM class. First to arrive were those bodied by Park Royal; these became SMs 101–148 and were 38-seaters. Following shortly were SMs 449–538, bodied by Metro-Cammell-Weymann as 41-seaters. At about this time agreement was reached with the road staff to carry 56 passengers on all Merlins and Swifts, the balance beyond the seated capacity to be standees. In June 1971 this agreement was further revised to 60 passengers on single deckers and 80 on double deckers.

As expected, a notable effect of the SM arrivals was that the RLH class was taken out of traffic, the last being RLH 35 into Addlestone garage at 2309 hours on 31st July 1970. Fifteen of the class were sold to a dealer early in 1971; another passed to a Reigate scout group at the end of 1970 as a direct sale, and the residual RLH 44 was converted into a uniform clothing store and issuing unit, carrying on in this role until 1982. However, the first SMs had gone to Leatherhead garage in June 1970 and had enabled a small start to be made on RT withdrawals, which gathered momentum during the next months. One unscheduled withdrawal occurred when MB 101 was burnt out in a fire while on service 318 at Chipperfield on 25th September 1970. By the end of 1970 44 of the 48 SMs had been placed in service, four at the end of the Park Royal order having being stored. More than half of the Metro-Cammell order had also arrived at Aldenham, although few had been accepted into London Country stock and these were all in store.

Nevertheless, between February and July 1971 the second batch of SMs all entered service, and the RT fleet began to sustain major losses; many were put up for disposal, dealers eagerly snapping them up. Although the original London Country intention was to follow London Transport practice by introducing type conversion on a pre-determined date, it was necessary to bring in new vehicles ahead of the date in order to relieve vehicle shortages, of the type being replaced. This resulted in many SM vehicles being crew operated for a while before the official conversion date. In this, as in many other ways, the London Transport culture was gradually being replaced by London Country's own way of doing things, another reflection of which was the gradual removal of the decorative hub-caps from RTs, RFs and Routemasters. A modest start had been made on the actual updating of the fleet, and there was an impressive order book for vehicles still to come. It was very much a case of the lull before the storm.

The *Blue Arrow* service at Stevenage had produced an impetus to look more closely at future service patterns in this New Town, and a joint working party had already been set up by London Country and the Stevenage Development Corporation. A pointer to future developments occurred at the end of October 1970 when an early model Metro-Scania single decker, WOE498J, was used in Stevenage. Followed during the first week of November by the demonstrator VWD451H, which had already been used by London Transport. Both vehicles were offered for the public to ride on and to give their comments. As a result of these trials two vehicles were delivered during the summer of 1971 and placed in service alongside SM vehicles on what were by then being marketed as *Superbus* services in Stevenage, bearing a distinctive blue and yellow livery. This in turn was evolved after a curious experiment early in 1971 when SM 144 was painted with yellow roof and lower panels, with the window surrounds area in Lincoln green to the front and nearside, and in royal blue on the rear and offside. Various other SMs later gained full *Superbus* livery as services expanded.

As an indication of trains of thought towards the orthodox single deck stage service where Swifts might not be suitable, a brand new Ford R1014 with Plaxton bodywork intended for Midland Red (YHA320J) was inspected at Reigate during November 1970 before being delivered to its owner. This line of thought was not however pursued.

The first class of vehicle to be completely withdrawn was the RLH (referred to by staff as 'Lowloaders'), being replaced by new one-man single-decker SMs from 1st August 1970. Seventeen RLHs ran for London Country and they at least had time to gain their new gold fleetnames before withdrawal. They were required for routes 436/A, 461, and 463 and were based at both Addlestone and Guildford garages, but the complexities of interworking meant that they were also scheduled to work routes approved for RT operation. RLH 32 performing duty WY32 is seen at West Byfleet Station on the short 420 route to Woking. Geoff Rixon

With the amount of single-deck work across the fleet increasing the number of front destination blinds needed to accommodate all routes and terminals increased too. (Hertford garage had no fewer than eight different front RF blinds). This caused problems when vehicles were substituted, since the blind had to be replaced as well. By reducing the size of the area displayed more routes could be added to a blind, albeit sometimes by reducing the intermediate point information. Amersham was the first garage to be so equipped, from 20th February 1971, as demonstrated by immaculately turned out RF 553 at Rickmansworth Station. RF 553 had received body 8706 from former Green Line RF 310 in London Transport days, which explains the side route board brackets. *Colin Brown*

SM 144, used in the livery experiment at Stevenage, was joined by SM 143 transferred from Guildford and SMs 146/7/8 from storage, and after rumours as to their intended use they were put into service at Crawley in April 1971 on routes which had been taken over by London Country from Southdown. This was the first of a number of schemes during the 1970s under which the *Polo mint* area of London Country operation was integrated with neighbouring NBC operators. The original plans had involved the hire of five Bristol RELL6G vehicles from Southdown to operate the services, but this did not materialise, although a Southdown Leyland Leopard coach, 2716CD, was hired for the summer to operate private hire and excursion work from Crawley.

The year 1971 was one in which many NBC subsidiaries were forced to face a serious decline in traffic and London Country was, of course, not exempt from this. At the same time, the recent introduction of Bus Grant coupled with a need to place vehicle orders some time ahead of requirement meant that a number of companies found themselves embarrassed by having ordered vehicles for which they no longer had a need. So considerable had been the upsurge in orders caused by Bus Grant that a roll-on effect had produced the need to predict vehicle requirements two to three years ahead. This had already made itself felt in the delays caused to the orders placed by London Country at the start of 1970 and many companies were feverishly attempting to divert or delay their earlier orders. The

The Stevenage Superbus service to Chells, formerly part of route 809, commenced on 31st July 1971 using Metro-Scanias and SMs wearing a yellow and blue livery for use on this service. MS 2 *centre right* and SM 496 *right* are both seen at Stevenage Bus Station shortly after the introduction of the Superbus service. *Colin Brown*

The three Willowbrook-bodied Swifts stayed at Crawley all their working lives as did the Marshall-bodied vehicles at St Albans. SMW 3 is at Crawley Bus Station on one of the ex-Southdown routes. While the three Crawley buses received NBC livery very early in their careers, London Country's attractive Lincoln green and Canary yellow adorned the St Albans buses a while longer. The aluminium beading and AEC badges gave a nice finishing touch to members of the SMW class, but the beading was painted over in later years, the badges lost and, on the Marshall buses, sliding vents replaced some of the fixed windows following passenger complaints of stuffy interiors. SMW 3 shows the initial method employed by the company for coping with the difficulties of suffix letters. *Barry LeJeune*

Below **The light green livery first appeared on double-deckers with the delivery of the AF class, at the beginning of 1972, with the yellow extended to the area surrounding the lower deck windows. By now the fleetnames, fleet numbers and company logo were applied in yellow on practically all members of the company's fleet. AF 8 is seen at Godstone, the home of the class for its entire ten years or so of service, on its principal operation over that period, route 410. The wooden bus shelter, complete with its enamel-iron sign was typical of the rural area, a legacy from London Transport days.** Colin Brown

particular position of London Country, with a notably ancient fleet and a strong case for vehicle replacements, was to turn to its immediate advantage. Following a series of negotiations a further 77 vehicles were brought into the London Country fleet as surplus to the orders already placed by other NBC subsidiaries. Most of these were delivered direct to London Country.

First of these to be announced were 21 AEC Swift chassis with Alexander bodywork which were surplus to the orders of South Wales Transport. To dual-purpose specification within the established W-type body shell, these would provide useful updating to the Green Line fleet and enable some of the RFs to be withdrawn. South Wales Transport had also received fifteen AEC

One Strachan-bodied Merlin had been inherited from LT and in July 1971 it was re-classified from XMB 15 to MBS 15, staying at Tring to work the local route 387 where it was known by staff and passengers alike as the 'Yellow Peril'. Tring Station is two miles from the town and, since LNWR days, there has been been a local link connecting the two points. *Colin Brown*

Swifts with bus bodywork, three dating from 1969 and twelve in course of delivery, which were no longer required. The three 1969 vehicles, carrying Willowbrook bodywork, were taken out of service, and arrived with London Country between June and August 1971. The twelve new vehicles with Marshall bodies never entered service with South Wales (although they had been registered) and after repainting by the Bristol Omnibus Company, they were brought to Reigate which was now being used as a focal point for new vehicle deliveries. It should be noted, however that prior to the end of 1972 other sites were also used for vehicle acceptance. All 15 of these Swifts became the SMW class, the first three entering service at Crawley from 25th September 1971 and the other 12 gradually at St Albans from 2nd October 1971; they remained at these garages throughout their careers. The 21 Alexander bodied vehicles, designated as the SMA class, were not to arrive until the start of 1972.

Next to be announced were 11 Daimler Fleetlines with Northern Counties bodywork which were no longer needed by Western Welsh. Although London Country had shown its preference for Leyland Atlanteans in the orders which had been placed, these Fleetlines would at least have Leyland engines and so were acceptable. These too were not expected to be delivered until early in 1972, when they materialised as the AF class (although originally intended to be DF).

Midland Red was another company with a surplus of orders, which included 50 Leyland Atlanteans to be bodied by Metro-Cammell. Arrangements were made for them to be split between Maidstone & District (who took 20 of them) and London Country when they arrived in 1972.

The NBC in conjunction with British Leyland had meanwhile been progressing development work on the Leyland National single decker, and when orders for 1972 deliveries were announced during the preceding year, London Country was allotted 70 vehicles. This brought London Country's foreseeable vehicle intake to 327 vehicles in mid-1971, with 140 vehicles already delivered since formation.

Returning to the inherited fleet, in the interests of tidiness, the experimental Merlin XMB 15 was renumbered MBS 15 during July 1971, and a programme was completed to upseat the MBS vehicles to 33 seats following the removal of their Autofare ticket machines after decimalisation of the currency. Some of the last SMs going into service at Dunton Green in summer 1971 had replaced RFs as well as RTs and several surplus RFs were bought by Halls of Hounslow for work at Heathrow Airport. However, initial eagerness by dealers to buy RTs was waning, the market for these reliable machines now being saturated by newer examples of the type released by London Transport, who were also enthusiastically pursuing a one-man conversion programme. A further fire loss was RC 11, which caught fire at Kingswood on 16th August 1971. The type had continued to be problematic after being re-introduced to service on the 711 in October 1970 and later in August 1971 the survivors returned to the 727 route. Due to the difficulties encountered with this type they continued to necessitate spare vehicles being at hand which could have been better used elsewhere. The impending expiry of certificates of fitness led to the start of an overhaul programme on the RC class from September 1971. Further reductions in Green Line requirements meant that more refurbished RFs could be downgraded to bus work, in turn enabling some of the older RFs to be taken out of traffic. The small GS class finally ceased to operate on 30th March 1972 when GS 42, duplicated by GS 33 owing to many enthusiasts being in attendance, operated the last journey on route 336A. The GSs were not replaced and Loudwater Village, where one bus had been outstationed until its regular driver retired in 1971, never again saw a bus service.

During the autumn of 1971 the SMW class entered service as described earlier, and in November the RPs started to arrive. An initial allocation was made to the 727 route in December 1971, followed by many other Green Line routes during the first half of 1972, and RCLs and RMCs were displaced as expected to ordinary bus services, enabling RTs to be withdrawn. By this process all double deck work on Green Line service ceased except for three vehicles on route 709. From January 1972 the SMA class commenced delivery, and these vehicles replaced RFs on the 725 service between Gravesend and Windsor via Bromley, Croydon and Kingston. The pace was now hotting-up, and a further two Metro-Scania single deckers were delivered during March 1972 for use at Stevenage.

The AF class arrived during January and was put into use at Godstone during February 1972, displacing RMLs which in turn consigned further RTs to oblivion. By the summer of 1972 large numbers of RTs

Left **A total of 120 Atlantean double-deckers were delivered in 1972 as the AN class and all but one (AN 90) came in the new style of double-deck livery. It was lucky that they all came during 1972 since, towards the end of that year, the all-over drab green NBC livery was about to be launched, making these the last new buses to receive London Country's own individual livery. Obviously, it would have been wasteful to re-paint such new buses and they therefore carried this superb paint scheme well into the late 1970s. Park Royal bodied AN 34 was one of a batch sent to Guildford for the 17th July conversion of routes 408/A and 470 and is seen loading up in Commercial Road Guildford while working the local 408A.** Barry LeJeune

Below left **The last 30 of the batch of ANs were bodied by Metro-Cammell – try to spot the many detail differences in the front end styling from the Park Royal example shown above. It was found impracticable to fit fare boxes to the *Met-Cam* buses, thus a grand switch round took place. AN 110, seen at Uxbridge Station, was one such bus transferred to Luton to enable an earlier Park Royal bodied bus to be fare box fitted. At the time of the Garston/Luton AN conversion Aldenham Works had too much work in hand to manufacture the blinds, thus all ANs received route number and intermediate blinds made by ECO – the give-away was the rounded 3s – whilst retaining RT destination blinds. One of the disadvantages with omo is demonstrated here, as passengers were denied the convenience of boarding on the stand and were obliged to wait by the ever-closed doors in all weathers.** Colin Brown

were being assembled for sale, and also a small number of RFs had been sold. At this stage, however, withdrawals of RFs was slower as the need began to develop to retain them in order to cover early difficulties with the newer single deckers. The 90 Leyland Atlanteans, classified AN, also commenced delivery from March 1972 and their introduction throughout the system contributed to the rapid disappearance of the RT, both by direct and indirect replacements.

Meanwhile the *Blue Arrow* XFs had been taken off service from 11th March 1972 as

the *Blue Arrow* concept was incorporated into the *Superbus* network, and these vehicles served as a float during the overhaul of the XF class. April 1972 had seen the emergence of National green corporate colour and of the new NBC symbol to replace the individual LCBS symbol, and from October 1972 London Country had to submit to white as the relief colour on its vehicles in place of the bright canary yellow. XF 7 emerged from overhaul as one of the first LCBS vehicles to be seen in the new corporate colours. Subsequent repaints of all

classes also gained NBC *leaf* green and white, but it was to be some years before the attractive *Lincoln* green with yellow relief finally disappeared. The last examples to carry this livery were SM 514 and SM 517 at Dartford, both doing so until December 1980.

General vehicle shortages which arose from difficulties with supplies of spare parts had during 1972 begun to afflict London Transport to a serious extent, and the apparent carefree abandonment of RTs a year earlier had led to a situation in which there were not enough RTs to support requirements. In a surprise move, 34 of the RTs withdrawn by London Country passed back to their original owner in September 1972, and were hurriedly repainted red and pressed into service. Two of them were amongst the final allocation when RTs came out of London Transport service at Barking in April 1979.

The autumn of 1972 saw the arrival of the 30 Atlanteans diverted from Midland Red, which pushed further RTs towards withdrawal, but most attention was poised for the 70 Leyland Nationals which were on order. Intentions for the use of these vehicles changed several times. The first two, pre-production vehicles, had arrived in the spring of 1972 and had always been intended for use at Stevenage on Superbus services, but they had several trips to and from the manufacturers before entering service in September 1972. The remainder had been due to go into Green Line service, so that in conjunction with the RPs and SMAs the Green Line network would have been completely updated, and earlier plans envisaged

Eastern Coach Works finishing the Leyland National shells to a Green Line specification. However, this plan fell by the wayside, as did a further plan for vehicles to be painted in two shades of green, and all 68 remaining vehicles appeared to the rather stark standard bus specification. This had been determined by higher powers, 21 vehicles (up to LN 23 with the original two) having dual-door bodywork and the rest being single-door. LN 3 and LN 4 found themselves diverted onto Superbus work and LNs 5 to 23 were set aside for bus work at Hatfield

and Dunton Green (after further delays whilst routes were surveyed for acceptance). Plans were made for the next 47 to be classified LNC and used on Green Line service but in the event were subject to change. Indeed throughout their career with London Country there had always been allocation problems due to their length and, as a result, no more of the long version were ever bought as new. LNs 8, 9, 10 and 11 were delivered direct to Nottingham City Transport, who borrowed them for use on a trial *park-and-ride* type service and they were to provide

further surprises in 1973. It was decided that twelve of the LNCs were, after all, to be used on ordinary bus services and even this figure was increased to thirteen. The Company was obviously viewing with some dismay their starkness of interior, a view that was to be shared by the luckless passengers who had to travel on the LNCs on the Green Line routes they worked. It was July 1973 before the order of 70 was complete, and September before all the vehicles had entered service (excepting LNB 70 in February 1974), those used as buses being classified LNB.

Above **During 1972 the three Blue Arrow XFs were overhauled and repainted for return to normal service at East Grinstead. XF 6 and XF 8 (seen here at Dormansland) received the then current LCBS light green and yellow, but XF 7, the last of the three to be repainted, emerged in the new standard NBC Leaf Green with white relief.** Mike Harris

Right **When RMCs were first scheduled for bus work under London Transport, all retained Green Line livery and, as they were all based at garages that also operated the type on Green Line duties, were interchangeable. Once they were all displaced from Green Line work in 1972 they gradually acquired the bus livery of Canary Yellow bands and the London Country fleetname. The prototype vehicle RMC 4 worked alongside the production batch and had a long association with Hatfield Garage, first going there in 1966. The non-opening upper-deck front windows and the three-piece blind layout identified the odd man out. The bus has just set down some passengers at Robins Nest Hill between Hertford and Essendon Corner while working on route 341.** Capital Transport

Chapter 3

THE NATIONAL ADVANCES

A T THE START of 1973 London Country held a total of 1,215 vehicles in stock, of which 422 had been delivered since the split from London Transport, the RT class had been halved, the RF class was being reduced and the RLH and GS types had been eliminated. The first production batch of Leyland Nationals was in course of delivery and a further order for another 77 was expected later in the year. There were also 23 Bristol LHSs with 35-seat Eastern Coach Works bodies on order and these, together with the Nationals, would of course make substantial inroads into the RF fleet. To enhance the coaching side of the business now being built up, five luxury coaches on AEC Reliance chassis with Plaxton full-coach 51-seat bodies (modified to 49-seaters by the Company) were on order for 1973.

Progress was however to be seriously disrupted by continuing difficulties with spare parts and with the performance of Swifts, Merlins and earlier Reliances. The temporary delicensing of such vehicles began to feature with increasing prominence in the monthly details of vehicle movements, and RFs and RTs which were being replaced by new vehicles found themselves pressed into use to cover shortages with newer classes. Nor was this a problem confined to London Country, and four RTs found themselves hired, on a rotation basis, to Alder Valley between May and November 1973 to assist with difficulties there. The irony was not lost that it was the yeoman warriors inherited from London Transport which helped to save the day during the next two years – a great credit to the London Transport overhauling system. As well as inhibiting normal operations, the vehicle shortages had the inciden-

tal effect of disrupting and substantially delaying programmes to repaint vehicles into the newly-dictated NBC house liveries – a situation in which regret was not evident.

Early in 1973 London Transport had made arrangements to sell their 47 XA (Leyland Atlantean) vehicles to China Motor Bus, having experienced continuing problems with the type in central London service. After several denials, London Country took its own three XAs out of

service on 31st January 1973 and these were re-united with their comrades and sold to the same customer in April 1973, an order being immediately placed for three new Atlanteans to replace them. Another LT-derived class thus disappeared. The 50 were to see around eight years of intensive service on some of the busiest services on Hong Kong Island.

Once again the specification for the Leyland National order was the subject of

Above right **The first of 543 Leyland Nationals to be owned by London Country went into Superbus service in September 1972 at Stevenage. LN 1, the first of the dynasty, is in the attractive blue and yellow Superbus livery.** Mike Harris

Right **Three more Atlanteans had been ordered to replace the XAs sold in 1973 – they finally arrived at East Grinstead in the summer of 1974 where they remained until the garage closed 7½ years later. They were Park Royal bodied like most of the 1972 AN delivery, but the most noticeable difference to the passenger was in the positioning of the offside staircase, which was further forward than on the earlier buses. They were the first London Country double deckers with three track number blinds. AN 123 is seen here at Horley.** Colin Brown

much adjustment. Originally for 34 long vehicles and 43 of the new 10.3 metre version, the order was changed so that it was entirely for the shorter type, and various totals were advanced for vehicles to suburban coach specification with improved seating and a flat high floor. Once again deliveries did not correspond to expectations, and a total of 45 vehicles were delivered with ordinary bus seating, although fifteen of these were refitted with moquette covered seats by Park Royal as a concession to Green Line requirements, the others had plastic seating. All of the first 45, originally classified SN, were designated as the SNC class, and numbers ran on continuously from the LNB and LNC series which had been used for the single-door vehicles in the 1972 order. Before delivery was finished, the new classification of SNB was introduced for vehicles of this type used on ordinary stage services. The remaining 32 vehicles were at last fitted with a more respectable style of seating, although the two-level floor was retained, and these too were classified as SNC vehicles. Their delivery, up to SNC 147, took until October 1974 to complete, by which time more of the original LNC series were being downgraded to bus work as LNB type.

Meanwhile the four Leyland Nationals hired to Nottingham had finished their work there, and reached Reigate in July and August 1973. Only LN 9 was to enter London Country service, however, the other three (LNs 8, 10, 11) being transferred to Hants & Dorset in September 1973, and there was not a great deal of surprise when one month later three Metro-Scania single deckers from the Hants & Dorset fleet turned up with London Country. These vehicles, the only other ones of the type to exist in the NBC, had been acquired by Hants & Dorset from Chisnell ('King Alfred'), Winchester when that firm had been absorbed a few months earlier.

The five touring coaches were a welcome arrival in the late summer of 1973, and to

distinguish them from the run-of-the-mill vehicle in the fleet, these special vehicles were not given any classification or fleet numbers. The twenty-three Bristol LHS vehicles also arrived from June to October 1973, and comprised the BL class, enabling RFs to be withdrawn from some lighter country routes and from some of those where physical difficulties prevented the use of larger vehicles. By their very nature many of these routes were those most susceptible to risk when county council subsidies were reviewed in the coming years. As matters turned out the need for Bristol LHS vehicles was to decline relatively quickly, just as it had done for the GS class twenty years earlier with London Transport in the Country Area.

The shortage of vehicles had meant that every serviceable unit had to be pressed into

passenger service, and a further shortage was thereby created in the training fleet. In order to help combat this problem, London Country hired three AEC Reliance coaches with Harrington bodywork from Maidstone & District. At the same period, due to London Country having some of the earliest *short* Leyland Nationals in production, a few SNC vehicles went on evaluation trials to other NBC subsidiaries including Hants & Dorset, East Kent and Maidstone & District. The Maidstone & District Reliances developed a number of mechanical problems, and only one of them, 117PKP, survived the winter with London Country.

The opening of 1974 saw orders for a further 30 short Leyland Nationals to suburban coach specification (up to SNC 177) and 30 more Bristol LHSs. The LHS vehicles would be to a special 7ft 8in

Above right **The first small Bristol buses entered service at Dunton Green and St Albans in October 1973 and a welcome change from the austere narrow pvc-covered seats of the Nationals was the fitment of moquette seats to give a reasonably pleasant interior but with a typical ECW look about it. BL 23 is standing at the Quill Hall Estate terminus while working from Amersham garage a few years later. Many London Transport bus stop flags continued to survive for some years after a start had been made on their replacement.** Mike Harris

Right **On 15th November 1973, MBS 15 was transferred back to London Transport after having been delicensed all year following certificate of fitness expiry. In its place, London Country received MBS 4 from London Transport, the only vehicle of the type to have received a full overhaul. This was rapidly repainted green and moved to Tring, though after only a few weeks it was despatched to Reigate, and spent the rest of its life in the southern areas.** Mike Harris

Large numbers of red Merlins were hired from London Transport, beginning in June 1974. After initial use on Derby Day the first batch were used at many garages, including Garston, which operated both the single-door and dual-door types.

Left **MB 115** was one of a batch of 50 low driving position single-door Merlins in the LT fleet, and displays the unusual lettering and layout of the Norbury Brothers blinds obtained in 1973. Poor quality linen led to their early demise, to be replaced during 1974 by much neater King & Flack blinds using upper-case lettering. Capital Transport

Below **MBS 34** captured at Edenbridge Hilders Lane terminus shows the superior King & Flack produced blinds. This bus was one of a batch of 49 originally introduced for London Transport's suburban flat fare schemes. Colin Brown

width for use on routes where the ordinary LHS was not a sufficient answer to restrictions. However, the 1973 order for Leyland Nationals was still in course of delivery.

The three Atlanteans to replace the XA class were also still awaited and they arrived in the late spring and were promptly sent to East Grinstead. The delays in new vehicle deliveries, combined with a further worsening of the vehicle defect position, necessitated drastic action. Some of the delicensed vehicles found themselves raided of parts which would enable others to return to service, and a number of Swifts, Merlins and Routemasters became delicensed at this stage, never again to return to service with London Country, developing into carcasses which were not cleared from their premises for several years. Thus, some of the vehicles received to replace ex-London Transport

units themselves achieved an early grave and the older, more reliable, vehicles outlived the new in such cases.

So severe were the problems, exemplified by the situation at Amersham garage in April 1974 where only four SMs were available for service against a scheduled requirement for 16, that arrangements were made to hire a number of Merlins which were surplus to London Transport's requirements. Twenty-four were taken on hire for immediate use on Derby Day in June 1974 and thereafter were scattered to provide general relief for shortages throughout the fleet. Many more Merlins were hired over the next two years, peaking at around 50 vehicles on hire at any given time in February 1975. The deliveries of the 1974 orders provided some relief to the situation. The Bristol LHS vehicles, classified BN but

with fleet numbers continuous from the BLs, arrived between August and November 1974, whilst the SNCs from the 1973 order were of some help, though the 1974 order for these vehicles did not appear until between February and May 1975. Some interest was generated by the arrival of five Ford Transits with Dormobile bodies for a new *Pick-me-up* service trial in Harlow during August 1974. The RC class, which had found a new home on the 723 route at Grays, was finally downgraded to bus use at Hertford from August 1974, appearing in a variety of liveries. In an attempt to avoid a recertification pile-up in 1975, MB and MBS vehicles began major overhauls, which were carried out by Park Royal and Marshall in the main. Further negotiations with Maidstone & District led to the acquisition of four Reliance coaches, including the survivor from the 1973/4

Right **Thirty narrow-bodied Bristol LHSs came in the autumn of 1974 and all replaced RFs over the following winter. Hertford's BN 47 is seen at Ware Park Hospital terminus on route 333 in August 1975. The Ware Park Hospital journeys were traditionally numbered 333B but the suffix was dropped to facilitate buses with three track number blinds.** Mike Harris

The RC class was demoted from coach to bus work from August 1974 and all went to Hertford garage to replace RFs. Various liveries were carried and the then new local coach NBC livery can be seen on RC 1, *below,* **at Blakes Corner, Barking prior to transfer to Hertford. Full bus livery is worn by RC 4,** *centre right,* **standing in Harlow Garage. Some had an off-white waistband painted over the central relief band on both the local coach variants and the few still in Lincoln green coach livery. Some carried** *London Country* **fleetnames, some** *Green Line,* **some neither, a remarkable variety for such a small class of vehicle.** Mike Harris / Philip Hopcroft

hirings, in August 1974 – these vehicles were classified T (for training) and gave much needed help to the training fleet until 1977.

During October 1974 a count of the London Country fleet showed that 342 vehicles were delicensed, more than a quarter of the fleet. Peaks were noted in the SM class (55 delicensed out of 138), the RP class (34 out of 90) and even the respectable RMC (17 delicensed out of 69). Exactly 100 RTs remained owned, though not all available for service – the vehicle position meant that the number of RTs sold during 1974 could be counted on the fingers of two hands. RF withdrawals and sales were continuing at a steady rate, partly due to the fact that most vehicles were now beyond economic repair, and partly because of the unsuitability of the type to cover the problems which were occurring.

Left **Summer 1974 saw the acquisition of four AEC Reliance coaches from Maidstone & District, following the hire of some the previous winter. They were the only Harrington-bodied vehicles ever owned, and were used solely on driver training work and surprisingly they lasted up to four years with LCBS.** Steve Fennell

Bottom left **RT 3752 was the only member of its class to be fully re-painted in the 1972 lighter green livery – it was the last of 56 RTs to be overhauled at Aldenham between February 1971 and April 1972. It first went to Chelsham but like many RTs it gravitated to Garston by June 1974, staying there until it became the last normal RT withdrawal on 13th April 1977 upon CoF expiry. (A few others were recertified and are depicted later in this book). It is pictured covering for an RML at Leavesden on route 306 in 1975.** John Miller

Bottom right **As RTs continued to soldier on covering defective newer vehicles correct via blinds were often not available and they were fitted with Routemaster side blinds on which the displays were not as deep. RT 604 is a great credit to the Dartford engineering staff who have applied masking to the via box and have covered the now redundant route number box.** J.G.S. Smith

There was not to be a great deal of change in the situation during 1975. London Country found themselves obliged to carry out recertification work on some of the London Transport Merlins on hire in order to continue having these vehicles available, and although a new Central Works was now in course of construction at Tinsley Green, Crawley, dependency meanwhile on outside sources remained high. The reduced proportion of LT-derived units in the fleet also reduced the extent to which it was feasible or economic to call on Chiswick or Aldenham for help. Fifty Leyland Nationals – 25 to suburban coach specification and 25 pure buses were on order for 1975, but a further order for Bristol LHSs was cancelled as County Council subsidy cuts accelerated the reduction in fleet requirements.

However if London Country was in desperate straits, some other operators were by now in a position to offer help, and there

began one of the most intriguing spells so far seen in the Company's history. The first inkling of this was the appearance of a Southdown Leyland PD3 on London Country premises, and after a certain amount of negotiation three of these vehicles were purchased in May 1975, classified LS and put into service at Godstone where they covered RML shortages until September 1976. Further Leyland PD3s surplus to the needs of Ribble were tracked down at Leicester and at Willowbrook's at Loughborough and formed the start of an LR class totalling 20 trainer vehicles by the end of 1976. They released other training vehicles for passenger service; however, none of the LRs themselves ran in passenger service with London Country. None of the 1975 order for Nationals arrived until 1976, and as the vehicle position declined again in the autumn of 1975 arrangements were made to hire vehicles for passenger service from a

number of operators, bringing unusual colours to many suburban towns.

First into use were six Bristol MW6G semi-coaches hired from Western National (Royal Blue) at Dunton Green from 27th October 1975 until 26th November 1977, covering SM shortages. They were not fitted for one-man operation thus had to be run in service with a crew. When their hire had been completed a mixture of BLs and SNBs covered their workings. Six Leyland PD2s from Maidstone Borough Council ran at Dartford from 8th November 1975 until 4th September 1976, covering RMCs mainly on route 499, and five Daimler Roadliner single deckers replaced MBSs on 460 at Staines from 22nd November 1975 until 3rd October 1976, being then covered by new SNBs. The Roadliners came from Bournemouth Transport, who also provided five Daimler Fleetline double deckers at Leatherhead from 24th November 1975 until 18th March

During 1975 two small classes of second-hand buses were acquired to help relieve shortages.
Above left One of the three Leyland PD3 'Queen Mary' double deckers that went to Godstone garage where they retained their traditional Southdown livery with London Country fleetnames applied.
Above right The LR class were also PD3s, but this time Burlingham bodied vehicles from Ribble used solely for driver training and painted in all-over yellow with a red fleetname. Colin Brown

In addition to the London Transport Merlins, numbers of other buses were hired for varying periods of time between October 1975 and March 1978. In the south east area Royal Blue (but all-white liveried) coaches worked from Dunton Green and special sets of blinds were made for them; they were not equipped to take ticket machines and so were crew operated. Two different vintages of Bristol MW were used, the bodywork variations being evident in these views of Nos. 1437 *left* and 2270 *below*.
R.C. Riley / Mike Harris

Right **The Eastbourne AEC Regent Vs were allocated to Swanley for route 477 which had some interworkings at Orpington with local route 493 as illustrated in this view.** Peter Plummer

Below left and right **Special blinds were produced for the Maidstone Leyland PD2As at Dartford garage. Maidstone Corporation Nos 15 and 17 are seen at Joyce Green Hospital terminus.** Mike Harris

Bottom left **The longest-lived hire was of Bournemouth Fleetlines, which worked from Leatherhead garage over a period of 2½ years. They replaced Park Royal ANs that were suffering problems in 1975. Their generous blind boxes were just the right size for RT rear blinds. Some of the buses continued to advertise the joys of Bournemouth.** J.G.S. Smith

Bottom right **Bournemouth supplied Daimler Roadliner single deckers to Staines to cover an MBS shortage, but when they left brand new SNBs replaced them, and MBSs never returned to the garage. Bournemouth Corporation No. 52 is in South Street, Staines in February 1976.** Mike Harris

Right **Harlow was chosen for the Southend Leyland PD3 operation so that RTs could be made available to prop up allocations elsewhere and also to be handy for Southend when PD3 replacements had to be made. The Southend buses used the blinds out of the RTs but they did not fit very well and soon became torn and awry, the intermediate panel falling into disuse. RTs never returned to Harlow; when the PD3s left in January 1977 RMLs took over. The buses were usually to be found on routes 339 and 397/A but the complexities of interworking meant that odd journeys were scheduled on Harlow's AN farebox routes as illustrated with Southend Corporation No. 345 on route 810A at the Templefields industrial area.** Mike Harris

Below right **During 1977 Maidstone Borough Council Atlanteans were hired to run alongside the RTs, RMCs and RCLs at Chelsham on routes 403 and 453.** Colin Brown

1978; the number declined toward the end of this lengthy hire period which culminated in a batch of brand-new ANs replacing them. An Ipswich Borough Transport AEC Regent V was inspected at Harlow late in October 1975 but no hires resulted; however three Eastbourne Borough Council AEC Regent Vs were hired for use at Swanley from 5th January to 12th June 1976, in this case covering RMCs on route 477. Harlow again featured from 29th March 1976 when 10 Leyland PD3s of Southend Transport were hired to operate the crew services there, in this case replacing RTs to prop up allocations elsewhere. The PD3s, which had previously been hired by London Transport for use at Croydon on route 190, finished at Harlow on 28th January 1977, and were replaced by RMLs made available from one-man conversions at Windsor. In all the hirings, serviceable vehicles of LCBS's own fleet were released to cover shortages at other garages. The hired vehicles were frequently swapped back-and-forth with their owners for maintenance purposes.

January 1976 saw the opening of the long awaited Central Repair Works at Crawley, and quite soon afterwards improvements could be seen in the vehicle situation. Nevertheless the scale of the problem meant that it took a substantial period of time to clear. Orders were placed for 1976 delivery as the 1975 Nationals were coming in, and a further 32 (later increased to 36) Leyland Nationals to slightly improved specification (SNB 228–263) were added to the order book. For once, these all arrived within the calendar year and helped to make it possible to return some of the hired vehicles as well as (by complex re-allocations and route reductions) to face up to realities by withdrawing the unpopular RC class in its entirety on 29th January 1977. Four of the RCs were selected for retention as training buses (to replace the T class) but this did not prove very successful and indeed were never used as trainers at all. Two further coaches were added to the fleet in February 1976, being second hand Reliances from National

Travel (South East), and in June these (together with the five from 1973) were classified for the first time, becoming P 1 to P 7. Another order was for 14 Bristol VRT double deckers, later increased to 15 to cover AN 98, which had been destroyed by fire while in service on 15th December 1975.

National deliveries early in 1976 had enabled many RFs to be withdrawn, and the Southend PD3s had helped to stop the gradual reduction of serviceable RTs. Indeed by May 1976 only eight RTs and eighteen RFs were formally scheduled for service. Seven RTs were at Chelsham for route 403 (Wallington – Warlingham Park Hospital) which was also worked by RMCs and one

was at Luton on route 360 (Luton – Caddington), though this lasted only until September. However many more were in use to cover defective Routemasters, notably at Garston and Windsor, and a survey showed that nearly twenty Routemasters were then tucked away in a cannibalised condition, all being covered in service by RTs. The RFs were scheduled at Garston, Hemel Hempstead, Staines and Windsor – although, again, several were helping out at other locations. The Nationals delivered later in 1976, together with service alterations, enabled all the scheduled operations of RFs to be removed by 29th January 1977, the last official operation being on route 309.

Many livery styles appeared on the RFs during their period of operation with London Country. This selection shows RFs without advertising, in the traditional way. In the mid-1970s many RFs had advertisements plastered on them, sometimes astride the central band, and often obscuring the fleetname. A few RFs at Hertford then received small fleetnames towards the rear.

Facing page pictures

Left **RF 592 in Lincoln green livery with yellow window surrounds – the classic RF country bus – is captured at Sevenoaks Bus Station working on route 413, an early rural casualty.** John Bull

Below **Some RFs gained the lighter green livery with yellow window surrounds in 1972 while a few received full NBC livery such as RF 310 seen at Byron Gardens, Tilbury. RF 310 had started life as RF 529 but was renumbered in 1956 when it was upgraded to Green Line duties.** Mike Harris

Bottom left **RF 221, seen opposite Sidcup Garage, is also in the NBC livery but looks a vast improvement on RF 310 simply by the addition of a white window surround. Some front blinds at Dartford were fitted with large route numbers to avoid the problem of changing blinds when a vehicle was substituted.** Peter Plummer

Bottom right **Modernised RF 39 had been downgraded to bus status in October 1972 and was given the canary yellow band and revised fleetname which in this case has been applied amidships. Unlike those modernised RFs down-graded in LT days this one had retained the brackets for the side route boards. It is seen at the somewhat stark surroundings of Harlow Bus Station** Capital Transport

This page pictures

Top right **Windsor's RF 120 has received the lighter green livery with the yellow waistband and is seen at Wexham Park Hospital. Where required the King & Flack produced blinds were given three lines of intermediate point data.** Mike Harris

Right **RF 88 in a green and white livery has received the NBC style fleetname above the windows.** John Miller

Below **RF 202 has been given a white waistband with the Green Line fleetname and was subsequently preserved by the company.** Peter Plummer

Below right **RF 54 looks decidedly odd in Lincoln green with a white waistband and green fleetname while working on Green Line duties at Hyde Park Corner on 10th April 1977. It is a great credit to the reliability of these elderly vehicles that they continued to be used to cover unreliable newer types on such arduous duties right up until the time of their withdrawal.** Mike Harris

The Bristol VRT order materialised in the spring of 1977 as the BT class and, after early speculation that they would replace the last RTs at Chelsham, they all were despatched to Grays, mainly for route 370. Here it was RCLs that were mainly replaced, several moving to Chelsham where they joined a mixture of RTs and RMCs and even a batch of five Leyland Atlanteans on hire from Maidstone Borough Council. These latter showed that the vehicle shortage was still not quite over, and they worked at Chelsham from 5th March until at least 21st October 1977, the last being officially returned to Maidstone on 26th November. In spite of an official removal of RTs from the schedules at Chelsham in May, a small recertification programme was still necessary to meet anticipated requirements for a short time and so, during summer 1977, four RTs (604, 981, 1018, 3461) and two RFs (202, 221) received garage recertification. This meant that RT 604, RT 1018 and RT 3461 became the only members of their class ever to carry the full NBC livery into passenger service. RT 2230 and RT 2367 had also received this livery, but were used only as training buses.

During 1976 it was clear that firm decisions would have to be taken to dispel the various relics of unserviceable Merlins and Swifts languishing at many garages. It was also the time to consider the fact that nearly all the Routemasters would sustain certification expiry during the next three years. Apart from those Routemasters already reduced to hulks for want of spare parts, it seemed unlikely that it would be economically viable to undertake major work on the Routemasters, either within London Country or by invoking London Transport help. Accordingly an early decision was taken to allow for the replacement of the Routemasters over the next three years and, subsequently discussions were opened with an interested customer for the purchase of the redundant buses – London Transport itself. The latter had found it desirable to

Above left **The small class of Bristol VRTs, the BT class, entered service on route 370 from Grays in summer 1977. Initially the blind boxes were full depth but soon became masked as service changes became more frequent and more displays had to be included. BT 4 is seen loading up on Romford Ring Road in August 1977. The class was sold after just three years of service to the Bristol (Avon) Omnibus Company.**
Mike Harris

Left **Just five RTs ever received the NBC livery. Three at Chelsham following re-certification in spring 1977 RTs 604, 1018 and 3461 could be found in passenger service. Trainers RT 2230 and RT 2367 were the other two of the class to carry the new livery. An immaculately turned out RT 1018 is working one of the few Tatsfield journeys on route 403. The last to work in passenger service was RT 604 but it suffered an engine failure in mid-June 1978 and was not repaired thus this stalwart class, which had helped the company out to a considerable extent in the dark days of the mid-1970s, passed without any ceremony.**
Peter Plummer

Right **More BNs arrived in the autumn of 1977 and some went to Hertford to cover SNBs that were about to replace RMCs on route 395, some to Dunton Green to help oust the hired Royal Blue MWs, and two went to Leatherhead to replace the last RFs at that garage (54 and 79). Route 416 became their principal route as illustrated by BN 56 at Leatherhead Station.** Colin Brown

Below **HM The Queen's Silver Jubilee was in 1977 and two silver-painted ANs (5 and 41), sponsored by advertisers, worked at various garages around the network during that year. AN 41 promotes the delights of Watford's Mac Market while stopping at Watford Junction on the ever-busy 321.** Colin Brown

consider maximising the Routemaster fleet for crewed routes and to propose an early removal of the DMS class of Fleetlines.

Accordingly, and in addition to the orders already in hand, London Country ordered yet another 60 Leyland Nationals for 1977, later increased to 90, which included twenty not required by Midland Red. The speed with which these vehicles were now being produced by the manufacturer meant that all 90 (SNB 264–353) arrived between May 1977 and January 1978 (apart from one in March). Double-deckers were not so easy to obtain and 24 Leyland Atlanteans (AN 124–147) did not arrive until spring 1978.

At certain times during London Country's existence the fashion for all-over advertisement buses gained popularity, mostly in the 1973–76 period with a revival from 1984. Whether it is artistic, tasteful or garish is a matter of opinion but it was a good source of revenue to the Company. RMC 1516 advertising Fine Fare Supermarkets is seen at Hemel Hempstead Bus Station in June 1974 working on the 330 trunk route to Welwyn Garden City. This RMC gained notoriety in January 1972 when it was deroofed in a low bridge incident and following a rebuild at Aldenham was not refitted with luggage racks. It had been a forerunner in the all-over advertising field as it had previously carried a special livery for Welwyn Department Store. Mike Harris

An option was taken up on 14 Bristol LHS chassis which had been built to coach specification and which were surplus to a dealer's requirements. In spite of there being no real need for these small buses the chance to acquire yet more new vehicles was obviously too attractive to pass up, and so they were bodied to 7ft 8ins size by ECW as further members of the BN class. During the summer of 1977 yet a further class of bus was placed into service, being the RN class of 10 AEC Reliances with 64-seat Plaxton bodies (partially with three-and-two seating) purchased from Barton Transport of Nottingham. They were reseated to 60 and placed onto school contract work, of which London Country was gradually acquiring a greater amount.

Two classes to experience decline in 1977 were the FT and the MS. The five FT Ford Transits were withdrawn after their dial-a-bus route was replaced by a conventional BN operated route at Harlow in April – all were sold to Midland Red later in the year. The MS class of Metro-Scanias had been presenting maintenance problems, not least because of the high cost in obtaining spare parts for such a small fleet. Accordingly they gradually fell by the wayside and were replaced by Nationals. Only four of the seven were running at the year's end and all were withdrawn during 1978. In fact they were all advertised for sale during 1977, although some were still in use, but there were no takers and they went for scrap in August 1980.

This was not to be the end, however. For some time there had been high-level discussion as to the future image of the Green Line network. The attempts to upgrade the network by the use of the RPs and SMAs had not been helped by the high failure rate to which these classes had become prone, and the very reverse had happened, with substantial gaps in service due to vehicles not being available. The Leyland Nationals originally ordered to retrieve the situation had hardly been the epitome of luxury comfort, though the later suburban coaches had gone some way to retrieve the situation once their teething troubles had been sorted out. By this stage the early LNCs had all been removed from Green Line work in favour of bus use, and a few RPs were beginning to

venture onto bus work. A major decision was taken that the Green Line fleet was to be completely revamped with vehicles no more than five years old. Such vehicles were to be to a high standard of comfort and reliability, and arrangements were made to lease vehicles at the rate of 30 per year so as to enable the replacement of the entire Green Line fleet within five years, and a constant renewal policy thereafter. AEC Reliance chassis were selected to fulfil this function, with an initial 1977 contract being negotiated for 15 with Plaxton bodies (to become the RS type) and 15 with Duple bodies (the RB class), numbered as one series.

The arrival of these vehicles from early in 1977 breathed fresh life into the fleet. The standard of vehicle finish coupled with the availability of bus grant meant that an earnest campaign could begin to restore the image of Green Line to the higher levels it had earlier enjoyed. So far as the fleet was concerned, the immediate effect was to enable RPs, and later SNCs of the various types, to be reduced to ordinary bus use. Except for certain vehicles which had fallen victim to the spares shortage, the SMA class soldiered on throughout this process, however. These 30 coaches entered stock during 1977, together with the BNs and SNBs referred to earlier. It is not easy to separate the effects of so many new vehicles arriving in the fleet as, during 1977, there were so many route alteration schemes, including four garage closures and many one-man conversions. The result was to achieve a much-changed balance in the fleet by the end of the year. Routemasters were displaced from such trunk routes as 339 (Harlow – Warley), 341 (Hertford – St Albans), 405 (West Croydon – Crawley), 409 (West Croydon – Forest Row), 414 (West Croydon – Horsham), 441 (Staines – High Wycombe), and quite a number of SMs had been replaced and much of the shortage of certain types had been covered. Works facilities were still not really adequate to cope with the amount of recertification work needed, notably on the SM class. The better reliability of the Leyland National meant

that a good number of Merlins and Swifts never did receive their recertification and were sold off without ever returning to service.

Plenty of Routemasters had been delicensed during 1977, either because of failure or following one-man conversions, but November 1977 saw the first formal withdrawals for disposal. Over a period of several weeks a total of 68 Routemasters (twenty RMCs, ten RCLs, 38 RMLs) were withdrawn and sold to London Transport in the closing days of December. Many of these buses were among the worst examples of their breed and some had been out of service for considerable periods of time. Of the total of 68, there were 21 (two RMCs, two RCLs and 17 RMLs) that were only fit for scrap, and were re-sold by London Transport to scrap dealers without actually passing onto LT premises. The remains were then crated up and brought back to London to go into stock as spares for the existing LT Routemaster fleet. The rest of the RMLs were rapidly re-painted red and put into passenger service (or in a few cases, onto training duty). The RCLs were considered too good to be trainers and they had their platform doors removed and went into passenger service in August 1980, whilst the RMCs went into the training fleet, except that RMC 1499 became a staff bus for a short period. It is a matter of conjecture whether London Country would have withdrawn Routemasters so soon had the spare parts shortage not manifested itself over the 1974–77 period. The Company was caught with a batch of good vehicles that needed parts and engines, which only London Transport was really able to supply. LT themselves were short of parts during this period and little could be spared for the needs of another operator, and so increasing numbers of RMCs, RCLs and RMLs had been cast aside by London Country through no fault of their own. The faithful but very tired RT had been kept on almost to the point of exhaustion.

Counting training and hired vehicles, at the end of 1977 London Country was operating 30 different classes.

Top **In 1979 wrap-round adverts rather than all over livery adverts began to appear on ANs and in 1980 they also appeared on SNBs and SNCs. The advertising style became known as Unibus and among buses so treated in 1981 was Dorking's SNB 74 which featured Happy Eater restaurants and is seen here in the delightful surroundings of Leigh on route 439.** Barry LeJeune

Above left and right **RF 594 was converted into a mobile recruitment centre in summer 1973 and was fitted with tables and cupboards. It visited many locations and here it is seen at Hemel Hempstead Bus Station hoping that a new recruit will turn up. By early 1976 it was repainted into an unusual livery of green roof, window surrounds and wheel arches, with main panels white and renamed a 'Staff Employment Unit'.** Capital Transport / Colin Brown

Right **This Matador breakdown tender was acquired from International Wreckers Ltd in 1976 and numbered M1. It is seen at Garston Garage in October 1976.** Philip Hopcroft

39

Chapter 4

THE INHERITANCE FADES AWAY

THE FOUR-YEAR period 1978–81 saw the transformation of the London Country fleet from a very mixed one, with much LT inheritance still in being, into a modern one – very much an NBC fleet – although still retaining some little individualities of its own. The scale of this transformation is shown by the figures – 529 new vehicles delivered, comprising 170 AN class double deckers, 190 Leyland Nationals (all in 1978/9) and 169 coaches.

Orders for 1978 comprised 55 Atlanteans which were added to the 24 already awaited; another 30 coaches were expected on lease and 30 more BNs were ordered. However the latter BNs were cancelled when BLMC were not prepared to construct them with automatic gearboxes, although some relief was available when 22 Leyland Nationals were transferred from an order now surplus to Maidstone & District's requirements. Delivery of the combined 1977/8 AN order took the class numbering from AN 124 to AN 183 between March and September 1978, but the remaining 19 buses were held up as Park Royal Coachworks was unable to meet the order. The body order was transferred to Roe in Leeds, thus delaying delivery until early 1979 and in turn giving the last few Routemasters a few more months with London Country. Although many of these ANs were used for a major service revision at Crawley, replacing mostly MBSs, Routemaster withdrawals resumed in the autumn of 1978 with routes such as 347/A and 411 receiving ANs. The 30 coaches, again split equally between Plaxton and Duple on AEC Reliance chassis, took most of the year to arrive and generally replaced RPs, many of which never ran again after CoF expiry.

It seemed that it was the Certificate of Fitness expiries during 1978 and 1979 of so many vehicles that dictated events. Even with the Central Works at Crawley in full swing, it was quite unable to cope with the sheer volume of work. A move to ease this situation came in February 1978 when a Northern Area Works was opened within a part of Garston (now renamed Watford) Garage. Henceforth the use of outside contractors and of London Transport declined. Even so, some help had to be sought and Willowbrook's in Loughborough overhauled a few ANs during 1978, and Wadham-Stringer at Portsmouth carried out protracted overhauls on the AF class during 1979. When CoFs on Routemasters, Merlins and Swifts expired, as well as on some RPs they were generally just put into store and never

Above left **The ANs were delivered in London Country's pleasing livery, in 1972, just prior to the imposition of the NBC corporate green, although some members of the class acquired the NBC style fleetname as worn by AN 82 at Harlow Bus Station in September 1978. The original fare box concept was designed to speed boarding, by insertion of one or two coins only, but successive revisions required a minimum of four coins for the 18p fare.** Colin Brown

Left **1978 saw the resumption of double-deck deliveries in quantity and eventually 170 basically identical ANs came into the fleet, in most cases seeing off Routemasters. At Effingham, new AN 125 stands adjacent to traditional London Transport infrastructure.** Ian Pringle

Right **In June 1977 RP 1 entered works for overhaul, which included modifications to the inadequate heating system and a new livery. RPs intended for further Green Line use re-appeared in a modified form of the 'local coach' livery with white top and a white band below the windscreen. But CoF expiries overtook the overhaul programme – remaining members of the class being stored, never to return to service – between June 1977 and July 1979 just 44 (of the class of 90) were overhauled. From August 1978 some were given bus livery (starting with RP 73) producing a quite attractive look. A further livery variation appeared from June 1981 when some in bus livery had their white bands removed making them look very drab, with their high window line. RP 53 is seen in the bus livery working on route 436 in May 1981. By this time 436 was marketed as *Weyfarer* but a decision had been taken not to provide dedicated brand name liveries.** Geoff Rixon

Centre right **By 1978 a cheaper version of the Leyland National – the B variant – became available. London Country acquired 168 of them from September 1978 to December 1979. Amersham's SNB 438 loads up in High Wycombe High Street in April 1980. Route 365 was originally numbered 442 until re-organisation of the town's services on 1st October 1977.** Mike Harris

Bottom right **An interesting experiment was carried out by Amersham garage in summer 1979 when SNC 159, in dual purpose green and white livery, received a green roof re-paint which considerably improved its appearance. It was joined by similar SNC 158 from Hemel Hempstead in 1980. However, officialdom frowned upon this enterprise and both buses lost their white areas returning to all-green in April 1981, but not before SNC 159 had been captured approaching Amersham Station while working on route 353.** John Boylett

dealt with, it being impossible to cope with all of them. They were of little value anyway as the Company was now standardising on Atlanteans and Nationals for its bus fleet. The relative ease with which Leyland Nationals in particular could be obtained at this time, coupled with a series of over-orders by some other NBC subsidiaries led London Country to review its needs for the future. Arrangements were accordingly made for the Company to receive an initial batch of 83 of the new, and cheaper, series B variant which had several of the original refinements removed or reduced to optional status. Later orders were for batches of 62 and 23, and indeed the whole 168 'B' models were received continuously from September 1978 to December 1979, the earliest ones coming into the fleet concurrently with the 22 'A' models referred to earlier. Fleet numbers reached SNB 543 and made London Country the largest operator of Nationals in the country, if not the world. For a while vehicles were allocated to whatever garages needed them as they arrived. Later, some sorting-out took place so that the series B vehicles were confined to garages whose allocations were either to be exclusively of that type or where a sufficiently large allocation occurred to allow the mixing of variants. One snag was that the series B vehicles did not

Left **Company-preserved RMC 4 was used on various special occasions, which included duplicating the final journey on 13th March 1981 of the last scheduled crew service of the company which was on route 477 from Swanley. On 20th June 1981 the coach was brought out as a tribute to retiring clippie Mona Blackman when she worked the vehicle for a full duty on route 719 and is seen here in Honeypot Lane. It was also used on 13th November 1982 on route 708 in celebration of Green Line's 50 years of operation to Aylesbury. By this time RMC 4 had acquired opening upper deck front windows.** Mike Harris

Below left **Nearing the end of its life with London Country a decidedly tatty RML 2352 stands at Gravesend's Valley Drive terminus on route 480, the last stronghold of class. The bus was sold to London Transport in January 1980.** Colin Brown

prove suitable for fitting with fareboxes, and as many of them were due to replace farebox-carrying MBSs, a number of allocation changes resulted. Nevertheless, it was MB, MBS and SM vehicles that largely found themselves ousted and, by the end of 1979, only a mere handful were left in service. The last few Metro Scanias also went in 1978, with MS 2 finally running in service at Stevenage on 20th October.

By mid-June of 1978 the last remaining RT in passenger service, RT 604 at Chelsham, was found to have sustained an engine failure. It had been intended that the last formal operation of both the RT and RF within London Country should be properly recognised. In the event RT 604 was never repaired and so that most legion of all types passed quietly away without ceremony

– although a few survived in the training fleet with RTs 981, 1018 and 3752 finally being disposed of in 1981. The RFs survived the year, with RF 202 at Northfleet and RF 221 at Chelsham. However the latter became disused by March 1979 and RF 202 was delicensed with a defect during October 1979. Fortunately, though, it proved possible for it to be repaired and it was restored in traditional Green Line livery and was used on special occasions from April 1980. The ECW-bodied prototype RMC 4 was also retained by London Country after all its fellows had gone back to London Transport, and it, too, received traditional Green Line livery by April 1980, and was used on special occasions. Both RF 202 and RMC 4 were much in evidence at events during Green Line's Golden Jubilee Year of 1980.

The nineteen ANs that had been transferred to Roe for bodying finally arrived early in 1979 and most were used to convert route 403, which had recently seen so many different types from the scheduled RMCs. Throughout 1978 and into 1979, Route-masters had steadily suffered withdrawal, largely due to CoF expiry, and an order was placed for 30 more Roe-bodied ANs (AN 203–232) for delivery later in 1979. These were intended to replace all remaining RMCs and RMLs which were now allocated only to four main routes (403 Express, 407, 477, 480). Expiries in 1978 had mostly affected the RCL variant, and a trickle of these found their way back to London Transport. However it appeared to the onlooker that there was no love lost between the two operators at this period. Largely due to the lack of effective replacements with the ANs held up, many Routemasters had to be kept running in passenger service right up to the last day that it would be legal to do so. Some buses going to LT were thus in somewhat less than tip-top condition, and indeed three RCLs were even sent back to London Country to be mechanically rectified. The Company, already at full stretch at Works with the overhaul pro-grammes, had to set up a small workshop within Grays garage specifically to prepare Routemasters for sale to LT, and this could hardly be considered a desirable course of action. Grays operational side featured early in 1979 when the very last RCLs in passenger service with LCBS ran, the last being RCL 2250 on 24th January which was the last bus to go back to LT in March 1979.

The large number of vehicles held for disposal, or awaiting overhaul, by spring 1979 was so great that accommodation was rented at the old Radlett Aerodrome site in Hertfordshire on the premises of Adams

Foods. Quite a number of Routemasters, RPs and ANs found their way there, the latter awaiting entry into works. Later, premises owned by Wadham-Stringer at Guildford and Beddington Commercial Motors were also rented for storage of withdrawn stock, principally SMs, SMAs and RPs.

London Country were obviously going to be unable to restore their entire remaining fleet of Routemasters to the standards that LT appeared to require and so a batch of withdrawn buses (3 RMCs, 6 RCLs, 8 RMLs) was sold in March 1979 to Wombwell Diesels. The first two to travel north were RML 2423 and RML 2424 in April, and indeed these were broken up by the famous scrap dealer. This seemed too much for London Transport

Over the years the various Routemaster classes and the preceding RTs proved to be very useful for shifting crowds attending sporting and other events.

Top right **RT 4742 and RT 3665 slumber in the parking area at Ascot in June 1974, which was to be their penultimate year of operation as Green Line 701 was withdrawn in October 1975.** John Bull

Centre right **Derby Week saw special route 406F providing an intensive service between Epsom Station and Epsom Downs, with RCL 2246 awaiting punters at the station. The number 406F was a remarkable survival from the Bassom route numbering system which ceased to be used in October 1934.** Peter Plummer

Right **Biggin Hill Air Display traditionally saw much duplication on routes 410 from Bromley North Station and 705 from Victoria. From 1975 the provision of a special service to and from Bromley, instead of 410, enabled a premium fare to be charged. RT 1012 and RMC 1502 lay over at the show in September 1974 waiting to return the crowds to Bromley. The body on RMC 1502 was formerly on RMC 1469, which was chosen to style the RCL class, and was fitted with a wide front blind box.**
Barry LeJeune

Left **RML 2354, seen in November 1977, was one of several Routemaster vehicles deployed around the fleet, at garages where conductors were available, to substitute for newer buses that were off the road. In some cases, such as with Hertford's 316, they represented a type that had never been previously used on the route or indeed at the garage. Hertford garage also temporarily hosts Harlow's AN 74.** John Bull

Below **The last two operational Routemasters (or Routemasters as they were described on the special blinds) with London Country were RML 2446 and RMC 1512. Both were used on an enthusiasts' farewell tour on 1st March 1980 over most of their recent haunts in the South East Area. The RML had a lower deck repaint specially for the tour and was the only RML ever to carry the NBC symbol on a white square. The RMC had the last laugh on the enthusiasts when it was pressed into service on the 477 on 5th March, the day before it was despatched to LT. The buses are seen here at Joyce Green Hospital.** John Bull

to bear, and an urgent agreement was reached in June for the immediate purchase, irrespective of the condition of the vehicles. The remaining fifteen of the seventeen Wombwell buses were re-purchased by LT before they had a chance to be collected by the dealer, and within a matter of weeks another 61 were taken, the majority moving over to the Victoria Docks for storage until LT could attend to them. This activity left London Country with just enough RMCs and RMLs to maintain their last routes until the ANs already ordered could be delivered. As these survivors reached their CoF expiry dates, they were almost immediately sent to London Transport. Various RMCs and RMLs had been used for a few years at certain garages where the types were not scheduled and even at some that were all omo. These were manned by the few remaining conductors who had not opted for voluntary

severance, and provided much interest to enthusiasts, running as they did on workings that should have been run by omo single deckers. In certain cases an enthusiast was even known to supply suitable destination blinds. The very last of these oddities, RML 2344 at Godstone and RML 2352 at Harlow, were recalled in August 1979 to prop up the RML allocation at Northfleet for route 480, the scene of many non-standard buses by this time. What was now considered usual practice, the thirty ANs were later arriving than expected, and they only entered the fleet between November 1979 and February 1980. This meant that a handful of Routemasters had to be kept after the original contracted date of 31st December 1979 as the day when all should have been despatched to LT.

London Country's eleventh year dawned with seven RMCs and six RMLs still in

passenger service. The type was still able to provide surprises with both Chelsham and Swanley, both RMC operators, had one RML apiece as a spare bus. Neither garage had ever operated this variant before, and the icy weather of that winter certainly did not endear them to the conductors, resulting in them being used as little as possible. CoF expiries and new AN deliveries soon enabled these survivors to be withdrawn, and RML 2446 was the last to run in passenger service, on route 480 on 16th February. RMC 1512 at Swanley continued to run on the 477 throughout February, and to commemorate their passing London Country organised an enthusiasts tour on 1st March using RML 2446 and RMC 1512, running over their last haunts. However the RMC had the last word when it was pressed into service yet again on 4th and 5th March, but this really was the final occasion as on the very next day, together with the last of its brethren, it moved away to London Transport.

Right **Incredibly two buses from Dartford garage, SM 514 and SM 517 were still running in Lincoln green and yellow livery in 1980. SM 517 is pictured at Joyce Green Hospital on local route 499 in June 1979.** Mike Harris

Below right **The Merlins came to the end of the road in 1980. Dorking was the last garage to work the MB variant at the end of February 1980, while MBS 424 became the last Merlin to work for the Company on 20th November 1980 on route 495 in Gravesend. The bus is seen some time before withdrawal working on companion route 496.** John Bull

Rapid introduction of so many new buses and coaches by the end of 1979 had a considerable effect on many classes, and six of the eight XFs had been withdrawn, along with many MBs, MBSs, SMs, SMAs and RPs. The year 1980 opened with just two XFs, four MBs, ten MBSs and thirteen Routemasters, together with a small number of these types awaiting disposal, as the only survivors of the vast fleet taken over from LT ten years earlier. Even some of the earlier Leyland Nationals were delicensed, and some never returned to service with London Country, as they were of the longer version and therefore difficult to find homes for. A number of SMs had been converted for use as driver trainers late in 1979 in addition to one RP, but this idea was never perpetuated to any extent.

Without any ceremony, and hardly noticed in all the celebration of the Routemaster passing, the last MBs were delicensed when MB 87 and MB 109, both at Dorking, came off the road on 28th February. The remaining MBSs were gradually picked off during 1980 as replacements became available from fleet contraction. There seemed to be no concerted urge to remove such MBSs and SMs as remained serviceable, partly due to renewed problems caused by the recertification programme on early Leyland Nationals and by the replacement of the BL class. By the middle of November MBS 415 at Crawley and MBS 424 at Northfleet found themselves as the last examples of their breed in service. Although the former bus was not delicensed until late in the month, it was last used on the 14th, so it fell to 424 to be the last Merlin of all when it ran on route 495 on 20th November. XF 5 had been withdrawn in February 1980 and so it fell to XF 3 to become the last ex London Transport bus to survive in service with London Country into 1981.

Meanwhile yet another 60 Atlanteans had been ordered, increased to 61 when AN 99 became the second of its class to be destroyed by fire in August 1980. Thus AN 233 to AN 293, again Roe-bodied, came between

July 1980 and May 1981 and were used, often indirectly, to replace most of the non-standard vehicles in the fleet. One direct replacement was of the BT class of Bristol VRT double-deckers. It had been difficult to obtain spare parts for such a small class of vehicle, and so in the interests of standardisation they were sold off to the Bristol Omnibus Company at the end of 1980. Many of this batch of ANs were used to allow some busy routes such as 341, 405 and 406 to revert to double-deck operation, something they had always needed – at the time of their conversion to omo some years earlier there were just not enough double deckers to go around. This meant that Nationals could be used to replace remaining members of odd classes. Thus the BLs, most of the BNs, all the SMs and SMWs came to the end of the road, but SMA 1 soldiered on alongside XF 3, both until late in 1981.

The coach fleet received yet another five second-hand Plaxton Reliances in 1980, but

a portent of changes to come was the receipt of two each of Volvo and Leyland Leopard coaches, to compare the possible replacements for the AEC Reliance, now out of production. The Leopard was chosen and ordered with 30 joining the fleet in 1981 – they were not replacements but were needed to cope with expansion in the Green Line network. One other class to enter the fleet in 1980 was a surprising one – seven DMS Fleetlines were purchased from London Transport for driver training work, and reviving the tradition set ten years earlier, London Country retained their old LT fleet numbers! The DMSs remained for two years, after which they moved on to Midland Red.

As events turned out, XF 3 survived even the SMs, the last of which came out of service in April 1981. The exceptionally long life enjoyed by XF 3 can be traced back to the fact that in its early days it had been experimentally fitted with a Cummins engine by London Transport, which it subsequently

retained. Problems arose in August 1972, when XF 3 sustained its original certificate of fitness expiry – to overhaul the Cummins engine, or not? For more than two years it was stored and, after some months at Sparshatt's Portsmouth Works it re-emerged in December 1975, fitted with a Gardner engine and was recertified. This gave it a certificate of fitness valid until the last few days of November 1981. In the event enabling legislation introduced on 1st April 1981 in connection with the interim period of changeover to Freedom From Defect testing meant that the CoF lapsed, and that the vehicle would be able to operate until the last day of 1981, subject to the ordinary annual test being satisfied. As 31st December 1981 also became scheduled as the last day of operation at East Grinstead garage, special arrangements were made for XF 3 to operate the last trip of the year from the garage before it closed down.

However, on Christmas Eve 1981, XF 3 was rostered out of East Grinstead as EG8 and worked the 07.55 departure to Reigate and back on route 424. The weather was cold, and winter had already set in with a vengeance. On returning to East Grinstead, the driver decided that sentiment and practicality were not compatible even at a time of good cheer. XF 3 was taken out of service with defective heaters.

Curiously, in the late summer of 1982, London Transport was yet again overhauling Routemasters which they purchased from London Country in 1977/8. Whilst for London Country this had been a saga of *new buses for old* – for London Transport it turned into a tale of *old buses for new*. As later events unfolded, the Routemaster would seem to go on and on, almost for ever!

The remaining London Country years were to see many new coaches delivered, as detailed in a following chapter, but the intake of new buses fell to a steady fifteen per year for the 1983–5 period. From 1982 a new class of bus, the Leyland Olympian with

Top left **An unexpected purchase in 1980 was that of seven DMSs from London Transport for use on driver training duties. They were repainted NBC green with a yellow band but only stayed with London Country for a relatively short time. From late 1982 they were sold for further passenger service to Midland Red East and the vehicle shown here, DMS 631, seen at the Green Line Golden Jubilee Rally at Crawley in 1980, was the last to go in March 1983. Converted members of the AN class replaced them as trainers.** Barry LeJeune

Centre left **XF 3 was destined to be the last member of the class to be used in passenger service, running for the last time on Christmas Eve 1981 just a week prior to the closure of its home garage at East Grinstead. The bus is seen a few years earlier at Gatwick Road/Rutherford Way in Crawley on peak hour route 438.** Mike Harris

Left **On 24th April 1982 London Country took over from LT the responsibility for the Barnet to St Albans link, surprisingly keeping the 84 route number. The route was the first to use the new LR class of Leyland Olympian double-deckers. Brand new LR 5 is passing through High Barnet.** Geoff Rixon

72-seat Roe bodies, became the new standard double decker for the remaining years of the company with classification LR being re-used. Thirty were delivered in 1982 with the first examples entering service on 24th April on route 84, between St Albans and New Barnet, newly acquired from London Transport. Later deliveries went to Leatherhead, Reigate and Godstone and a complex reallocation exercise enabled AN 1-9 to be released for conversion to driver training buses. This enabled the DMSs and two AF trainers to be withdrawn with AF 3 and DMS 631 and DMS 640 surviving into 1983. The AFs had not proved as reliable as the ANs and four had been withdrawn in 1981. The allocation of LRs to Godstone enabled the remainder to be withdrawn with AF 10 being the last one in passenger service, surviving until early October.

Two stalwarts from the 1950s were finally withdrawn in 1982 – 581J (ex RLH 44), the mobile uniform issue unit, and towing bus RF 79 with the former being replaced by a suitably converted LNB 57. Further inroads were made with the small Bristol classes as routes were either approved for SNB operation or became subject to further service withdrawals. From May Amersham had five BNs and St Albans two with each garage having a BL trainer although, in practice the St Albans examples were often used as staff ferry buses. The need for the two St Albans BNs ceased from July 1983 when the turn at Whitwell was no longer used but the garage retained the BL. During 1983 three BLs and 27 BNs were disposed of. The practice of painting dual-purpose vehicles half-green and half-white was discontinued with Windsor's SNC 191 being the last example to be so treated after overhaul in August. The fad for advertisement buses continued with the use of the *Unibus* version and the all over version now referred to as *Colorbus*.

A further interesting development in 1982 was that London Country contracted to provide three buses on the London Transport Round London Sightseeing Tour. ANs 106, 110, 109 and 116 were painted into red livery with the first two buses being converted into open toppers. They were allocated to Leatherhead and at times when not being used on the tour were occasionally used on London Country services. They were joined in June 1983 by AN 10 and AN 11 in a special livery for use on the rival London Crusader's RLST. London Crusader, a newly formed subsidiary of the NBC, also required an open top vehicle and London Country hired an open top Bristol VRT until AN 5, a recent low bridge casualty, was eventually converted to an open topper. AN 10 was subsequently converted to open top for the 1984 season and AN 108 was painted red for the LT tour. AN 109 changed its allegiance in 1985 when it was repainted into *London Crusader* livery.

The new bus delivery for 1983 was a modest fifteen LRs which all went to Hatfield releasing ANs to Northfleet to replace SNBs on 495/6, albeit on a reduced frequency to offset the additional capacity. Routes 300 and 303 received LRs, displacing LNBs, in October after problems with overhanging trees had been overcome. By the end of the year Godstone's LR 30 became the first of the class to appear in *Unibus* livery. Also in 1983 some fourteen SNBs 122, 147, 174, 183, 186, 187, 190, 191, 192, 193, 194, 199, 201 and 203 were formed into a central pool, being given the garage code CP, and were moved from garage to garage to cover

Above right **Upon withdrawal in 1970 RLH 44 was converted into a mobile uniform store and numbered into the service fleet as 581J, lasting in this role until 1982 when it acted for a time as office accommodation at Stevenage Garage. The vehicle is seen at Chelsham in March 1975.** Colin Brown

Right **Certain RFs were converted into towing tenders, first remaining in Lincoln green livery but subsequently acquiring a yellow and grey livery with variations between buses. They were not given numbers in the service fleet and the last survivor, RF 79, was withdrawn in 1982.** John Bull

Amersham and St Albans garages were the last strongholds of the BN class. St Albans needed two for route 304 until July 1983, when the problem with a turn at Whitwell was overcome. BN 34 is seen with RS 8 and SMW 11 (which was not at all suited to National green livery) at St Albans garage in August 1980. *John Bull*

Godstone's LR 30 became the first Olympian, in December 1983, to carry *UniBus* livery advertising *Mixamate* concrete. The bus is in Bromley on a short working on route 410. *Colin Brown*

buses in the Central Repair Works. The composition of the pool changed in 1984 by the addition of SNB 253 and SNB 254, plus ANs 18, 19, 20 and 32 with vehicles becoming allocated to a particular area.

Between April and June 1984 a further fifteen LRs were taken into stock with four going to Leatherhead, six to Watford and five to Harlow. This year saw the demise of the LNBs with thirty being sold and LNBs 48, 50

and 64 being retained as trainers. LNB 24, which had been put into store, returned to Hatfield from November 1983 until January when it was converted into a private hire coach for the disabled financed by Essex County and Harlow councils. LNB 69 was in use at Reigate until September when it was switched to Grays for a school contract working as no other vehicle could be spared until the following February when it was replaced by a TD. After this it was converted similarly to LNB 24 for use in Hemel Hempstead.

A further fifteen LRs (61–75) were delivered in 1985 but these differed from earlier examples in that they were bodied by Eastern Coach Works rather than Roe. They arrived during April and May with six going to Hatfield, five to Watford, and two each to Harlow and Leatherhead. Four at Hatfield were used on the newly won tender for London Transport 313, two at Harlow were for Green Line 799 Stansted – Victoria journeys and others enabled SNBs to be released to use on LT tendered route P4. This route was worked from the National London Coaches base at Catford to which SNBs 399, 411, 412, 476 and 483 were allocated. The first four were in the all-over green livery, initially without fleetname but later they gained National London fleetnames while SNB 483 was in a striking white livery. The route required extra buses on a Saturday with SNBs being loaned from Chelsham.

By 1985 some NBC subsidiaries had started to deviate modestly from the imposition of corporate identity. As far as LCBS was concerned the most exciting develop-

In 1982 London Country was contracted to provide three buses in red livery for the London Transport Round London Sightseeing Tour. AN 109 is seen *right* in Trafalgar Square in April 1982 and *centre right* open-top AN 110 is at Aldwych in 1984. From June 1983 London Crusader, a newly formed NBC subsidiary, started a rival tour with London Country providing AN 10 and AN 11 in a dedicated livery, the latter being seen *bottom right* in Trafalgar Square. The ANs for both of these tours were garaged at Leatherhead.
Mike Harris / Colin Brown

ment was the adoption of a revised livery for the bus fleet. On 1st October AN 208 and SNB 361 appeared with a light green relief in place of the white and a white fleetname without the NBC symbol but this too was later changed to light green and looked a vast improvement. By the end of the year some 75 buses had been so treated.

The prospect of further London Transport tendered routes being acquired meant that additional double deck buses would be required at fairly short notice. The company decided to purchase second hand vehicles, the first of which came in 1985 from Southdown (Brighton & Hove) and consisted of eight Park Royal bodied Atlanteans of 1974 vintage which were virtually identical to the LCBS single door examples. They were placed in store until early 1986 when, upon repaint, they became AN 294 to AN 301 which meant that the company now had 299 ANs – AN 98 and AN 99 had both been written off after fire damage. Four more, AN 302 to AN 305, came in March 1986 and were placed straight into service at Chelsham without a repaint. An additional bus was also acquired to be canni- balised for spare parts. Starting in May the first of a batch of 31 Alexander *AL* single doorway 76-seat bodied Atlanteans were bought from Strathclyde PTE who delivered them in a repainted and refurbished state. AN 306 to AN 336 of 1974/5 vintage were of quite a distinctive appearance with panoramic windows but they were to prove to be unreliable in service. They were destined for use on more LRT tendered services at Hatfield for 298, Dorking for 293, and to a re-opened Swanley for route 51. Others went to Hemel Hempstead for 347/8 and St Albans for 321, these allocations being gained from Watford where LT tendered route 142 was allocated. A further batch of 1974 Park Royal bodied Atlanteans, AN 346–356, ex Northern General Transport, started to enter service in July with ten going to Chelsham for routes 197 and 403 while one went to Swanley to work on the 51. The gap in the numbering represented by AN 337–345 was for a

further batch of Strathclyde buses which were not delivered until after the Company's split.

The only brand new buses and, in fact, the last to be delivered to London Country in 1986 were twelve Mercedes L608D 20-seat minibuses. They were classified MBM – MiniBus Mercedes – and the first six appeared in a dark green and lime green livery for Borehamwood Bustler and the balance were in a dark green and yellow livery for the LRT tendered 268 service. As circumstances turned out MBM 5 had to be transferred to Addlestone at the end of March to work on route 264 following the hasty withdrawal of Mole Valley from stage carriage work. The others were allocated to Scratchwood Services on the M1 which was an outstation of Watford. Under new conditions minibus drivers were responsible under a lead driver for cleaning and re-fuelling their buses with the maintenance being contracted to Mercedes. The Borehamwood service started on 22nd March with the 268 following in May and the MBMs were joined by BN 66 used as a ferry bus.

Now in its seventeenth year the London Country fleet was easily recognisable as a National Bus Company standard one. All former London Transport types had been replaced and in the *border* towns it was not always possible at a quick glance to tell if a bus belonged to London Country or any other NBC operator using the green livery.

Above **A new livery was introduced in October 1985 incorporating the light green band which initially retained the white fleet name, which was subsequently altered to light green. From 4th December 1982 London Transport provided a service on route 201 when the Epping – Ongar section of the Central Line was reduced to operate during Monday to Friday peak hours only. Unusually, London Country worked one journey making the route a unique example of joint operation between the two companies. LCBS acquired more workings over the years but ceased to operate on the route when it was contracted to West's Coaches on 24th May 1986.**

Harlow's SNB 228 is seen working the route on the last day of London Country's operation. Mike Harris

Below **Prior to the split of LCBS on 7th September 1986, the company acquired various second-hand Atlanteans, including some 31 from Strathclyde PTE Glasgow, in order to cope with the additional work taken on with the London Regional Transport tendered routes. In the north-west newer double-deckers were drafted to tendered route 142 and the second-hand Atlanteans were allocated to routes 321, 347 and 348. AN 310 is seen at Uxbridge Station on route 348.** John Boylett

During the 1960s in such towns the London Transport buses always seemed vastly superior to anything that the neighbouring operators could put on the road. As explained in a later chapter London Country's luxury coach fleet was something of which any company could be proud. Despite all the hype in 1970 about the age of the inherited, but nonetheless reliable fleet, the company had acquired some 63 Atlanteans, mostly for tendered routes, which were at the end of the NBC optimum life span of 12 years. In addition, it must be remembered, the company was also operating 118 of its own Atlanteans which were approaching 14 years old.

Not all of the inheritance had faded however and London Country stood out among its fellows in NBC, not least because of the fleet numbering system itself. Class letters within NBC were only shared with Eastern Counties, National Welsh and Crosville, but with all three the numbers were in common series. It was only London Country that continued LT practice of starting at one for every basic type. An NBC standard fleet it may have been, but there was still room for tradition. The 118 ANs referred to above perpetuated the London Transport three box blind arrangement at the front and most of the fleet still carried the London Transport style stencil holders for the painted garage code and running number.

Above **In the 1986 season neither London Transport nor London Crusader wanted to use London Country's staff or vehicles on their Round London Sightseeing Tours. London Country enterprisingly deployed the four open-top ANs (5, 10, 106 and 110), which were repainted into a green and white livery, on its own Green Line Sightseeing Tour with the buses carrying the Green Line fleetname. From 8th** June eight daily departures from the National Gallery were provided with a fare of £4 for the 1½ hour tour. AN 5 is seen crossing London Bridge. John Boylett

Below **By the 1980s vehicles in the training fleet had received yellow bands and very smart they looked. RP 50 and AN 4 stand side by side at the new Crawley premises.** Colin Brown

51

Chapter 5

THE ROUTE NETWORK IN 1970

RML 2335 in the London Country lighter green livery stands outside its home garage of Godstone while working on route 409. The sighting beacon on the nearside front wing with which all of the Godstone Routemasters were originally fitted is just visible. The damage to the dome is typical of many buses and despite the employment of specialised tree cutting vehicles is caused by overhanging branches. Although most of the service on 409 comprised shorts from Croydon to Caterham or Godstone, an hourly projection continued south to Forest Row in East Sussex, the only point in that county to be served by an LCBS bus route at the time. Colin Brown

THE STORY of the restructuring of the bus route network is characterised by three things. First, the widespread adoption of one-man operation, very quickly at first, virtually doubling in three years; second, a policy of co-operation and consolidation with neighbouring operators which resulted in several routes getting buses from a different operator; and third, probably the most important in terms of financial effect, involvement with local authorities in the route structures and levels of fares. It will be seen that there was to be some variance in services provided in later years, depending on the level of subsidy provided by the county supporting them.

The basic route network inherited by London Country had changed little since the formation of the London Passenger Transport Board in 1933. The main trunk routes were in many cases the same and over the years as industry and towns had expanded additional local services were provided to suit their needs. The system still operated within the arbitrary boundaries

defined by the London Passenger Transport Act of 1933. An unfortunate effect of this legislation was to cause a noticeable divide through the middle of border towns – Hitchin, Guildford and Gravesend were examples. The area was bounded by Crawley, Guildford, Windsor, High Wycombe, Tring, Luton, Hitchin, Bishops Stortford, Brentwood, Tilbury, Gravesend, Wrotham and East Grinstead. A number of projections just beyond the area had been withdrawn during the decade prior to London Country's take-over – Country Buses no longer went to Ascot, West Wycombe, Ewhurst, Coryton or Four Elms, but they still ventured to Aylesbury, Letchworth and Forest Row. Although construction of the New Towns had resulted in many new routes, these were mostly self-contained. In many cases a journey across the town centre often meant changing and it could be that the next mode of transport would be the train. Until 1958 this did not really matter – there were plenty of passengers to go round. The heyday of public transport ended abruptly in that year.

The budding motor car industry, which had been stifled by post-war raw materials and fuel shortages now went into top gear. As the economy perked up, standards of living rose. The motor car, quick, convenient and giving unheard of freedom, became the desirable thing to own. Weekend leisure travel by bus became a day trip by car. Following the disastrous strike of 1958 there were major cuts to bus services. A seemingly vicious circle of more cars, fewer buses and yet more cars was accompanied by the growth of television, which bit deep into evening and weekend travel. The scale of the problem is illustrated by the fact that in the early 1960s the car ownership rate in Harlow was twice the national average. Apart from the introduction of *Green Rover* tickets little was done to attract or retain custom. Economies of operation were not practised to any large extent – of the one-man operated routes most had been previously crew single-deck with only a few examples being converted from double deck to one-man RF operation.

In the mid-1960s, following the introduction of the RMCs and a general downward trend in vehicle requirements, RFs were rendered surplus and a start had been made on conversion of some double-deck routes to one-man single-deck. Examples of routes so treated include 313 (St Albans – Enfield), 342 (Colney Heath – Dunstable), 402 (Bromley – Tonbridge), 439 (Dorking – Redhill) and 460 (Staines – Slough). No doubt there were many other candidates for such treatment but as no new vehicles were forthcoming the opportunities were somewhat limited. Another economy in the mid 1960s was the conversion of the remaining crew operated RF routes to one-man operation (391/A St Albans local, 447/A/B Reigate local and 458 Slough – Uxbridge). As events turned out the first two were subsequently destined to be operated with Merlins. London Transport's

Reshaping Plan of 1968 envisaged larger capacity single-deck vehicles working as *pay the driver* on rural routes and by automated fare collection on short in-town routes. The first of these buses had entered service on the route 447 in March 1968. At the time Trade Union objections blocked their use to convert crew routes, but in November 1968 these objections were overcome and both types entered service in the way that had been intended. MBs (conventional omo) took over from RTs on rural routes 305/A, 455 (High Wycombe – Uxbridge corridor). MBSs took over from RTs on route 430 (Reigate – Redhill) using the new *Autofare* method of fare collection. Two Bell Punch ticket dispensers were installed immediately behind the driver on each side of the vehicle. Farescales on this and all subsequent Autofare routes were simplified, in the case of route 430 to just two fares, 6d and 1/-. More Autofare routes were introduced in 1969 at Hemel Hempstead, Tring, St Albans, Welwyn Garden City, Harlow, Gravesend, Slough and Watford. A further minor operating economy was achieved during 1969 when some 12 crew-operated routes were converted to one-man operation on Sundays using single-deck buses surplus on that day.

On 29th December 1969 London Transport introduced a new service for factory workers at Stevenage. This revolutionary, though not unique, idea was a bold

step in a bid to woo the motorist out of his car and on to the bus. Three XFs painted in a livery of blue and silver operated a service under the name *Blue Arrow* from Chells to the Industrial Area. The buses were timed to match factory starting and finishing times. Buses did not observe bus stops but picked up and set down at road junctions convenient for passengers' homes and at factory entrances within the Industrial Area. Each journey carried its regular complement of Season Ticket holders, there being no ordinary fares. Couriers were carried on Mondays in order to issue Season Tickets. Three days after the Blue Arrows started all Country buses and Green Line coaches were taken over by London Country, the Blue Arrows forming their only double-deck one-man allocation. It must be remembered, however, that double-deck one-man operation was not legalised until 1969. The

Amersham garage has been fitted with new London Country signage. On 20th February 1971 it became the company's first 100 per cent omo garage. All remaining RTs were ousted and the principal omo allocation at the garage was SM, of which SM 479 stands on the forecourt displaying a short-working 'lazy' blind. On the same date Green Line 710 was truncated to run to Uxbridge only and ran for the last time on 13th October 1972. The Green Line compulsory stop flag is unusual in that it has been fixed directly to the building. Steve Fennell

Left In *Blue Arrow* livery, XF 6 tours the Stevenage Industrial Area. The route number blind displayed A1 and A2 which corresponded to running numbers SV61 and SV62. Only two buses were ever used for this service, although the blinds optimistically provided numbers up to A6. John Boylett

Below LT produced the initial publicity for the *Blue Arrow* service which they operated for just three days (29th–31st December 1969). The XFs ran for a brief period with London Country fleetnames and London Transport legal ownership lettering. In a break from the traditional LT style of publicity of the time London Country soon produced various cartoon style material.

COMING TO STEVENAGE

BLUE ARROW

Starting December 29

CHELLS–STEVENAGE FACTORY AREA

↑ NO WAITING FOR BUSES
↑ GUARANTEED SEATS

Let us meet you and take you to work

Who's missing out on the Blue Arrow run?

Work and back, door to door for two bob a day

company had just over 300 bus routes at 1st January 1970, of which just over one third carried suffix letters. The vehicle requirement was for 892 buses (563 crew, 329 omo) on Mondays–Fridays, 642 (383 crew, 259 omo) on Saturdays, and 196 (104 crew, 92 omo) on Sundays. The percentage of omo, 37, 40 and 47 respectively, was to change dramatically within three years.

Speculation was rife in the early part of 1970 as to the future direction of London Country. With several towns served by both LCBS and other NBC concerns, wholesale switching of routes from one operator to another and several garage closures were suggested. However, it must be remembered that LCBS was basically at that time a hived-off part of London Transport. No other NBC Company operated vehicles similar to London Country, scheduling was carried out in a unique way, and conditions of employment and rates of pay were also very different. It was to be a few years before LCBS operations and vehicles were to become sufficiently similar to other National Bus undertakings for any integration to take place.

Upon its inception London Country was in a very unhealthy financial state. A large number of routes simply did not show a profit. Traditionally the system had been based on cross-subsidisation with the profitable routes supporting the loss makers. Over the years, however, the system failed to work as the number of loss makers far exceeded those making a profit. A policy of 100 per cent one-man operation was to be embarked on. In addition, local authorities were now empowered to subsidise loss-making rural routes for which there was a social need and LCBS asked for subsidies for a number of routes.

A major disadvantage with one-man-operation is the time taken to load up, and to be successful it is desirable that the majority of passengers have some sort of pre-paid ticket. At the time the vast majority of passengers were required to pay a cash fare. Weekly tickets had been available in part of the Northern Area under LT but by the time of the take-over only about 50 per week were issued. An experiment was carried out in St Albans with pre-paid tickets. On 4th May 1970 a self-service ticket machine was installed at the northbound 304, 355, 365 stop in St Peter's Street to enable passengers to buy their tickets in advance. The machine was removed on 16th August 1970 due to the fare increases from that date. Results from this experiment were never published, but use of the machine is

Routes 304, 355 and 365

BUY TICKETS IN ADVANCE

starting Monday May 4

At Stop 8 in St. Peters Street an experimental self-service machine will sell 6d. tickets for use on Routes 304, 355 and 365 between St. Albans and Wheathampstead.

Tickets may be used together for either a 1/- or 1/6 fare.

known to have been disappointing. A significant proportion of sales was probably to enthusiasts who kept the tickets. The fares revision – the first general one with London Country Bus Services – was an increase of about 11 per cent. As an extension to the well established Green Rover facility a *Golden Rover* ticket was introduced, at 15/- (75p), giving un-

TRAVEL THE ROVER WAY
These tickets are available on Mondays to Fridays after 09xx and any time at Weekends and Bank Holidays

GREEN ROVERS
8/- (40p) Adult   6/- (30p) Child
For a day's unlimited travel on all London Country buses
Buy them on the bus

GOLDEN ROVERS
15/- (75p) Adult   11/- (55p) Child
For a day's unlimited travel on all London Country buses and Green Line coaches (except route 727)
Buy them on the bus or coach

Above On 16th August 1970 a Golden Rover ticket giving unlimited availability on both buses and Green Line coaches, except initially route 727, was introduced to complement the well-established Green Rover facility. The company promoted the facilities over the years and this leaflet dating from October 1970 is interesting in that it quotes the decimal fare equivalent values well prior to the change-over in February 1971.

Left In a move to speed boarding times on one-man operated buses a machine was installed by the appropriate stop in St Peters Street, St Albans in May 1970. No further such machines ever appeared and it must be concluded that the experiment was not considered successful.

The new order came to London Country in the form of Swifts, the first of which were used to convert route 418 to one-man operation on 27th June 1970. A brand new SM 110 is seen opposite Leatherhead garage. The first SMs to be delivered did not carry the new London Country logo below the windscreen.
Colin Brown

limited bus and Green Line Travel for one day (except on route 727), and a campaign was launched to publicise them.

The first stage in the one-man programme occurred on 27th June 1970 when route 424 (Reigate – East Grinstead) was converted using the existing XA and XF vehicles, this being made possible by recent the legislation permitting one-man operation of double-deck vehicles. On the same day route 418 (Kingston – Great Bookham) lost its RTs in favour of SMs. Continuing LT policy, some more routes were converted to omo on Sundays, this time in the Amersham and Hertford areas. The Sunday service on routes 307 and 319 (Hemel Hempstead) ceased, the latter being a short-lived experimental service which local residents had requested, but rarely used in the event. Sunday reductions were to be a feature of subsequent years. More omo was introduced on the first day of August, again using SMs, to eliminate the only low-height buses (RLH class) in the fleet at Guildford and Addlestone. SMs also ousted many RTs from Town Services at Crawley, this being the first conversion of in-town local services to conventional omo, the idea of Autofare for this type of route now being abandoned – the experiment had not been a success and was never to be repeated.

Continued expansion at Stevenage resulted in an RT route to the new area of St Nicholas from 12th September 1970. The number 809 was chosen, probably because only one of these already existed, whereas there were already three 800s and three 801s – the Stevenage Town Services were

decidedly complex, and LT's route numbering policies have rarely been easy to comprehend. LCBS simplified things a little since, but the anomalies continued.

On the first day of November, elderly and handicapped persons' passes were introduced in Stevenage. These permitted half-fare travel during the off-peak period on Mondays to Fridays. The local authority met all the costs involved. It was the first such scheme involving LCBS and eventually spread throughout the area. Many different schemes appeared, some involving tokens and others free or reduced-rate travel. This resulted in several anomalies at authority boundaries, and some still exist, dependent on the policies and the politics of the local authority involved.

The major event of 1971 was, of course, Decimalisation which involved quite a lot of

expense for London Country. Decimal Day on the buses was 22nd February, six days after everyone else, to enable sufficient decimal coinage to circulate. This plan backfired somewhat, old pennies and three-penny pieces virtually disappearing within days. A by-product of Decimalisation was the removal of the Autofare machines. The use of the machines had caused a number of

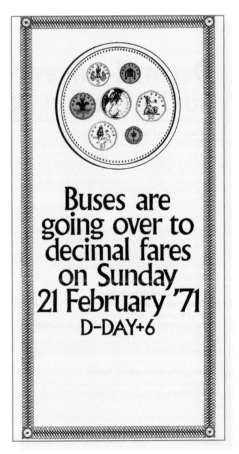

Buses are going over to decimal fares on Sunday 21 February '71 D-DAY+6

New Route 433

HORSHAM - LAMBS FARM - GREENFIELDS ROFFEY - HORSHAM

On and from June 27, a new route 433 will be introduced to Greenfields Estate.

This route will be a circular service with buses running in a clockwise and anti-clockwise direction.

The route, operated by double-deck vehicles will run via Rusper Road, Lambs Farm Road, Greenfields Estate, Shepherds Way, Roffey Corner and then follow routes 434, 473 to Horsham Carfax.

Left **London Country's first new route was the Horsham local 433 which was RT worked by Crawley garage.** Letters subsequently appeared in a local newspaper complaining of the unreliability of the service but unlike London Transport whose policy was to reply to such letters the new company chose not to do so. In the mid-1970s due to both vehicle and staff shortages local newspapers across the entire network contained many such letters.

Right This leaflet was produced to advise passengers of the impending conversion to decimal currency. All conductors and driver-operators were given training and ticketing systems had to be revised to suit the new currency. The Gibson machines which were used by most bus conductors at the time were not amended and some obsolete fare values were used to represent new values – for example the 11d was issued as a 1p ticket and the 1s 2d value represented 7½p. Notices were displayed in the buses but the new arrangements must have been confusing to both conductors and passengers. Following the release of Setright Speed ticket machines due to the one-man conversion of the remaining Green Line routes and the provision of more Almex machines on one-man operated buses the Gibson machines were phased out over the next few years.

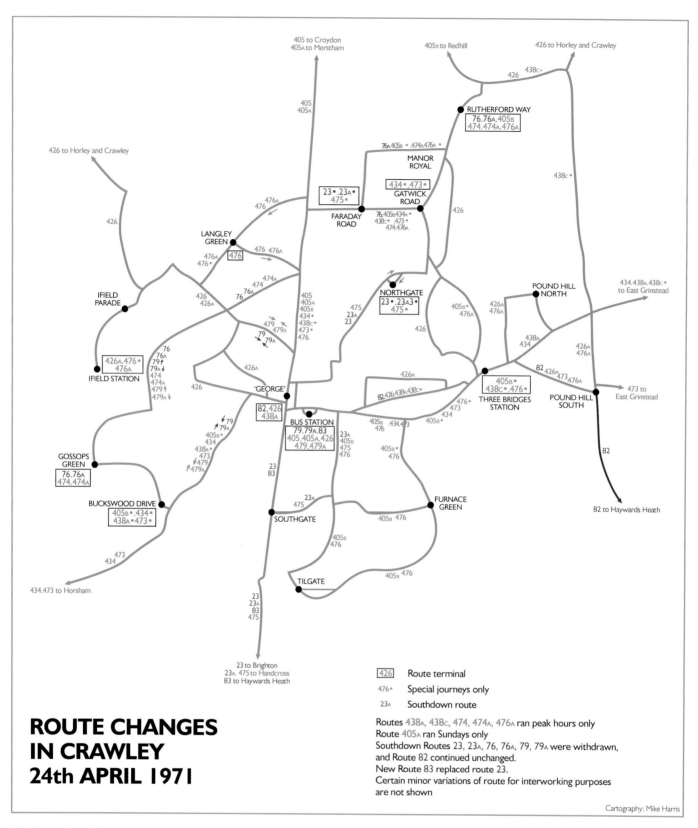

**ROUTE CHANGES
IN CRAWLEY
24th APRIL 1971**

Legend:
- 426 — Route terminal
- 476• — Special journeys only
- 23A — Southdown route

Routes 438A, 438C, 474, 474A, 476A ran peak hours only
Route 405A ran Sundays only
Southdown Routes 23, 23A, 76, 76A, 79, 79A were withdrawn, and Route 82 continued unchanged.
New Route 83 replaced route 23.
Certain minor variations of route for interworking purposes are not shown

Cartography: Mike Harris

The first occasion, of what was destined to become many, where there was a change of operator on routes in the London Country area occurred at Crawley on 24th April 1971. Although a small development, it was perhaps a confirmation that London Country was here to stay; there had been much gloomy speculation that the company would not survive on its own. It made a lot of sense to combine facilities in one town where two operators each had a garage.

The small Southdown garage in Crawley was closed, routes 23A, 76, 76A, 79 and 79A became London Country 475, 474, 474A, 479 and 479A respectively. Southdown 23 (Manor Royal, Crawley and Brighton) was withdrawn, with just a two-hourly 83 (Crawley and Haywards Heath) to cover part of it. Very little change occurred to the town network in Crawley for the next few years, and the complicated pattern continued with the ex-Southdown routes merely superimposed. New housing developments to the

south-west of the town caused new routes 478 and 429 to be introduced in 1972 and 1976 and, in 1977, most buses on 405 were projected from the Bus Station to either Northgate or Southgate to cover the daytime service on 475. Otherwise the network survived largely intact until the C-Line scheme of 1st July 1978.

London Country set about changing the traditional LT order by the introduction of new buses and, where scope existed, exchanging routes with neighbouring operators. On 24th April 1971 Southdown's local routes in Crawley passed to London Country and, until the C-Line revolution of 1978, remained unaffected by other town services. AEC Swift SM 143 in the pleasing original livery takes on passengers in Crawley Town Centre in May 1971.
Barry LeJeune

operational problems, particularly their unreliability on a moving vehicle and the inability for other types to substitute for the MBSs. It was decided that converting them to accept decimal currency was not worth the expense and the MBSs were converted to conventional omo from 21st February. The machines were put into store at Hemel Hempstead garage, where they remained for about ten years until a decision was taken to sell some of them off to enthusiasts at garage open days. A bus fares revision took place on 3rd July and while the 3p minimum fare was retained its availability was adjusted to apply for one half-mile stage only thus passengers wishing to travel two stages faced a rise of 1p to 4p.

The small takeover of Southdown's local services at Crawley from 24th April 1971 seemed revolutionary at the time, but it was only the first of a considerable number of border route exchanges to achieve economies of operation. In this case Southdown's small garage in Crawley was closed, RTs came to Gossops Green and SMs to Northgate and Handcross, the latter becoming at the time the most southerly point served by London Country.

On 20th March 1971 some Stevenage local routes received alterations and SMs were introduced on the Chells section of route 809. For a few weeks these were conventional omo but from 8th May 1971 fareboxes (the first on LCBS) were fitted. Following local surveys among the public a new livery of yellow and blue was adopted and the service was marketed under the name *Superbus* from 31st July. The Chells 809 became an unnumbered Superbus service and was speeded up to run direct to and from the Town Centre – 'fast, frequent and cheap' became the slogan. Publicity was plentiful and loadings exceeded all expectations. Frequencies were doubled on all days of the week and the flat-fare

Publicity material for *Superbus* appeared in a bold, distinctive style using the corporate yellow and blue colours. To emphasise the frequency it was expressed in seconds – 7½ minutes may have been somewhat more user friendly. The Chells service started on 31st July 1971 and the frequency was subsequently increased and the fare reduced.

New SUPERBUS service starts on July 31st...
travels to where the action is every 450 seconds for 6p (children 4p)

Yes! SUPERBUS service swings into action on July 31st between Chells, Stevenage Town Centre and the Industrial Area. And a SUPER bus service it is! yellow-and-blue roomy single deckers, proud 'SB' insignia will run eight times an hour, speeding you from Chells to the Town Centre

*Service interval varies late eve

Leave your car at ho[me]
and give us your driving a[nd]
parking worri[es]
Enjoy the super-convenien[ce]
super-spe[ed]
of reliable SUPERB[US]

— it's the service tha[t's]
setting the pace for the 7[0s]

minutes. For work-people early morning and late afternoon services will run on to the Industrial Area. The flat fare of 6p (Children's services excepting) for the travelling all heart...

Your SUPERBUS times...

FROM CHELLS TO TOWN CENTRE				FROM BUS STATION TO CHELLS			FROM INDUSTRIAL AREA TO TOWN CENTRE AND CHELLS					
MONDAY TO FRIDAY		SATURDAY	SUNDAY	MONDAY TO FRIDAY	SATURDAY	SUNDAY	MONDAY TO FRIDAY				SATURDAY	
							NORTH		SOUTH		From Industrial Area NORTH	SOUTH
0620	1605▽	0620	0712	0608	0608	0700	0654	1609	0709	1617	0652	0752
27△	12△	30△	Then every	Then every	Then every	Then every	0724	24	32	32	0802	
35	20▽	40	30 mins until	7½ mins until	10 mins until	30 mins until	39	39	47	47		
42▽	27△	50	1042	2000	1030	1030	54	54	0802	1702		
50	35▽	0700	Then every	and every			0809	1709	17	17		
57△	42△	10	15 mins until	15 mins until	Then every	Then every	24	24	32	32		
0705▽	50▽	20	2012	2330	15 mins until	15 mins until	39	39	47	47		
12△	57△	30▽	Then every		1900	2000	54	54		1802		
20▽	1705▽	40△	30 mins until		Then every	Then every	0902			1902*		
27△	12△	50	2342		10 mins until	10 mins until	09					
35▽	20▽	0800			2300	2330						
42△	27△	10			30							
50▽	35▽	20			2400				* Monday to			
57△	42	30			0030				Thursday only			
0805▽		40										
12△	Then every	50										
20▽	7½ mins until											
27△	2057	Then every										
35△		7½ mins until										
42△	Then every	1912										
50	15 mins until	Then every										
	2342	15 mins until										
Then every		2312										
7½ mins until	Then every	Then every										
1535	10 mins until	10 mins until										
42△	2312	2312										
50▽		0012										
57△		42										

Those journeys marked run on to the Stevenage Industrial Area
△NORTH ▽SOUTH

GO BY BUS—
YOUR SERVICE IS GETTING BETTER ALL THE TIME!

LONDON COUNTRY BUS SERVICES LTD
DANESTRETE · STEVENAGE · TEL STEVENAGE 54561

This scene in Luton was taken immediately before the complete withdrawal of route 364 which linked Flamstead and Hitchin. RF 593 is working on route 366 to Welwyn Garden City and, following the withdrawal of the weekday 365, lost its limited stop status as the destination blind shows the wording *Limited Stop* having been blanked out. RF 290 is bound for Hitchin, a link which had been established by F.C.H. Motor Haulage & Engineering Co Ltd, who sold out to National in 1926. Steve Fennell

became 6p. In February 1972 the fare dropped to 4p. The success was such that the usefulness of *Blue Arrow* was reduced, and in March the XFs were replaced by SMs and the service itself came off in September. With this stage more *Superbus* vehicles were introduced into the fleet and the 809 section to St Nicholas came into the network. Route

numbers SB1 (Chells) and SB2 (St Nicholas) were adopted and so was the 6p fare again, this to become standard throughout the town in October on all routes. However on 19th November the Sunday *Superbus* fare went down to an unprecedented 3p, with pensioners and children travelling for just one penny!

The changes of 7th August 1971 were to be of far-reaching consequence, even though the routes concerned would not have been missed by many. Infrequent rural routes 329 (Hertford – Knebworth, Nup End), 381 (Harlow, Epping – Toot Hill), 807 (Stevenage – Letchworth via Weston) together with the odd rail replacement route 351 (Buntingford

The London Country bus services running into Bedfordshire were still intact by the autumn of 1971, but reductions in support by that county caused a speedy deterioration. The main services to Dunstable came from the St Albans direction and from 8th January 1972 they were changed so that 342 now ran only on Saturdays, with 343 extended from Markyate to Dunstable on Monday to Saturday. This was in consequence of the conversion of these routes to one-man operation. From 19th February 1972 route 337 north of Studham and the whole of route 352 were withdrawn. Route 364A comprising of the main route from Hitchin to Kensworth, projections to Whipsnade Zoo and the supplementary service, formerly numbered 343A, from Studham to Dunstable was withdrawn. Route 364 was diverted to omit Woodside running from Luton to the nearest point outside

LONDON COUNTRY BUS ROUTES IN BEDFORDSHIRE AUTUMN 1971

AC-DELCO WORKS

337•.342•
364A•

337•.342•
352.360•
364A

DUNSTABLE

342
360•
364A•

352

337

342
364A

KENSWORTH
'Farmers Boy'

364A•

WHIPSNADE
ZOO

364A

364A

352
DAGNALL

STUDHAM

364A•

343
MARKYATE

342
343 364

342•.343•
364

FLAMSTEAD
VILLAGE

337

337 to
Hemel Hempstead

CADDINGTON
360•

360

WOODSIDE

LUTON

321.360
365.366

LUTON
AIRPORT

364A
364

VAUXHALL
WORKS

365
366

321

364A
364

364. 364A
to Hitchin

365 to St. Albans
366 to Welwyn Garden City

321 to St. Albans
and Uxbridge

342 to St. Albans
343 to Brookmans Park

- - - Bedfordshire County Boundary

352 Route terminal

364A• Special journeys only

NOTE: The Summer only services to Whipsnade Zoo are not shown

Cartography: Mike Harris

Bedfordshire which was Markyate. From 15th July 1972 the Monday to Saturday service on 365 was withdrawn with the limited stop service 366 revised to serve all stops into Luton. The cessation of the Sunday

remnant of 365 together with the remaining sections of 337 and 364 was on 7th July 1973. With the loss of so much work around Luton it was not surprising that the London Country garage closed in 1977.

Independent operator Court Line took over sections of route south and west of Dunstable and Jey-son Coaches took over the 364 between Luton and Hitchin. Both operators eventually collapsed

with United Counties stepping in. The Dunstable journeys on the 360 ceased from 28th June 1975 so as to provide a bus for a new route 365 to Kimpton and Codicote, described elsewhere in this

section. From 4th December 1976 the remaining section of 360 from Luton to Caddington was passed to United Counties.

The group of rural bus routes in the Longfield area suffered heavily after 1970. The Saturday only 452 was the first to go from 20th February 1971. Then from 8th January 1972 reductions in financial support by Kent County Council caused the complete withdrawal of routes 451, 489 and 489A but a new 490A (later renumbered 489) was introduced between Gravesend and Ash via New Barn thus covering some sections. However, Fawkham Green and Meopham were never again served by London Country and, by 1980, Betsham and Westwood had only two buses per day.

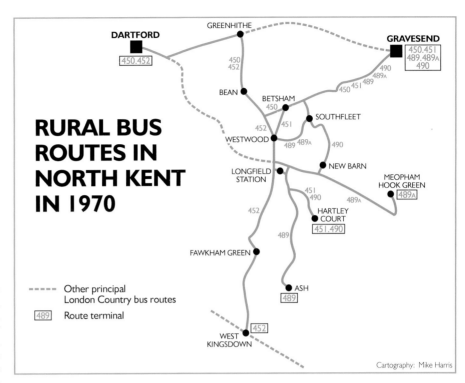

RURAL BUS ROUTES IN NORTH KENT IN 1970

Cartography: Mike Harris

– Much Hadham via Ware) all ceased to run. An independent operator took over the 381 and LCBS was to return a few years later to the 329 roads. In view of a considerable amount of speculation over further proposed route withdrawals, the Company issued a statement to the effect that "the County Councils have received three months formal notification of the Company's intention to withdraw loss making rural routes, but have been invited by the Company to enter into discussions on the possibility of making a grant for any of the routes which they may wish to be retained. No final decision has been reached on the withdrawal or curtailment of any route, and will not be until final decisions are reached by all the Local Authorities concerned as to whether they wish to make a grant to maintain any of the routes involved. It would therefore be premature at this stage to assume that any particular route will be withdrawn or curtailed". Whether it was the long-winded statement or the financial considerations, it is difficult to say, but Bedfordshire and Buckinghamshire County Councils declined to make grants towards the threatened services, and during February 1972 a number of cuts were made. The following routes or sections of routes were withdrawn: 337 (Studham – Dunstable), 352 (Dunstable – Dagnall) and 364A (Whipsnade – Luton). Route 364 was diverted away from Woodside and ran non-stop between the County Boundary (near Aley Green Turning) to Luton. Passengers could no longer make local journeys within Bedfordshire. It would seem that County Council support, or rather the lack of it, was recreating similar anomalies to the 1933 legislation.

Route 359 was withdrawn between Great Missenden and Aylesbury and diverted to Chesham. Various revisions and service reductions were made in the Amersham and Chesham area. The changes to routes 337 and 364 led to their complete demise in July 1973, caused by loss of traffic sources. Another rural loss-maker to disappear at this time was the 494 (East Grinstead – Oxted).

In Kent, LCBS rural services based in Gravesend and Sevenoaks were severely

pruned from 8th January 1972. The last GS worked route, the 336A (Rickmansworth – Loudwater), ran on 30th March, having become totally uneconomic taking receipts as low as £6 a day. Following Hillingdon Borough Council's decision to withdraw their subsidy, route 309A was withdrawn and route 309 severely pruned between Rickmansworth and Harefield from 30th December, only to be restored six months later after a council re-think. A rather different attitude prevailed few years later when Hillingdon sponsored their own bus service (LT route 128) in the area! In the 1972 climate of withdrawals a surprise was the extension of route 384 to Baldock, from 14th October, in the evenings and on Sundays for the benefit of visitors to the large Lister Hospital in North Stevenage. It was the first service of *London* buses to Baldock since LT withdrew in May 1936 and lasted just over four years.

The advance of one-man operation continued through 1971. On 20th February routes 303/A (Hitchin – New Barnet), 353 (Berkhamsted – Windsor) and 362/A (High Wycombe – Ley Hill) were converted, using SMs. These virtually eliminated RTs from Hatfield and High Wycombe garages and made Amersham the first all-omo garage. More SMs went to Dartford and Swanley from 3rd July bringing mass omo to the area and leaving in the main only routes 477 (Dartford – Chelsfield and 499 (Dartford local) with crew operation. The last SMs entered service at Chelsham and Dunton Green on routes 403A (Tonbridge – West Croydon), 453 (Chelsham – Caterham) and 454/A (Tonbridge – Chipstead via Weald), and by this stage 50 per cent of the fleet had become one-man operated.

London Country had a disproportionately much larger number of long serving operating staff than the former LT Central Area. Some of the very senior staff started their careers before the formation of London Transport with companies such as East Surrey, National and Green Line. The first issue of *London Country Matters* contained an article on a driver and conductor who had worked together as a crew for some 38 years! Under Trade Union agreements inherited from LT there was no compulsory redundancy for conductors – where there were surplus conductors following omo schemes many left the company with voluntary redundancy payments while others were offered driver training, coin box handling, courier duties, or were used to cover shortages at adjacent garages. In some cases surplus conductors enabled crew operated vehicles to be substituted to cover newer vehicles suffering reliability problems.

Large numbers of omo-fitted buses were delivered from late 1971 and through 1972. First were the SMW class, used to achieve much omo at St Albans on routes 338/A (St. Albans – Radlett), 343 (Brookmans Park – Markyate), 358 (St Albans – Borehamwood) and 361 (St Albans – How Wood) from 8th January 1972. They also replaced RFs at St Albans on route 342. One month later, London Country's first purpose-built omo double-deckers entered service on route 410 at Godstone garage, that garage's first omo allocation. It was, however, the AN type that was to become the standard double-deck omo vehicle and the 120 delivered in 1972 saw off a great many RTs. Of the 120 the first 90 were bodied by Park Royal and the balance by Metro-Cammell. Routes 310/A (Hertford – Enfield) were the first recipients in April

In the early months of 1972 the one-man conversion of all double-deck coach routes, except the 709, permitted the cascading of the Routemaster coaches to certain bus routes, thus enabling many RTs to be withdrawn. RMC 1513 is seen in St Albans working on trunk route 330A to Welwyn Garden City. The suffix letter, which denoted an alternative routeing via Lemsford Lane in Welwyn Garden City, was dropped from 7th February 1973 when all journeys were numbered 330. Steve Fennell

1972, followed by 408 (Guildford – West Croydon) and 470 (Dorking – West Croydon) in June. The latter conversion involved the cut back of these routes from Chelsham, with an increased service on route 403 as a result and making the latter service a major stronghold of RTs for some years to come. July saw RT operation at Garston and Luton garages much reduced with ANs on routes 321 (Luton – Uxbridge), 385/A/B (Watford locals) and express route 803 (Maple Cross – Welwyn Garden City). Also in July a small number went to Crawley for the recently

acquired ex Southdown routes 474/A, 479/A and works services 438A/C. It was found that the Metro-Cammell batch were not suitable for farebox operation thus some earlier ANs were fitted with fareboxes for use on revised Town Service networks at both Harlow and Stevenage from 14th October where a flat fare of 6p applied. The farebox system was to gain much favour and fareboxes were fitted to buses operating local routes 495/496 at Gravesend and 446/A/B at Slough, these using MBSs. The last few ANs were used on a small omo conversion, of

Grays area routes 328/A/B in February 1973. At the time of the conversion the opportunity was taken to get rid of the suffix letters with route 328A becoming 329 and 328B becoming 373.

The first ANs displaced RTs from busy routes 310/A at Hertford on 29th April 1972. The new image came to the area in quantity as Green Line 715/A also gained new coaches on the same day. AN 10 loads up in Fore Street Hertford as journeys to Sele Farm Estate did not serve the Bus Station. This bus was subsequently sent to Stevenage to be fitted with farebox equipment. Capital Transport

Left A service revision of 8th January 1972 saw twelve Marshall bodied SMWs replace RTs on routes 338/A, 343, 358, 361 and RFs on 342. The new livery suited them well, as illustrated by SMW12, passing St Peter's Church, St Albans. Capital Transport

Right A momentous day in the north-east was 14th October 1972, when the town networks at Harlow and Stevenage went over to operation by ANs fitted with Johnson fareboxes with a flat fare of 6p. The 'Unifare' (a name not used for long) system featured a no-ticket, no-change policy. Buses used for the farebox system were Park Royal bodied and some vehicle transfers took place in which new Metro-Cammell bodied ANs (not suitable for farebox wiring) went to Hertford, Garston, and Luton garages in exchange for Park Royal buses going to Stevenage and Harlow. Yet again large numbers of RTs fell by the wayside. Both towns' networks were operationally separate from the surrounding country services, seeing a considerable expansion of the 800-series of route numbers to cope with all the new route variations. Both networks remained essentially unchanged until letter-prefix numbering schemes took over in 1980. In this view, AN 67 loads up at Stevenage Bus Station in July 1974 catching a passenger actually inserting a fare into the red farebox. The seemingly simple destination blinds fail to make clear that the bus passes the Bus Station twice on its circuitous journey to Lister Hospital. John Bull

Below From 4th November 1972 a new route 478 in Crawley provided a one-bus shuttle to connect the newly-developing areas of Broadfield and Southgate West. Crawley had one SMA allocated for private hire work, but it was habitually used on the 478 and is seen here at Crawley Bus Station. Barry LeJeune

By this stage four garages (DG, GF, MA, WY) were all-omo and in addition CM, CY, DS, EG, HA, HE, HF, HG, HH, LH, LS, RG, SA, SV, TG were all-omo on Sundays with SV on Saturdays as well. A comparison with the operational requirements at LCBS's formation may be of interest here. The Monday–Friday total had dropped to 818 (253 crew, 565 omo), on Saturdays it was 595 (170 crew, 425 omo) and on Sundays 180 (25 crew, 155 omo), giving percentages of omo of 69, 71, 86 respectively, a healthy saving over that applying three years previously.

Apart from omo, much else had been done since 1970. County and Borough Councils had been reminded of their statutory duties, some Town networks had been restructured, Stevenage had a *Superbus* service and the farebox system had been adopted. It was now the time to set about consolidating the network.

Chapter 6

TAILORING THE BUS SERVICES

THE PERIOD 1973 to 1977 was a time when both rural and town services became supported by County Councils, in some cases with a *local identity*, something that was to become common in later years. It was also the time of the mass introduction of Leyland Nationals all over the fleet, and some of these were to be used for new omo conversions, especially in 1977. Their three-track route number blinds were to cause the re-numbering of a great many suffix-lettered routes, and this trend extended to routes not even operated by this type of bus. A total of 77 suffixed route numbers either disappeared or were absorbed by their parent route numbers during this five-year period, some going as

During 1973 and 1974 very many suffix lettered routes were re-numbered or simply lost their suffix to be absorbed into the main route. Various anomalies of course occurred, but it was allegedly to avoid problems on buses fitted with three-track number blinds. Virtually all suffix letters around Hemel Hempstead disappeared from 7th July 1973. The number 316 had been discontinued since 1965; 316A did not become 316 as might have been expected, but 322 simply because one end of it went to Highfield, as did the 322. Here RT 3130 is seen at Two Waters garage prior to working a journey on 322. Fred Ivey

part of route-change schemes. In general the principle was to give an en-route deviation a different number, for example, 457A became 452 because of a half-mile difference in Slough, and the parent number if at least one of the termini was the same (341B became 341). There were of course anomalies and the numbering system continued to perplex. Hatfield, one of the first garages to receive Leyland Nationals, had coped with routes such as 303A and 340B by the simple expedient of including the suffix letter on the main route blind. This practice caused the length of the blind to be considerably extended as each destination had to be repeated with the appropriate suffix. In order to achieve the correct presentation of the suffix the practice of saving length by using over lapping displays could not be employed. A few routes were gratuitously re-numbered (for example, 300 to 375) to allow the original number to be used elsewhere, so that a pair of routes could have similar or adjacent numbers to reduce the amount of blind changing when interworking.

Fares continued to rise and the serious inflation from 1973 accelerated the process. 1975 saw the heaviest fare increases, those of July being an increase of 66 per cent over January 1975 levels! A major loss of traffic was the inevitable result and service levels declined from then on. Costs continued to rise and in 1977 four garages were closed, coupled with route revisions and omo conversions. By the end of 1977 the network could be worked by 10 per cent fewer vehicles than in 1973. Fares increases in June 1973 had seen a short-lived experiment whereby a penny surcharge was made on all

EXACT FARE PLEASE

Routes 446 & 446A
are operated by FAREBOX buses
at flat fares of

7p adult, 6p child
from 09 30 to 16 00 and after 19 00 on
Mondays to Fridays and all day Saturdays,
Sundays and Public Holidays

8p adult, 7p child
before 09 30 and from 16 00 to 19 00
on Mons. to Fris. (except Public Holidays)

NO CHANGE IS GIVEN

so please have the exact fare ready
as you board and

DROP IT INTO THE FAREBOX

➤➤ **LONDON COUNTRY**
Associated with the National Bus Company

The peak hour 1p surcharge on buses was introduced with the 3rd July 1973 fares revision and proved to be unpopular and confusing to passengers. The Slough locals 446 and 446A were converted to fare box operation on 14th October 1972. This panel illustrates the complicated arrangements surrounding the peak surcharge. Altercations between passengers and drivers were apt to occur if the bus due immediately prior to 16.00 hours had been cancelled!

Deliveries of buses with 3-track route number blinds led to problems of displaying suffix letters. Some of the first Leyland National routes had suffix letters, and this Hatfield example *right* (LN 69) appears to cope fairly easily with its 303A route number. The amount of information required to be displayed has necessitated this Aldenham produced blind to break with the LT-established standard by using upper case lettering for the intermediate points. Some destinations had to be duplicated – with and without suffix letters – to reduce blind lengths most suffixes were either given new numbers or incorporated into their parent routes. A route such as 331A became 337 which, at the time, did not use buses with three track number blinds. On 16th February 1974 Grays route 300 was replaced by 375. The 300 was immediately re-used to phase out 303A as illustrated by LN 5 *below right* displaying somewhat grubby route numbers. Collin Brown / Mike Harris

peak-hour fares. What this was supposed to achieve is not clear, but it certainly slowed down boarding of one-man buses even more and caused some arguments; the scheme was abolished in 1975.

Until the summer of 1975, apart from the suffix renumberings and a few withdrawals of bad loss-makers, little major change had occurred to the route network. The London Transport practice of simply reducing headways and withdrawing or severely curtailing evening, and Sunday service levels rather than to reappraise the needs of a town or area had been continued. However, in February 1974 local services in Welwyn Garden City were reorganised using a new series of route numbers (840 to 848) which provided a kind of local identity. Variations in routeing all carried a different number, an improvement over the use of 324 and 340A for many of the sections. A Sunday only 849 connected several areas for the summer of 1974 but did not come back in later years.

BUS 379

A London Country, Hertfordshire County Council Bus Experiment.

● STEVENAGE BUS STN.

● KNEBWORTH

● DATCHWORTH

● BRAMFIELD

● HERTFORD BUS STN.

» LONDON COUNTRY
Hertfordshire C.C.

The year 1975 had seen the beginnings of real County Council involvement in local bus services. Hertfordshire produced a series of *Rural Bus News* publicity which was posted in many rural locations to publicise the County supported improvements such as the new 379 and a Sunday service on route 317A. Kent on the other hand provided less support than ever and from 30th August Edenbridge was thence served by only route 485 from Westerham, which was extended to

Left **A bright spot in an otherwise dismal year was the introduction, on 31st May 1975, of route 379 – was one of several new facilities supported by Hertfordshire County Council – restoring a service between Hertford and Knebworth lost in 1971. The northern destination of Stevenage was more helpful than the previous Nup End of the 329. This handy plastic card contained a timetable on the back.**

East Grinstead, with the 434 being curtailed at East Grinstead and 465 from Oxted being completely withdrawn. Also from 30th August revisions occurred in the Dartford and Gravesend areas. In Dartford routes were shuffled about, mainly due to the introduction of a one-way traffic scheme, which resulted in some buses missing the town centre, and some routes swopping terminals or routeings and the number 467 disappeared. In Gravesend some terminals were interchanged and a new route 482 appeared as an amalgam of some route 480 journeys and some on 488. On Sundays the basic 480/482/488 cycle became unidirectional with 482 running just from Erith to Singlewell, then 488 Singlewell to Denton and 480 Denton to Erith. Buckinghamshire again reduced their support of the

Left **On 31st August 1974 a 'dial-a-ride' minibus service started in Harlow, mainly aimed at residents of Old Harlow, where narrow roads precluded normal bus services. Sponsored by the Department of the Environment and Harlow Development Corporation the service, known as *Pick-me-up*, utilised five Ford Transit FTs with Dormobile bodies seating 16 passengers. Buses were in radio contact with Control at the bus station and passengers used roadside telephones to ask for a pick-up. The service was run for an experimental period of two years and was backed by a massive publicity launch, including door-to-door leaflet distribution. Although loadings were good, overheads meant an overall financial loss and from 4th September 1976 the service was rationalised into a fixed route conventional service still provided by the FTs. However, this was only a temporary measure, since from 2nd April 1977, the service to Churchgate was taken over by BNs under the route number 809. Eventually it was incorporated into the main town network – and so from a small beginning, part of the Transits' catchment area was subsequently served by Atlanteans!** Capital Transport

Centre left **The introduction of Leyland Nationals to Green Line services enabled the better refurbished RFs to take over bus duties which allowed other members of the class to be withdrawn. RF 194 is working on route 469 which linked Staines and Virginia Water via Thorpe.** John Bull

Below **Independent operator Jey-son coaches abandoned its Friday and Saturday route between Codicote and Luton via Kimpton at the end of June 1975 and at very short notice from 4th July London Country started an RF operation from Luton garage, indeed the last new route to be scheduled for RF operation. The 365 was an interesting service, being previously served by several independents and originally by the famous Birch Brothers. The bus for LCBS's allocation came from the withdrawal of the occasional journeys on 360 between Luton and Dunstable via Caddington, and the Saturday service was crew-operated due to staff rostering reasons. In early 1976 the 365 was one of the first to receive the new plain B type Nationals (from SNB 203). It passed to United Counties operation, as route 45, in December 1976 only to come back again as part of a joint UC/LCBS route 44 in October 1977! The number 365 had been previously associated with the Luton area as it was one of the services withdrawn in the Bedfordshire cuts of 1973.** J.G.S. Smith

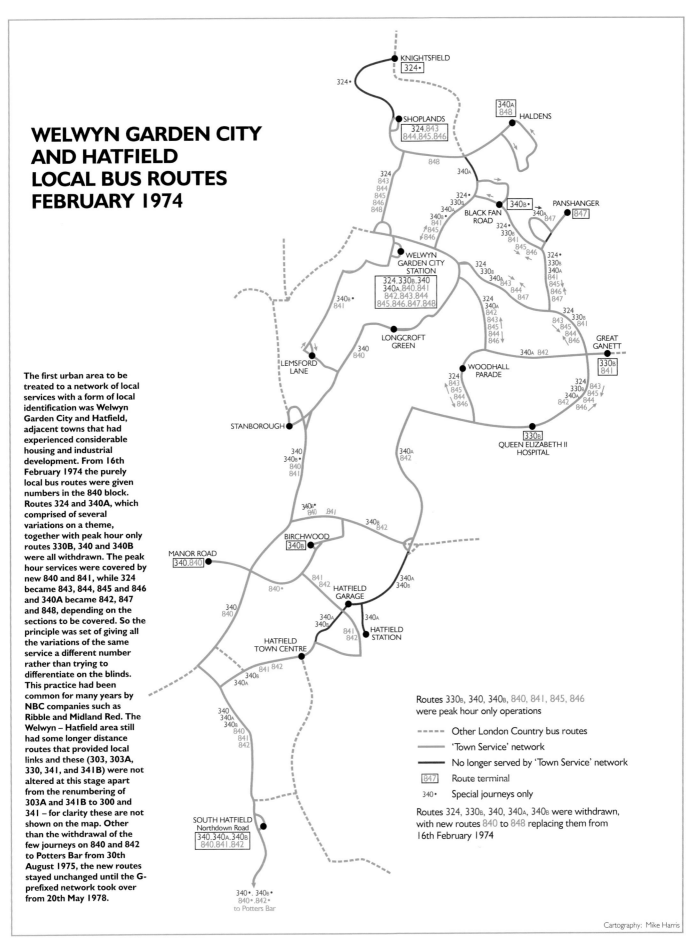

WELWYN GARDEN CITY AND HATFIELD LOCAL BUS ROUTES FEBRUARY 1974

KNIGHTSFIELD
324 •
324 •

SHOPLANDS
324.843
844.845.846

340A
848 HALDENS

848

340A

324 •
330B
340A
BLACK FAN ROAD
340B •
340B •
841
845
846

340B •
847 PANSHANGER
847

340A

324 •
330B
341
845 846

WELWYN GARDEN CITY STATION
324.330B.340
340A.840.841
842.843.844
845.846.847.848

324 •
330B
340A
841
845 846
847

324
330B
340A
843
844 847

340B •
841

340
840

LONGCROFT GREEN

324
330B
340A
843
844 847

324
340A
842
843
845
844
846

324 330B
843 841
845
844
846

GREAT GANETT
330B
841

LEMSFORD LANE

340A 842

WOODHALL PARADE

324
843
845
844
846

324
330B
340A
842
845
844
846

STANBOROUGH

340
340B •
840
841

340A
842

330B
QUEEN ELIZABETH II HOSPITAL

340B •
840 841

340B
842

340A
842

MANOR ROAD
340.840

BIRCHWOOD
340B

841
842

HATFIELD GARAGE

340A
340B

840 •

340
840

340A
340B

841
842
HATFIELD STATION

HATFIELD TOWN CENTRE
841 842

340A

340
340A
340B
840
841
842

SOUTH HATFIELD
Northdown Road
340.340A.340B
840.841.842

340 • 340B •
840 • 842 •
to Potters Bar

The first urban area to be treated to a network of local services with a form of local identification was Welwyn Garden City and Hatfield, adjacent towns that had experienced considerable housing and industrial development. From 16th February 1974 the purely local bus routes were given numbers in the 840 block. Routes 324 and 340A, which comprised of several variations on a theme, together with peak hour only routes 330B, 340 and 340B were all withdrawn. The peak hour services were covered by new 840 and 841, while 324 became 843, 844, 845 and 846 and 340A became 842, 847 and 848, depending on the sections to be covered. So the principle was set of giving all the variations of the same service a different number rather than trying to differentiate on the blinds. This practice had been common for many years by NBC companies such as Ribble and Midland Red. The Welwyn – Hatfield area still had some longer distance routes that provided local links and these (303, 303A, 330, 341, and 341B) were not altered at this stage apart from the renumbering of 303A and 341B to 300 and 341 – for clarity these are not shown on the map. Other than the withdrawal of the few journeys on 840 and 842 to Potters Bar from 30th August 1975, the new routes stayed unchanged until the G-prefixed network took over from 20th May 1978.

Routes 330B, 340, 340B, 840, 841, 845, 846 were peak hour only operations

- - - - - Other London Country bus routes
───── 'Town Service' network
───── No longer served by 'Town Service' network
847 Route terminal
340 • Special journeys only

Routes 324, 330B, 340, 340A, 340B were withdrawn, with new routes 840 to 848 replacing them from 16th February 1974

Cartography: Mike Harris

NEW ONE MAN BUSES

SERVICES 301·302

Times and Fares STARTING 31 MAY 1975

» **LONDON COUNTRY** Associated with the National Bus Company

Amersham area rural services and service levels were reduced on many routes from 29th November 1975. Continuation of services in this area seemed in serious doubt now, and all were losing great sums of money. One route to be completely withdrawn was the 459 which linked Uxbridge to Richings Park Estate. In August 1974 main route 458, from Uxbridge to Slough, had been diverted away from a weak bridge in Iver Lane to run through Bangors Road South which had been previously served only by the 459. This diversion had rendered the 459 largely superfluous but an independent operator did provide a limited service to Richings Park for a period. In Surrey from the same date, route 416 was withdrawn between Leatherhead and Esher, being covered by the local independent *Mole*

Valley. The last example of outstationing ceased when route 412 became entirely worked from Dorking garage and the parking facilities at Holmbury St Mary were no longer used.

An interesting innovation was the introduction on 15th November for the pre-Christmas period of a free *Shopperbus* service between Watford Junction and the town centre. Financed by Watford Borough Council and the local Chamber of Commerce, a frequent service of MBSs (for ease of loading and unloading) was provided. The BR station car park at the Junction was free during Saturday shopping hours, the idea being for shoppers to park their cars at Watford Junction and travel into central Watford on the bus, thereby easing traffic congestion in the town centre. Surveys,

Most of the remaining crew work at Hemel Hempstead garage went over to omo from 31st May 1975, mainly using a batch of SNB Nationals recently demoted from Green Line work by improved versions arriving. The leaflet for the 301 and 302 conversion featured the usual LN 7, with registration letter altered by hand to the then current N mark. Inside the full faretable revealed that it cost only 40 pence to travel from Watford to Aylesbury. Substantial fare increases had yet to take hold – eight years later it would cost £1.40 for the same journey. Operationally the vehicles used on town and country services were separated, which would cause problems before long when vehicle shortages became prolific. The SNBs for the 301 and 302 were fitted for standard omo, while those for the 320, 334 and 377 were farebox-fitted, as were the MBSs already operating on routes 314/A/B/C and 344. The farebox system was the precursor of the major upheaval of January 1977 for town services.

Above **The Hatfield and Welwyn Garden City local identification schemes saw some routes being publicised by individual timetable cards, distributed in their catchment areas. A further Summer Sunday route 849 serving Stanborough Lakes appeared in May. LN 13 takes on passengers at Haldens on route 848 which linked this area to the Railway Station and was a far simpler, user friendly service than the complex 340A which it replaced.** Ian Pringle

Left **RF 154 is seen at Hosey Common en route for Edenbridge on route 485 which was timetabled to interwork with routes 464 and 465. The RF was one of the refurbished members of the class down graded to bus status in April 1968 and given this attractive yellow waist-band. London Transport removed the roof board brackets at the same time but other members of the class so treated by London Country retained them. The routes serving Edenbridge had remained basically unchanged since 1946 but the period of stability was soon to come to an end. From 30th August 1975 Kent County Council's reduced financial support meant that Edenbridge lost routes 434 and 465, retaining only the 485, which in its revised form, re-established a through link from Westerham to East Grinstead lost in 1935.** Mike Harris

however, showed that a large percentage of users arrived by public transport (mostly BR). The service was nevertheless continued every year because of its popularity, Leyland Nationals taking over in 1979.

The first change of 1976 was on 3rd April when the entire network at Grays was reshuffled. Cuts were considerable, mostly in frequencies but routes 329, 357, 370A, 371A and 371B were all withdrawn. Route 323 became a more important route, replacing all the previous route 370 journeys to Chadwell St Mary. New route 324 took over route 370A with corresponding reductions to other routes. Although services were simplified,

vehicle types were not, almost all routes being mixed one-man and crew operation.

Two schemes in the North West Area in May and September 1976 saw off most suffixed numbered routes in the area. Some improvements were made to routeings in Hemel Hempstead and there were various changes to school facilities at Watford and Amersham. Barnet lost almost all its London Country buses and routes 306 and 311 lost RMLs in favour of SNBs. The start of the school term in September saw the famous group of suffix-lettered *School Specials* in Watford renumbered into the 830 series with the 833 and 835 retaining crew operation. The 352 service to Bucks Hill was lost but a limited facility for shoppers was added to route 319. The new Bus Station at Luton

Above **The first programme of service changes in 1976 occurred at Grays on 3rd April and, setting a future precedent, featured considerable frequency cuts, many of them in peak hours. The 370 lost its Chadwell Morant Road journeys to a revised 323. A line up of RCLs and RMCs in both the Lincoln green and NBC green liveries stands outside Grays garage. The RCLs had a long association with Grays first being allocated in July 1965 until December 1967 and returning in October 1969 until January 1979.**
Capital Transport

Below **An improvement in Grays was the introduction of a town *midibus* service. Numbered 399 and BN operated, it served several estate roads that had not previously seen buses. The northern loop had a flat fare of 11p; the southern loop 7p which was too close to the town centre to attract sufficient passengers and lasted just seven months. From 1st July 1978 the Jesmond Road section of the loop was served by separate route 396, linking with Little Thurrock, leading to SNBs replacing the BNs due to high passenger loadings.** Ken Glazier

The first scheme to use prefix letters for a town service network occurred at St Albans from 30th October 1976, but was only a late change from plans to replace routes 325, 354, 391/A with a group 820-825. Timetable booklets were issued with route S6 listed first, reflecting the late change, as it was due to have been 820. Both old and new City services were worked by MBSs – MBS 302 loads up in St Peters Street and despite the destination blind is heading for the Cotton Mill Estate loop before returning to New Greens Estate. The correct lazy blind display has not been selected by the driver and, while regular passengers knew at which stop to board, this user unfriendly sloppy blind setting probably encouraged strangers to take a taxi. The St Albans S-route scheme was unlike some later ones in that it did not take over cross-town services provided by country routes such as the 341, which continued to run to Marshalswick Estate as before. Ken Glazier

caused all routes to abandon the traditional Park Square terminus from 4th September. The Luton local route 360 to Caddington lost its RTs but oddly kept crew operation on SNBs. Similarly at Stevenage RTs on the 303C were replaced by crew-worked RP coaches released from a reduction on the Green Line 716 service. It did not take long for conductors to be dispensed with, and Luton lost the 360 to United Counties. Withdrawal by London Transport of route 224 south of Colnbrook caused certain journeys on LCBS 460 to be diverted through Horton Village in May.

Following the Welwyn Garden City scheme of 1974 with a new set of route numbers, it was the turn of St Albans to gain a local identity on 30th October 1976. It had been planned to replace local routes 325, 354 and 391/A (all one-time Autofare routes) with a new network numbered 820 upwards, but the City and District Councils wanted something that would distinguish *their* local services from all others in the City. In consequence, a late decision, after publicity was prepared, was made to adopt a letter prefix and numbers S1 to S6 appeared on the local MBSs, which provided the entire S-route allocation. The City's colours of yellow and blue were used on publicity and on certain bus stops, but no identity as such appeared on the buses themselves. As will be

ST. ALBANS BUS SERVICES

Starting 30 October

LONDON COUNTRY ➤➤
a **NATIONAL** bus company

🦌 HERTFORDSHIRE COUNTY COUNCIL

Route 498 passed to Maidstone & District from 30th October 1976 in exchange for London Country's extension of 480 to Valley Drive in Gravesend. RML 2340 is on the stand at Gravesend Clock Tower prior to working a journey to Coldharbour Estate on the old 498 and is being overtaken by RML 2342 on route 488 running from Swanscombe to Denton. Both are local routes that would have been ideally suited to one-man fare box operation. The route number 498 was restored to London Country on 1st April 1978 when all town services came to be worked by the company. R.C. Riley

Right The withdrawal of London Transport's route 224 south of Colnbrook in May 1976 meant that the link from the Bath Road to Staines was lost. Surrey County Council supported a Monday to Saturday direct link from Poyle to Staines via Moor Lane numbered 467 which started on 27th November 1976. But the Monday to Friday service lasted just ten months. SNB 240 stands at Poyle Coleridge Close terminus in September 1977. Interestingly, London Transport's 224 arriving from the Uxbridge direction referred to the location as *Colnbrook* Coleridge Close. Philip Hopcroft

Below The re-numbering of local town services in Hemel Hempstead on 8th January 1977 was the second to use prefix letters, but was notable in being the first really comprehensive attempt to separate out the town sections of country routes and incorporate them into a cohesive network. It was the second phase of the local *bus experiment*, the first being the introduction of a townwide flat-fare system 18 months earlier. This scheme introduced separate sets of numbers for daytime and peak hour services; daytime routes were numbered H1 upwards, peak hour routes from H11 upwards. Other similar schemes elsewhere have followed this pattern, sometimes with another series (21 upwards) for school services. The existing MBS and SNB fare-box buses were retained, the flat-fare at inception of the H-network being 13 pence. MBS 408 is seen approaching the Apsley Mills terminus on route H16 in June 1978 by which time the flat-fare had risen to 18 pence. Mike Harris

seen, letter prefixes for town service schemes came to be widespread in later years.

On the same day a long-overdue co-ordination scheme came into effect at Gravesend between LCBS and Maidstone & District, thus sweeping away the 1933 boundary. The 482 (Erith – Singlewell) was withdrawn and the long established 480 (Erith – Denton) was extended into M&D territory at Valley Drive, locals 487 and 488 were also revised. To compensate M&D, their routes 307/308 were extended westward over London Country route 498 which was withdrawn. The latter change turned out to be short-lived as London Country took over of all M&D local services at Gravesend in April 1978, when the 307/8 became London Country's 497/8.

An interesting set of three services began on 27th November 1976, all for differing reasons. The 429 was of the traditional *New Town* type route connecting Crawley to the developing Bewbush Estate, and was of a temporary nature pending further development of roads and housing which would allow it to be incorporated into the rest of the town network. The 467 was supported by Surrey County Council and provided a direct link on Mondays to Saturdays from Poyle to Staines consequential to the withdrawal of London Transport's 224 south of the Bath Road to Staines and Laleham in May 1976. The route was not a success, being reduced to a Saturdays only service after just ten months, although county council funding

saw it last until May 1980. There were few places of habitation over its entire length and after being denied their link to Staines for some six months presumably the residents of Poyle had made alternative arrangements. The third new route was the 465, marketed as *Village Bus*, providing a shopping link for many small communities with Oxted, the only town of any size in a large rural area without long and expensive journeys to, say, Croydon or Redhill. Its success was assured by the subsidised 15p flat fare that applied. The existing local 464 route had also acquired a reduced 11p maximum off-peak fare since September.

In the autumn of 1976, British Rail had made plans to abandon Sunday services over several lines in Southern England but in the event never implemented the proposals. LCBS however, had made application to

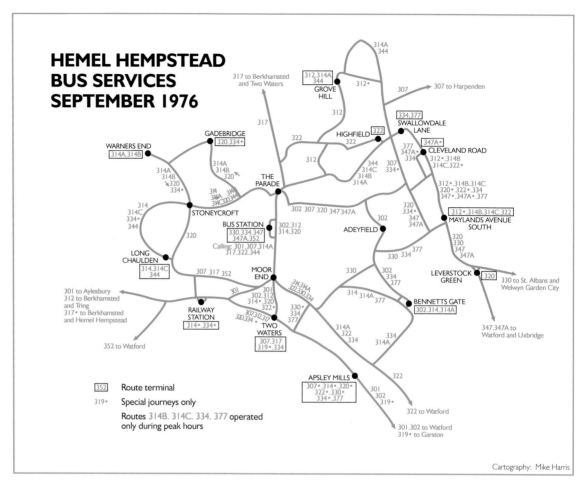

HEMEL HEMPSTEAD BUS SERVICES SEPTEMBER 1976

Cartography: Mike Harris

By September 1976 the network of routes in Hemel Hempstead had become extremely complex, even though suffix lettered routes had been renumbered previously. For example, the numbers 314, 314A and 344 meant something different depending on the direction of travel, and other variations were superimposed. Longer distance routes 302, 312 and 322 operated across the Town Centre to various suburbs, this over the years being the gradual response to demand as new estates were built. Although the purely town routes had been converted to flat-fare fare-box operation in May 1975 there was still a mix of conventional omo and double-deck crew operation alongside the fare-box buses. From 8th January 1977 existing fare-box town services 314/A/B/C, 320, 334, 344 and 377 were withdrawn together with the town sections of 302, 312 and 322 which were cut back to the Bus Station, except for a few peak hour journeys on 302 to Grove Hill. The new route network utilised numbers HI to H6 for daytime routes and HII to H15 for peak hour routes. The map of the H-routes reflects the situation by April once certain modifications had been made.

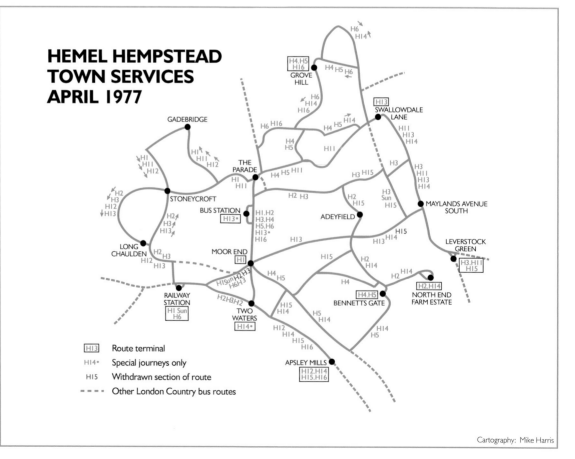

HEMEL HEMPSTEAD TOWN SERVICES APRIL 1977

Cartography: Mike Harris

70

Right and centre right **The Martins Wood area of Stevenage** was served by routes 813 and 814 from 14th October 1972, but from 29th January 1977 they were incorporated into the Superbus network as route SB3. Some of Stevenage's existing ANs gained 'SB' stickers but retained green livery. However from 2nd July 1977 these ANs were swopped with existing yellow and blue single deckers from route SB2 and thus yellow SMs came to work the SB3. AN 70, seen on the very first day on SB2, displays the 'SB' logo in the intermediate points blind box but is yet to receive any stickers. During 1977 several SMs received repaints and some of the Superbuses were included in this programme. To avoid future problems when buses needed to be transferred in or out of Stevenage, the opportunity was taken to paint them green, with just yellow and blue 'SB' stickers carried on the vehicle sides as seen on SM 498 in Danestrete. The yellow Superbus livery, as carried by the bus in the background, became increasingly rare and eventually disappeared. Colin Brown / Mike Harris

run a Sunday route (900) between Guildford and Sevenoaks via Dorking, Redhill and Westerham if the cuts had taken place.

Further economies were in prospect for 1977 and involved shutting four of the smallest garages in the system – Romford, Luton, Tring and High Wycombe. Despite reassurances that there would be no cuts prior to the closure of Luton garage, routes 360 and 365 were transferred to United Counties operation, as routes 6 and 45, from 4th December 1976 at short notice.

The year 1977 was to see London Country's original plan of 100 per cent omo take a giant step forward, even though it was accompanied by an overall vehicle reduction of six per cent. The first major scheme of the year was on 8th January when all routes in Hemel Hempstead were changed. The in-town projections of trunk routes 302, 312 and 322 were cut back to the Bus Station, and a local identity town network was set up with routes numbered H1 to H6 for daytime routes, H11 to H15 for peak-hour works services. Various complaints were made about the cessation of some cross-town links and of the vagaries of the flat fare system, worked by farebox-equipped SNBs and MBSs at 13p per ride. A journey from, say, Bennetts End to Warners End (formerly 314A) now meant a change in the Town Centre from H4/5 to H1 – the journey time increased and the fare doubled! However there was an improved frequency on some sections of route and the new North End Farm Estate gained a service for the first time.

Right **Thankfully, during their final days, the RTs were** never allowed to get to the quite appalling appearance that was achieved by some RMLs. RT 4792, however, had clearly seen better days when photographed at Hoddesdon in April 1977 while substituting for an AN. Route 316 was introduced on 29th January 1977 and replaced route 310A and part of route 327 and was the last new route to see RT operation, albeit unscheduled. The bus has been fitted with an AN route number blind and an RMC via blind which is not as deep as the RT box and did not include a 316 display thus the Hertford engineering staff have improvised as best they can. Ian Pringle

Left **One of the last routes to be scheduled for RF operation was the 458 between Slough and Uxbridge which officially lost the class from 8th January 1977, leaving just the 309 and 335 Chalfont shuttle to RFs for a few more weeks. RF 610 does good business in Slough while working a short journey to Iver in the mid-1970s.** Mike Harris

Luton garage closed after service on 28th January, the two remaining bus routes moving out to Garston (321) and Hatfield (366). The quaint extension of the 384 to Baldock disappeared, and so did the express route 812 connecting Potter Street with the Town Station in Harlow. Stevenage locals 813/814 came into the Superbus system as route SB3. A new route 316 started on 29th January covering parts of withdrawn 310A and 327 between Hertford and Enfield, and was notable as the last LCBS route to be introduced to see RT operation, albeit unscheduled. Official RF operation was to

have ceased in January on routes 309 and 458, but the last officially RF-worked service turned out to be a replacement for the cutback 335 between Gerrards Cross and Chalfont (Latimer Lane), supported by Chiltern District Council from 29th January to 26th February only. Very few local people seemed to lend their patronage.

Tring garage closed its doors after service on 1st April and from the next day its services were worked by Hemel Hempstead, with route 312 being covered by revisions to the 301/302. The spring and summer saw adjustments to several routes in the Harlow, Redhill, Dorking, Grays and Dartford areas as well as the closure of Romford garage, which only operated one Green Line route. One development, however, was the introduction of *Ramblers Bus* 417, operating on Sundays and Bank Holidays from Dorking to many beauty spots in the surrounding Surrey countryside. This route proved a success and appeared in subsequent years –

good publicity and bargain fares have all played their part. Route 309 was withdrawn between Rickmansworth and Harefield early in September in favour of the Hillingdon Council sponsored LT route 128 with buses in a dedicated livery.

The last day of service from High Wycombe garage was on 30th September. Some local staff had transferred already to Alder Valley or left LCBS employment for other things. Routes were plagued by service cuts and many staff did not wish to transfer to Amersham garage – it was, after all, many miles from their homes in the High Wycombe area. The new network commenced the next day almost entirely with SMs, which replaced RMLs, on local 326 and the High Wycombe – Penn section of 363. The High Wycombe – Totteridge section of the 363 route was handed to Alder Valley. Cuts in service levels were yet again made to rural routes west of Amersham and Chesham and not a lot remained.

Right **During the summer of 1977 the 417 *Ramblers Bus* started to operate, based on Dorking, and due to its success similar ventures were started in other parts of the network. The route performed a vast clockwise circular incorporating rural villages and beauty spots in the area as depicted by BN 44 at Coldharbour. A small diversion to include Shere was made from the 1981 summer season.** Barry LeJeune

October 1st also saw a co-ordination scheme with United Counties near Hitchin. Their route 82 (Hitchin – Welwyn) passed to London Country as 314, running on to Welwyn Garden City, while Hitchin local 383 passed to United Counties as their 80. A joint route between both companies introduced a new low number to LCBS, with route 44 (in the UC series) between Luton and Stevenage via Kimpton – loadings were very good. Weston village regained its link with Stevenage, lost in 1971, with a Thursday and Friday shopping service off route 384. At Staines the Monday–Friday service on the 467 came off after less than a year but a new route 451, connecting Laleham with the new Civic Centre at Knowle Green as well as Staines, restored a bus service, albeit limited, to Worple Road.

It was, however, the straightforward omo conversions that were a main feature of 1977 with well-known routes 330, 339, 341, 370, 395, 405, 409, 414, 441 and 499 all losing their Routemasters. The service requirement on the bus network at the end of 1977 had gone down to 724 (75 crew, 649 omo) on Mondays–Fridays, 575 (49 crew, 526 omo) on Saturdays and 165 (8 crew, 157 omo) on Sundays, representing a percentage of omo of 90, 91 and 95 respectively. Quite an advance! Even so, eleven garages still had a scheduled crew operation, working routes 347/A (Hemel Hempstead – Uxbridge), 403 (Wallington – Warlingham Park Hospital), 405B (Redhill – Crawley works journeys), 406 (Kingston – Redhill), 407/A (Slough local), 411 (West Croydon – Reigate), 477 (Dartford – Chelsfield) and 480 (Erith – Gravesend), plus odd journeys on another seventeen routes.

Substantial changes in the west of the London Country area took place on 1st October 1977 with the one-man conversion of routes 441/C in the Staines – High Wycombe corridor coupled with reorganisation of services upon the closure of High Wycombe garage.

Top right **RML 2444 above left stands at the delightful setting of Hedgerley Village shortly before the conversion.** Philip Hopcroft

Centre right **High Wycombe Garage was a stronghold of RMLs for local routes 326 and 363 until its closure after traffic on 30th September 1977. RML 2440 appears to have had some front panels re-painted and has acquired a fleet number in NBC style grey.** Peter Plummer

Right **After less than a year of exclusive United Counties operation on route 45 (previously LCBS 365), the link between Codicote and Luton, was extended to Stevenage from 1st October 1977 and both companies combined to work joint route 44, the first time that London Country had used such a low route number. Each company worked three round trips, London Country's contribution being with RPs from Stevenage garage, whose RP 73 is travelling through Old Knebworth in April 1980. The leaflet issued for the changes emphasised the fact that the services were designed principally for shoppers – the phrase:** *These experimental services are sponsored by Hertfordshire County Council and could be modified if they do not meet users' requirements* **was a great improvement on** *Use it or lose it.* Mike Harris

Chapter 7

LOCAL NAMES & CONTINUAL CHANGE

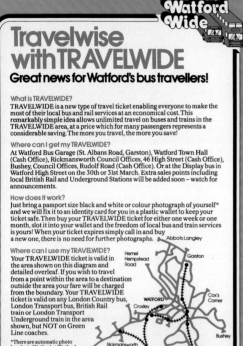

Travelwise with TRAVELWIDE

Great news for Watford's bus travellers!

What is TRAVELWIDE?

TRAVELWIDE is a new type of travel ticket enabling everyone to make the most of their local bus and rail services at an economical cost. This remarkably simple idea allows unlimited travel on buses and trains in the TRAVELWIDE area, at a price which for many passengers represents a considerable saving. The more you travel, the more you save!

Where can I get my TRAVELWIDE?

At Watford Bus Garage (St. Albans Road, Garston), Watford Town Hall (Cash Office), Rickmansworth Council Offices, 46 High Street (Cash Office), Bushey, Council Offices, Rudolf Road (Cash Office). Or at the Display bus in Watford High Street on the 30th or 31st March. Extra sales points including local British Rail and Underground Stations will be added soon – watch for announcements.

How does it work?

Just bring a passport size black and white or colour photograph of yourself* and we will fix it to an identity card for you in a plastic wallet to keep your ticket safe. Then buy your TRAVELWIDE ticket for either one week or one month, slot it into your wallet and the freedom of local bus and train services is yours! When your ticket expires simply call in and buy a new one, there is no need for further photographs.

Where can I use my TRAVELWIDE?

Your TRAVELWIDE ticket is valid in the area shown on this diagram and detailed overleaf. If you wish to travel from a point within the area to a destination outside the area your fare will be charged from the boundary. Your TRAVELWIDE ticket is valid on any London Country bus, London Transport bus, British Rail train or London Transport Underground train in the area shown, but NOT on Green Line coaches.

*There are automatic photo booths in Watford at Watford Junction Station, The Co-op (Gade House) and Woolworths.

THE EARLY 1980s had consolidated London Country services into networks which revealed a relationship to County boundaries, largely supported financially by the Counties. Good housekeeping, service planning and scheduling gave London Country a comprehensive network, although service frequencies were often reduced, sometimes severely, especially in evenings and Sundays. Very few places had actually lost their bus service, something that cannot be said for the country generally at the time. More local identity schemes were introduced, notably at Crawley in 1978

Left **Several urban areas were treated to *Travelwide* tickets, giving unlimited travel within specific areas. They became quite popular and reduced boarding times on a fleet that was now close to full one-man operation. The Watford area extended from Abbots Langley to South Oxhey and Maple Cross and included travel on London Transport bus, Underground and British Rail services. Introduced on 31st March 1979 to coincide with the *Watfordwide* scheme the rates were £3.30 per week or £13.00 for one month.**

and Watford in 1979, with much local consultation beforehand and since – increased traffic and better reliability have been the outcome. Involvement with the nation-wide MAP (Market Analysis Project) of the NBC caused London Country to join forces with neighbour Alder Valley to revise the networks on the western side of the area. The aforementioned good planning had resulted in London Country achieving a reasonably efficient network, and the Company came out of MAP relatively unscathed, unlike Alder Valley. In addition to the Crawley and Watford *brand-names* schemes, the three MAP networks also received these, together with the town networks at Stevenage and Harlow, being treated to letter-prefixes route numbers in 1980. In most cases, vehicles received local identity fleet names but, unlike several other NBC operators, retained their London Country name as well.

One-man conversions slowed down after the speedy progress during 1977, and it took

until March 1981 to remove the last crew operation. One area of expansion that was explored was school contract work. From a small start in September 1977 at Dorking, many garages gained contract operations, often in competition with private operators. The fact that a school bus could often be utilised to provide rural shopping services during the day made some financial savings for the Counties. All five neighbouring NBC operators as well as London Transport featured in route exchanges, the latter ceasing to serve such places as Chertsey, Leatherhead and St Albans at the behest of their GLC masters. The political accident that created the GLC boundary gradually caused an arbitrary cutback of LT services to closer-in points irrespective of passenger objectives, and was reminiscent of the 1933 boundaries that LCBS inherited. At least London Country continued to provide services from within its boundaries into nearby towns within the GLC area.

Fares increases continued to occur, twice during the years 1979 and 1981. Percentage increases were slightly higher in counties with lower revenue support, Buckinghamshire, Berkshire and Kent, while in Surrey and Hertfordshire fairly modest increases were made – indeed in the general revision of 4th October 1981 fares in Hertfordshire did not go up at all. This was to set the scene for future fare revisions. Many

Left **From November 1972 Aldenham outshopped RMLs in the new NBC leaf green and white livery which featured grey fleet numbers and wheels. RML 2451 stands at Uxbridge Station in September 1973 on the lengthy route 347 to Hemel Hempstead. This route was not a traditional trunk route but had emerged in the 1950s by the linking up of various shorter routes. Routes 347/A were jointly operated by Garston and Two Waters garages and had the distinction of being the last crew operated routes in the northern area, finally succumbing to omo in September 1978.** Colin Brown

Top right **The Short Nationals were first delivered in 1973 and were numbered on from the LN class. They were classified SNC or SNB and the company went on to obtain a vast number of them and they were used across the network on a variety of routes. Newly delivered SNB 359 is seen on route 418 at Surbiton on 21st October 1978, its last day of operation, being replaced by routes 476/8/9 which also absorbed the 481 and part of 419.** Geoff Rixon

Centre right **London Country buses first approached Sutton from the Banstead direction on 1st October 1977 when route 422 from Redhill replaced Green Line 711. It was joined by 418 from Leatherhead and 420 from Walton-on-the-Hill in April 1982 when London Transport services were withdrawn and in August 1982 the 422 was extended from Redhill to Crawley. AN 187 is seen in Crawley heading for Sutton on route 422 in the new livery with the light green band and fleetname which first appeared at the end of 1985.** Barry LeJeune

Right **Borehamwood local BW1 was planned to be jointly worked between London Country and London Transport but in the event the route started on 21st April 1979 being exclusively London Country worked.** J.G.S. Smith

urban areas had *Travelwide* tickets introduced, the first being Crawley in September 1978, later joined by Harlow, Watford, Gravesend, Hemel Hempstead, Slough, High Wycombe, Amersham, Guildford, Stevenage, Welwyn Garden City/Hatfield and Thurrock. These gave unlimited travel for either a week or month on all London Country bus services within each area, in addition some areas included Green Line, other operators bus services and British Rail availability. Although some attempt at standardising the prices was made they tended to vary according to the size of area of availabililty. A dual flat-fare system (inner and outer zones) was introduced at St Albans from 30th August 1980. During 1978 the *National Wanderbus* ticket was introduced by the NBC at £2.40 and, after non-availability on Green Line at first, became available on most services. Four years later it had been

and booklets were produced for small local areas or even individual villages or towns in the County and a countywide public transport map was first published in 1982.

The special *Ramblers Bus* 417 from 1977 continued in subsequent summers, and was joined in the summers of 1979 and 1980 by a similar operation around the beauty spots of west Kent, numbered 418 and was based on Sevenoaks. Although well publicised locally, and by the Ramblers Association and local groups with leaflets detailing selected walks in the countryside, it never became as popular as the 417. The River Lea forms the boundary between Hertfordshire and Essex. Between Hoddesdon and Waltham Abbey the area had been developed as a Leisure Park with various attractions based on the river and the adjacent countryside. From the summer of 1980 a Sunday and Bank Holiday route 318 operated, marketed as the *Lee*

Valley Leisurebus, with various journeys timed to enable people to visit each of the attractions without the aid of a car. On all three of these routes special day tickets at bargain rates were available for unlimited journeys.

Border exchanges with London Transport from 28th January 1978 formed the first bus service changes of the year. London Transport's 237 to Chertsey was curtailed nearer to the GLC boundary and a new London Country 459 ran from Addlestone and Chertsey to Sunbury and Feltham. As compensation, LCBS gave up the Berrylands deviation of the 418 to LT who covered the section by the extension of their 211 from Kingston to Tolworth. Later in 1978 the 418 was replaced by routes 476/8/9 which also replaced the 481 and part of the 419 in the Epsom area. This gave an increased frequency from West Ewell to Kingston and enabled more buses to pass the garage at Leatherhead in service thus saving on dead running. LT changed the timetables for their services in the Banstead area (80/A, 164/A, 280/A) and to Leatherhead (265 for 71) from 31st March 1979, but this was only a prelude to giving up the services. Leatherhead was last served by LT on 26th September 1980, but LCBS had already introduced their part of the package on 31st August with an extension of the 468 from Chessington to Leatherhead coupled with improvements to Green Line 714. It took until 24th April 1982 for the Banstead area services to pass to London Country, with 418 from Sutton to Leatherhead and 420 from Sutton to Walton-on-the-Hill. LT only reached Banstead with a few buses on the 164 after that date. In the northern area between the operators there was a minor switch of routeings east of Waltham Abbey from 31st March 1979,

From 20th May 1978 regular routes G1–G4 and peak hour routes G11–G14 replaced the 840–848 Hatfield and Welwyn Garden City local routes. The letter W was clearly reserved for Watford thus G for *Garden City* was chosen. LNB 62 at the Cherry Tree works on the short G4 route to Panshanger formerly numbered 847. *Mike Harris*

increased to £2.97 (the maximum fare on any NBC stage carriage service at the time) and represented enormous value, especially as the *Golden Rover* had increased by this time to £2.75, thus becoming less attractive. Special fares promotions during the Februarys of 1981, 1982 and 1983, to promote bus travel, had a disappointing effect, but isolated fares bargains, mostly on rural routes in Hertfordshire for journeys into nearby towns for shopping, did become popular and were supported by the County. Indeed Hertfordshire became quite a model for others to copy, with their whole-hearted support for public transport. Many leaflets

followed by a major switch from 24th April 1982 when LT 84 to St Albans was taken over by LCBS, using the same route number. A reciprocal swap caused LT to take over the Potters Bar to Enfield section of LCBS 313. A proposal for joint operation between the operators involved a town service in Borehamwood – route BW1. In the event London Country worked the whole service from April 1979 following a dispute with staff at LT's Edgware garage, who would have worked the

end depot was closed and their local 307/8 routes became LCBS 497/8, reversing the changes of 1976. Part compensation was given to M&D as their Borough Green depot took on more work locally, including responsibility for almost all services in the Wrotham area – LCBS no longer ran any buses there but kept a token coach link for another two years. A by-product of the Gravesend switch was the take-over by London Country of the duties on several

National Express seasonal services in the area, an activity that was built upon in subsequent years.

Two lettered route schemes occurred in 1978, the first being a fairly minor one in the Welwyn Garden City and Hatfield areas in May when the 840–848 group was replaced by new routes G1–G4 and G11–G14. The prefix G (for Garden) was used as the letter W was reserved for Watford in the following year. Many new Atlanteans had replaced RCLs and MBSs at Crawley during spring 1978 and from 1st July they were thus all in position to inaugurate *C-Line*, the brand name chosen from submissions by local schoolchildren, and covering all Town Services. The system was launched with vast publicity and local traffic increased dramatically, in some cases service levels were higher than had applied previously. Ten local routes were withdrawn and the new prefixed system took over with C1–C8 for daytime routes, C15–C17 for works routes and a new sequence (C21, 22) for schooldays routes. This pattern of numbering has characterised the lettered route systems subsequently introduced.

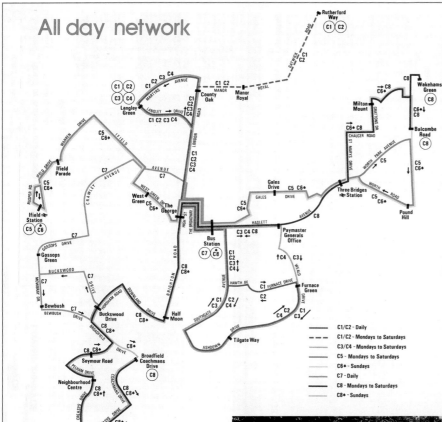

All day network

Left **The C-Line network in Crawley was introduced on 1st July 1978 and was the first major revision to receive a local identity name. The name C-Line was adapted from the suggestion *Crawline* made by a local schoolboy and featured extensively on publicity and vehicles. For a few months prior to the change a fleet of 23 new ANs gradually replaced MBSs and RCLs on local routes. This was the first local identity network to use the 20s block of numbers for school specials.**

Below **The C-Line scheme at Crawley involved a new pattern of routes with a 20 pence flat fare. All routes with the exception of the schooldays C21 were AN worked. AN138 with *C-Line* stickers is seen on the C7 to Bewbush.** Colin Brown

LT share. Even LT bus stop flags and LT-style timetables were displayed and blinds were fitted to Edgware's BLs before the starting date, which had to be deferred for three weeks due to the dispute. All the route exchanges with LT were in co-operation with the appropriate County Councils, who had in each case favoured London Country due to their lower operating costs. The somewhat monolithic structure of LT and the often restrictive, and sometimes inefficient, operational methods coupled with higher rates of pay resulted in high operating costs, which caused the Home Counties to look to others to provide services where financial support was required.

The first day of April 1978 saw a series of service reductions in north west Kent, the prime reduction being the 401 link between Dartford and Sevenoaks, which was curtailed at Eynsford where through passengers were required to change to a train for Sevenoaks. Maidstone & District's Graves-

One-man conversions resumed in the autumn of 1978 as omo double-deckers were once again available and the last RML routes in the Northern area, 347/A (with 347A becoming 348) were converted together with 411 in the South, while the 406 received single deckers which proved to be inadequate. Most of route 403 was converted to omo AN operation early in 1979 following which there was a further year's pause until more buses became available.

On 27th January 1979 there were some quite severe service reductions around East Grinstead giving a most complex local route structure. The 409 was diverted away from the main road through Newchapel and Felbridge to run via Felcourt and Baldwins Hill. Surprisingly, an experimental Sunday service was worked on local routes 428/9 but this lasted only until October, being hardly

used at all. Indeed revenue on the routes in the area never amounted to very much and services continued to decline until the actual closure of the local garage at the end of 1981. Unusually, London Country took over responsibility for a service from an independent operator when new route 474 joined the 434/473 routes to serve Colgate and Pease Pottage on the Crawley and Horsham section in lieu of Tillingbourne's service 451. This happened again in March 1979 with a Tuesday route 354 between Much Hadham and Harlow, following the cessation of Blue Diamond Coaches' service.

For some time the local authorities in the Watford area had been complaining about local services, with some justification it must be said, and their poor reliability. They had after all seen a period of vehicle and parts shortages in the mid-1970s and there was

even a suggestion that the Council would take over the operation of the town's bus services. In the event of course they co-operated with London Country to devise the *Watfordwide* network that took over on 31st March 1979. Local routes were numbered W1 to W11 and most trunk routes were revised to fit in with these, several being terminated in the pedestrian-orientated Town Centre. Several areas of Watford now had a bus service for the first time – Sherriff Estate and Woodside (W11), the south side of Holywell Estate (321) and eventually a link was provided beyond Watford Heath to Carpenders Park. The whole idea was to base all services on the Town Centre but the removal of several cross-town connections caused some complaints. In compensation for this a vastly improved reliable service was provided to some areas. The Little

Top **From 27th January 1979 London Country served new territory between Horsham and Crawley when route 474 replaced part of Tillingbourne route 451 through Colgate and Pease Pottage. MBS 420 heads a convoy through Colgate.** Barry LeJeune

Right **The *Watfordwide* scheme saw all buses at Garston (renamed Watford) garage carrying the brand name irrespective of whether they were employed on the local W routes or the trunk routes. The buses initially carried a small green brand name sticker but this was changed in 1980 to the bold style depicted in this view of St Albans garage forecourt in July 1981. There is some confusion with the blinds, as under the scheme the Rickmansworth journeys became 327 with the 321 running to Holywell Estate. The passengers for the 84 wait patiently by the ever-closed door in what seems a rather unsafe queuing arrangement. Who would have thought at the time that in less than a year the 84 would be a London Country route?** John Bull

Bushey route formerly served by 301/2 had suffered late running buses from Aylesbury and Hemel Hempstead being curtailed at Watford Town Centre or Bushey Station but with the revision W9 provided a far more regular service. The drivers were pleased with the revised system which gave them adequate recovery allowances in terminal time and the number of passengers overall increased. A determined effort to improve reliability had been made, but as subsequent economies of operation were implemented reduced stand times and cross-town interworking gradually eroded some of the initial advantages.

On 1st September 1979 the annual round of service revisions at Grays meant the withdrawal of six routes and the introduction of seven new ones. Although in the main this was merely *shuffling the pack* (something at which London Country was indeed becoming very adept) it did restore London's green buses to Orsett with routes 378 and 389. The 369 took over Eastern National's 269 between Grays and Brentwood, but a reciprocal change caused LCBS 339 (Harlow – Warley) to be curtailed at Ongar, thus not quite completing the circuit around London by London Country bus services. On the

same day routes 392/3 (Harlow – Welwyn Garden City) were withdrawn west of Hoddesdon with this section being covered by new route 324. This change effectively meant that all of Harlow's bus operations operated almost entirely within Essex. The different route numbers and different frequencies highlighted the fact that the Herts/Essex county boundary had inconveniently intervened. In Surrey route 412 was extended to Ewhurst and Cranleigh, considerably outside LCBS's area – it never caught on, though, and lasted just two years. Late in October the last remaining bus service into East Sussex ceased when the 409 was removed from Forest Row. An express bus service took over much of the traditional 409 between Croydon and East Grinstead, and the 411 gained a diversion through Old Coulsdon, allegedly to support LT's 190 on this section.

The year 1980 was undoubtedly the busiest one yet for route changes – five brand-name systems were introduced together with a myriad of other service alterations. During the year there were modifications to the C, H, S and W routes, in most cases connected with the serving of developing housing areas. At Stevenage in April all

the 800-series route numbers, together with the *Superbus* network (latterly not too evident due to the repaint programme, which had removed most of the yellow-and-blue buses from the town), succumbed to *StevenageBus* covering the whole town with SB-prefix route numbers. At the end of August a similar exercise affected Harlow with the *TownBus* system of T-prefix route numbers. The old 800-series numbers that LT had started in 1954 for new routes in the New Towns from now on came to be used only for routeing oddities, notably for school routes.

More one-man operation came, this time to routes 403 Express and 480, while the 407/A crew operations disappeared under the Thameslink revision. The Sunday crew service on 477 and 493 became one-man in November, leaving just the weekday 477 as the last crew route. It lasted only until March 1981 when schedule changes removed the possibility of buses passing on the narrow section near Crockenhill and the safety requirement for conductors to assist a possible reversing manoeuvre no longer applied. Meanwhile more ANs had restored top decks to busy routes such as the 341 and 406.

Above **Yet further changes occurred in the Grays area from 1st September 1979 with routes 323, 324, 328, and 371 being replaced. The RCLs were withdrawn from Grays in 1978 but a handful returned during the autumn and remained until January 1979. RCL 2241 is seen at Alexandra Close terminus on route 323 in May 1978.** Peter Plummer

Below **From 1st September 1979 the 412 was revised in conjunction with Surrey County Council to be extended beyond Holmbury St Mary to Cranleigh and Ockley with Sutton Village continuing to be served by double running. The Dorking to Ranmore section was covered by bifurcations on route 425. Newly delivered SNB 507 is seen at Holmbury St Mary heading for Cranleigh.** Barry LeJeune

(revised to become a limited-stop service) and 403 (extended to Cheam, covering the local 408/470 service within the GLC area). Some quite severe rural service cuts were applied to routes such as the 425 and 462, 464 and 465. Much chipping away at evening and Sunday services occurred in 1980, and for example Sunday buses last ran on routes 310, 326, 329, 416, 433 and 488. At the end of November yet another new scheme altered services between Crawley and East Grinstead. Route 426 (unchanged since May 1937!) gained a grand cross-country diversion from Horley to partner route 424 to East Grinstead, following the halving of that route's frequency. Most Southdown buses south-west of East Grinstead were removed, and London Country provided a replacement in the form of route 474 through West Hoathly and Sharpthorne – the first bus to these villages had been operated by East Surrey back in 1927.

Nevertheless, as if all the other changes were not enough, MAP altered the network all the way down from Amersham to Guildford, and buses of both London Country and Alder Valley were adorned with local identity labels. In April *Chilternlink* covered LCBS routes from Amersham garage and Alder Valley from High Wycombe. At the end of May *Thamesline* was provided by LCBS buses at Windsor and Staines garages and by Alder Valley from Maidenhead. There were initial problems with the new operations at Windsor garage which culminated in a strike. The last day of August saw *Weyfarer* from Alder Valley depots at Woking and Guildford and from LCBS garages at Addlestone and Guildford. With this last scheme LCBS buses did not carry the *Weyfarer* names externally, following a Company decision that local

Services in Kent yet again experienced reductions, in April and in November. Although no places actually lost their buses, there were often fewer of them. A similar exercise occurred in both April and December of 1981, about which more later. An economy in operation in summer 1980 was the takeover of M&D's local 55 route between Sevenoaks and Kemsing – it was amalgamated with LCBS's own 421 service under the numbers 457/467.

Practically the whole network in East Surrey was restructured at the end of August 1980. Main changes included the 414 (cut back to Dorking or Capel in favour of the 714 to Horsham), 470 (withdrawn altogether except for a school facility), 408

Above **Why the odd route number 999 was chosen is a mystery!** The service ran just from 29th October 1979 to 25th April 1980 and was a contract operation for Marconi in Borehamwood. The electronics company had a recruiting drive in the St Albans area and the new bus service was designed to carry workers from various estates around the city direct to work each day. Relatively few staff were in the event recruited who actually needed bus transport so it did not last long. Hatfield garage provided the vehicle, in this case RP 84 that is seen in St Albans Saint Peters Street on the very last day of service. John Bull

Both Stevenage and Harlow, as in 1972, were treated to a grand revision of their town networks in 1980. In Stevenage the SB-prefix, hitherto used for *Superbus* services, was continued but now stood for *Stevenage Bus* – the *Superbus* idea had been allowed to fade away somewhat as vehicles had needed replacement or re-painting. For Harlow the prefix letter **T** (for *TownBus*) was used as H was already in use at Hemel Hempstead.

Top left **AN 48** in Stevenage shows off its new *local identity*, the logo being in the old *Superbus* colours of yellow and blue. Steve Fennell

Centre left **AN 2** adorned with *TownBus* stickers stands at a very informative bus stop flag at Harlow Town station. The via blind box contains both destination and intermediate point information. Ian Pringle

Bottom left **The introduction of local identity schemes** meant that many of the 800-series numbers fell out of use, but in many cases contract operations for schools and colleges were allocated numbers in the 800-series. Route 841 linked Hatfield Polytechnic with Balls Park College in Hertford and was introduced from 30th August 1980 as a limited stop service over part of route 341. RP 24, complete with a blue limited-stop destination blind, is seen at Hatfield Polytechnic. The route was absorbed into the main 341 in January 1984. John Boylett

Left **MAP came to London Country in 1980 and first involved services operated by Amersham garage in a joint scheme with Alder Valley. While some route numbers were removed, the main feature of** *Chilternlink* **was the use of route numbers in the 300-series by both operators and joint operation of some routes. A new allocation of ANs was provided for Amersham garage to work some of the LCBS participation and one of these, AN 113, is pictured in Chesham on the 362. This long established route gained a peak hour extension beyond the traditional LCBS area between High Wycombe and Marlow.** Steve Fennell

Below left **On 31st August 1980** *Weyfarer* **created a change in service patterns around Woking and Guildford and, while Alder Valley adorned their buses with the new identity, LCBS did not. A lengthy London Country excursion outside their traditional area took the 459 to Knaphill, while the short 437 was extended at both ends to link Guildford and Weybridge, albeit by a roundabout route. Following the demise of King & Flack,** *Weyfarer* **blinds had to be obtained from different manufacturers resulting in some unusual displays. Initially some SNBs were loaned to Addlestone garage in September 1980 because of the late delivery of new blinds for the SMs and RPs. This meant that the latter types were restricted to such unaltered routes 408A and 436, often causing embarrassment when vehicles interworked onto other routes. So, in practice, SMs and RPs hardly ran in the first weeks of the changes. The** *Weyfarer* **network was further enhanced from 25th April 1981 when the 436 from Guildford to Staines was sensibly extended to the better traffic objective of Heathrow Airport. RP 53 is seen at the airport carrying the less than pleasing style of destination blind.** Geoff Rixon

identity brand names had gone far enough. The Market Analysis Project had been devised over the years by the NBC, modelled on an original Midland Red idea – ironically an idea that eventually helped to speed the split-up of Midland Red into small companies. Extensive surveys were carried out on and off buses to try to determine passenger requirements from which various sample networks could be devised. It was then up to the operators and the Local Authorities to choose a route system that could try to be viable financially while covering as many as possible of passengers'

needs. Inevitably in most cases nationally, services overall were reduced and in these cases they were no exception, although as has been noted, earlier economies by London Country meant that they were affected to a relatively small degree. London Country achieved new destinations outside their traditional area, and now reached Marlow, Booker and Great Kingshill with Chiltern-link, and Knaphill and Lyne with Weyfarer. There was a certain amount of actual joint operation of routes around High Wycombe, and Alder Valley routes all received numbers in the 300-series. Much cross-town running

of local town routes occurred at High Wycombe but, strangely, at Guildford the traditional dividing line in the middle of the town was perpetuated. Hardly any stretch of road on the London Country side of post-MAP was left unserved, although the remaining Saturday service on 467 (Staines – Poyle) disappeared.

Much of 1981 was taken up with more minor alterations, mostly by tinkering with routeings and frequencies, often to save the odd bus here and there – it all helped to make small economies but the multiplicity of timetable changes caused many of the area booklets to become out-of-date quickly. Even so, a few new areas came to be served – Biggin Hill Valley on a 410 diversion, the new housing estates of Cock Lane and Claymoor in High Wycombe (397) and Bricket Wood near St Albans (381). The seemingly endless service reductions took place at East Grinstead in April and around Gravesend in December, the latter including a new pattern of service again upsetting the traditional course of route 480, which had been stable for five years. Services around Sevenoaks were drastically reduced in April, but mitigation was at hand in the first allocation of double deckers to Dunton Green garage for nine years, so as to maintain capacities for schoolchildren's journeys. The long-established route 402 was withdrawn together with the main off-peak service route 454, which were covered by existing Green Line 706 between Bromley and Tonbridge. A limited Sunday route 805 covered various places in the local rural areas, helping to cover the non-appearance

of the Sevenoaks *Ramblers Bus* that year – little traffic manifested itself and the route last ran in January 1982 and another country town lost its Sunday buses.

The one really major scheme of 1981 was in north and east Hertfordshire on 25th April. Following requests from the County Council, a number of lengthy cross-county links were instituted such as Waltham Cross via Hertford to Stevenage (390) or Welwyn Garden City (324). There were improved services to the major area hospitals in Welwyn Garden City and Stevenage from further afield and there were more even, and sometimes increased, frequencies on a number of routes between Hertfordshire towns. A service to the new Rosedale Estate in Cheshunt was provided by route 360 from Enfield, using buses running on and off the 310 – interestingly this service was entirely within existing LT territory. A number of new links were made by changes to Green Line services, described elsewhere in this book, including the town of Royston in the far north which also received an LCBS bus service in the form of route 188. It took over the number 188 from United Counties who had previously connected Buntingford with Royston just on Wednesdays. London Transport's country buses had earlier ceased to serve Royston in 1935 due to problems encountered with the 1933 boundary arrangements. Also from 25th April an inroad was achieved when 436 was extended from Staines to Heathrow. The decline of the importance of the bus in the 1980s was demonstrated at Hertford when the large bus station dating from the mid 1930s was swallowed up in a development scheme. After temporary arrangements a new bus station, which was in effect a glorified lay-by, opened on 1st August 1981.

The biggest route change scheme of 1982 occurred right at the beginning of January, following the closure of East Grinstead garage on the last day of 1981. Ever-increasing losses in the area meant yet another reduction in frequencies, and operation of the local routes by garages distant from the area meant another change to the service pattern. Both Edenbridge and Handcross lost their London Country buses but a certain amount of double-decking on inter-urban routes helped to mitigate some of the cutbacks. Route 438 in particular was transformed from just a small peak hour service into a main Horsham – Crawley – East Grinstead trunk service with ANs, taking over from buses on other single-deck routes between Horsham and Crawley.

April saw the exchange of routes with LT in St Albans and Banstead, described earlier, and July featured the usual annual shuffle at Grays; this time four buses were removed on Mondays to Fridays. The Hertford and Stevenage and Crawley and Reigate areas both received minor timetable revisions, once again featuring thinning-out of evening and Sunday services with some being

The May 1981 changes in Hertfordshire produced a route 360 linking Rosedale Estate in Cheshunt to Enfield, where AN 113, now at Hertford garage, is seen loading up. John Boylett

withdrawn altogether and enabling an odd bus here and there to be saved. On 1st September the first Wednesday in the month route 854 to Chichester ran for the last time. More double-decking was possible on certain routes or sections of route by virtue of these savings. Indeed by September 1982 just over half of the 289 bus routes on the system had double-deck operation, either wholly or partially. From 21st August London Country buses reached another new destination when most 459s and all 461s were taken away from Feltham and diverted instead to Ashford. On the same day the Express section on the 403 was withdrawn, reducing to four (336, 408, 409, 419) the number of routes that sported the blue express destination blinds.

An interesting development occurred from 4th December 1982 when, as a precursor to complete closure the service between Epping and Ongar on the Central Line was reduced to Monday to Friday peak periods. A LT replacement bus 201 worked between Ongar and Epping with projections to Loughton and Buckhurst Hill but London Country provided one afternoon journey. This was the first example of a LT/LC jointly operated route after the failure of the BW1.

The traditional route numbering using the 300- and 400-series numbers was destined to break down even more over the coming years, an example was a Saturday only Slough to Colnbrook Market service which started on 30th October and was numbered 882. The market declined in popularity and it ran for the last time in March 1983. From 2nd November an omission in the Chiltern MAP scheme was

To replace the withdrawn section of Green Line 734 between Heathrow and Addlestone, route 436 was extended to Heathrow from 25th April 1981. It also served Stanwell which had never before been linked dierctly to the airport. London Country prominently displayed the *Weyfarer* name on this leaflet although reticent about showing it on their buses. Further expansion of services to Stanwell and Heathrow as well as an additional service on the 436 featured from 29th January 1983.

Hertfordshire County Council supported route 84 from 24th April 1982, which was awarded to London Country, restoring green buses to Barnet. Among the advantages stated in this leaflet was a co-ordinated timetable between St Albans and London Colney with routes 357/8, and the provision of *Outback* returns which effectively reduced fares as such facilities had not been offered by London Transport.

Left **An odd route number for an odd service. Route 854 was a 'first Wednesday in the month' operation from Guildford and Cranleigh to Chichester which ran from 3rd September 1980 to 1st September 1982, thus achieving just 25 journeys. The regular vehicle was RN 3, seen here at Alfold.** Mike Harris

Centre left **From the mid-1950s London Transport introduced express routes with fewer stops and a higher minimum fare to cater for longer distance passengers. Some routes were new while others ran over sections of existing routes using the appropriate route numbers – in all cases displaying distinctive blue and white blinds. The degree of success of express operations varied considerably and one of the longest survivors was the express section of 403, which ran between Warlingham and West Croydon on Monday to Friday peak hours only in the direction of the peak traffic flow. It ran for the last time on 21st August 1982 and is seen here some years earlier with Maidstone Corporation Atlantean EKP230C at Warlingham.** John Boylett

Bottom **During London Country's existence economies were achieved by the closure of no fewer than nine garages which were offset by the opening of three new ones. Crawley garage consisted of a very small shed which had been opened by East Surrey in June 1929 and by the London Country period was totally inadequate to cater for the services of the busy town and the coaching activities at Gatwick Airport. This situation resulted in most buses being parked in the open on adjacent land and new premises finally replaced it on 21st November 1982. This view, taken some ten years before closure shows a line up of RTs.** Steve Fennell

corrected when a Tuesday and Thursday 313 was introduced from Totteridge Drive to High Wycombe with BN operation.

On 29th January 1983 London Country took over more London Transport operations in the Staines, Weybridge and Kingston areas. LT routes 211 and 219 were withdrawn with reductions on 116, 203, 216 and 218 and London Country's 435 was also withdrawn. These changes were covered by 436 which was re-routed via Clare Road in Stanwell Village, 437 which underwent minor re-routeings and was extended from Weybridge to Kingston, a new 455 linked Chertsey and Heathrow via Shepperton, Sunbury and Ashford, and a new 456 linked St Peter's Hospital with Heathrow via

Right **RP 14 is in Thames Ditton on the 437, which in January 1983 was extended from Weybridge to Kingston to replace withdrawn LT route 219. The RP is perhaps in the process of being converted from Green Line to bus status as it carries only the National symbol.** Geoff Rixon

Centre right **The 1980s usually meant change, change and more change to bus services which often resulted in the demise of long established route numbers. A major scheme was introduced from 28th January 1984 in Hatfield and St Albans which resulted in the withdrawal of route 330 on the Welwyn Garden City – Hemel Hempstead trunk service. All buses ran as 340 which had previously been an evening and Sunday variation. LR 11 stands at Hemel Hempstead Bus Station.** John Boylett

Bottom **The Bishops Stortford – Harlow – Epping corridor lost traditional routes 718 and 720 from 2nd April 1977 and various combinations of bus and coach routes were provided in the area being subjected to frequent changes. A better solution was found from 12th May 1984 when the 329, 339, 702 and 712 were all withdrawn to be replaced by a series of express buses numbered 500 to 503. The express routes continued the tradition of using white on blue blind displays but this facility was not extended to the route track blinds as illustrated by SNB 168 in Station Road Epping.** Nick Agnew

Walton and Sunbury. The 459 was withdrawn east of Chertsey and 461 was revised to run from St Peters Hospital to Kingston via Walton replacing LT 211. LT introduced return fares on 218 which were inter-available with 437 between Hersham and Kingston. The 455 and 456 routes were the precursor of the successful 555/6/7 series of many years later.

The year continued with minor revisions in Crawley to serve new housing, The Fairway, and Stevenage with a seasonal 888 running from Stevenage to Knebworth House. June saw a revision in Hemel Hempstead in which the lunchtime Apsley Mills journeys were reduced to just one bus and a diversion on routes 405, 411 and 422 to

On 27th May 1984 a new *Rambler* bus 452 was introduced to link Sevenoaks to Ide Hill, Edenbridge, Hever Castle, Chiddingstone, Penshurst and Weald. The route was normally SNB worked but on certain occasions London Country's preserved RF 202 was used. The bus is seen standing outside Dunton Green garage. *John Boylett*

serve the new East Surrey Hospital at Earlswood. Route 411A was withdrawn away from Reigate to serve White Bushes via the new hospital. July 2nd saw the demise of routes 312 and 327 with Watford area reductions which should have been introduced with the Hemel Hempstead changes but were deferred following local authority objections. On the same date 342/3 was extended from Welham Green to the more useful objective of Potters Bar via Bell Bar which enabled the 303 to run via Brookmans Park. Timetable changes took place from 23rd July in much of the South East area which included the extension of routes 400, 401 and 421 from Belvedere to Thamesmead (Bentham Drive North) on behalf of LT Selkent. The start of the school term in September saw several new school routes in the 800-series and from 7th November London Country took over a local service, 868, in Harpenden which had previously been run by Kingsman Coaches on behalf of the County Council. County councils were becoming very adept at awarding contracts to smaller operators in the knowledge that if they became unable to meet their contractual obligations the large traditional operator could always be called in, often at short notice, to pick up the pieces.

Two things that were to become increasingly common as time went on were the provision of services to out of town supermarkets and the duplication of route numbers across the system. This was illustrated by the provision of routes from Holmer Green and Penn to Booker Asda numbered 356 and 357 respectively which ran for a month immediately prior to Christmas. The numbers followed on from Alder Valley's routes 350/1/4/5 which also served the store but, of course, the London Country numbers were duplicated in St Albans. The routes returned as free services in March 1984 but this time as 902 and 903, following on from Alder Valley's 900 and 901. These new numbers were destined in

turn to duplicate numbers in the Green Line Specials series as 902 started in 1985 linking Welwyn Garden City with Alton Towers and in 1986 a Langley to Alton Towers service numbered 903. The new 903 actually passed very close to the original 903 serving Beaconsfield and Amersham.

A St Albans and Hatfield revision on 28th January 1984 saw the 84 extended to serve Marshalswick and the cross country trunk routes 320 and the long-established 330 replaced by 340. The next major revision took place on 12th May at Harlow where an interesting feature was the numbering of a circular service T7A and T7C to denote anticlockwise and clockwise operation. The main change was to introduce a new series of route numbers for express operation. Express bus route 500 Bishops Stortford – Romford replaced 712, route 501 Harlow – Romford replaced 339, route 502 Harlow – Walthamstow via Loughton replaced 702 and route 503 Harlow – Walthamstow via Waltham Abbey replaced 329, which had served Waltham Cross, and a new LT 254 linked Epping and Waltham Cross. The advantage was that the former Green Line services and buses had different running times and the coaches, which were effectively doing bus work, did not serve all stops. The curious thing with this revision was that London Country took over Eastern National routes 47, 47A and 47B which linked Harlow with various villages in the area. The route numbers were not altered and London Country served places such as Toothill and Epping Green which they had abandoned as long ago as 1971. In compensation new Eastern National routes 57/A replaced the 338 journeys to Lower Sheering.

May 1984 saw the seasonal reintroduction of rambler routes 318 and 417 but this year they were joined by a *Chiltern Rambler* 327 based on Hemel Hempstead and 452 at Sevenoaks which performed a smaller circuit than 418. A very short-lived local 472 was introduced on Wednesdays and Fridays in

Sevenoaks on 16th May but it had been withdrawn before the end of August The number 472 had become spare in June 1983 when Mole Valley took over the long established special service to Netherne Hospital.

Windsor garage, which had opened in 1933, was closed after operations on 28th July to be replaced by new premises in Slough, coded SL, close to the Bus Station. The opportunity was taken to completely revise the Slough local routes and while more routes served Wexham Park Hospital no additional sections were covered. Routes 444/5/6/8, 481/4 were all withdrawn and a new series of routes numbered 90 to 96 took their place. They were seemingly numbered in that series as the Alder Valley routes in the area were all numbered below 100. The evening service on 458 was renumbered 58 and diverted via Chalvey High Street to provide a service to an area covered during the daytime by Alder Valley. The opening of Lakeside Tesco at Thurrock in October saw free routes T1–T7, which duplicated Harlow numbers, providing links from Grays, Chadwell St Mary, South Ockendon, Tilbury, Uplands Estate, Brentwood and Dagenham respectively. T8 from Herongate, T9 from Aveley, Usk Road and T10 from Bexleyheath, which was worked by Swanley, joined them in March 1985.

Further reductions took place in the Hertford and Hemel Hempstead areas from 26th January, 1985 again involving evening and Sunday cuts. A trend which has started elsewhere was expanded with evening and Sunday only routes H37 and H38 which covered sections of certain other routes. The 188 to Royston was withdrawn and 316 gained evening journeys to Enfield to cover a reduction on 310. Route 308 was severely dealt with, losing all service to Cuffley and Cheshunt being reduced to a circular based on Hertford linking Bayford, Epping Green and Little Berkhampstead with just two journeys on Tuesday and Friday. The County Council had got it wrong here and following protests the route was re-instated to Monday to Saturday operation between Hertford and Cuffley on an increased frequency from 15th April. The County Council exercised its option to change the operator on Hemel Hempstead rural route 317 which was awarded to B&B – Tates while the Tring local 387 was offered for competitive tender and awarded to Red Rover.

The results of a Guildford area bus study in conjunction with London Country, Alder

Valley, Tillingbourne, Blue Saloon and Safeguard were implemented on 14th April with the demise of London Country routes 407, 408A, and 425 with 412 being replaced between Dorking and Boxhill by a new 451. London Country worked G6 Guildford – Burpham – Merrow – Guildford circular, with G7 running in the reverse direction, absorbing the 436 shorts, and G8 Guildford – Merrow, Bushy Hill. The 425 was covered by a revision on Green Line 773 and Tillingbourne 22 and 25. From the next day changes in Essex saw schools route 840 withdrawn, the journeys covered by the joint LT/LCBS route 201. London Country retained the contract to run the former Eastern National 47 group routes with a completely revised 47A running from Abbess Roding to Ongar in place of Eastern National 34/A. Route 369 Grays to Brentwood and Shenfield was awarded to Ingatestone Coaches leaving London Country operating the peak hour Ockendon Station – Gatehope Drive section. Dartford, Northfleet and Swanley operations were also subject of revisions in April with the 486 taking over the Thamesmead journeys from 400/1 and 421. May saw the four rambler type routes returning and in July a new Wycombe Rambler, the 387 was introduced on a circular working from Amersham.

Further operations in rural areas were lost when the county councils awarded tenders to smaller operators. The Stevenage – Letchworth section of 382 was lost to Simmonds Coaches in May and from 31st August Harlow's 392/3 were lost to Golden Boy Coaches. The routes were also extended to Ongar replacing most of 501 which was reduced to a three day per week operation between North Weald and Romford. Route 370 was withdrawn between Tilbury Asda and the Ferry and on Sunday a new 378 linked Feenan Highway and Grays. Essex County Council contracted a Chadwell St Mary to Tilbury Ferry service to Highfield Minicoaches and, incredibly anyone wanting

to travel direct from Grays to Tilbury Ferry was obliged to use the train where, not so many years before, up to four buses per hour had operated! A curious un-numbered joint operation took place in Guildford to a Superstore at Burpham from 1st October until Christmas being jointly worked by London Country, Alder Valley and Safeguard with each participant running the route for one week in three. The final major alterations of 1985 took place on 26th October when the long established cross-country Green Line route 724 from Harlow to Windsor was withdrawn. An express bus 524 from Harlow to Watford was provided as a replacement but it took a revised route from Welwyn Garden City and Hertford enabling bus 334 and most of 324 to be withdrawn. At the

Above **Windsor garage had been opened by London General Country Services in January 1933 with undercover accommodation for all vehicles and was enlarged in 1936/7 to enable two garages in Slough to close. Unlike the simple East Surrey sheds the well designed frontage of Windsor was one of which the Royal Borough could be justly proud. Occupying a valuable site it was replaced from 29th July 1984 by new premises in Slough thus saving much unproductive running of garage journeys and presented the opportunity to recast the Slough local routes. Different cross linkings applied and although no new roads were served an improved service to Wexham Park Hospital was provided. The existing route numbers disappeared to be replaced, not by a local identity scheme, but by routes 90 to 96, which were chosen because the local Alder Valley routes were numbered below 100.** Nick Agnew

Below **Route 96, worked by AN 218 in Slough High Street, linked Britwell with the Town Centre and Wexham Park Hospital and replaced part of routes 448 and 482.** Mike Harris

Left On 31st August 1985 route 393 was lost through Essex County Council tendering to Golden Boy Coaches and companion route 392 was withdrawn. SNB 206 is passing through Katherines in Harlow a few years earlier. The origins of the 393 went back to 1949, when it linked Harlow to Hoddesdon, most of the route traversing lanes which had not previously seen a bus service. Mike Harris

Below Swanley garage was opened by East Surrey in October 1925 comprising of the basic shed with the administrative block in the foreground clearly showing London Transport design style. This view was taken just prior to closure, with operations being transferred to a new Dartford site on 19th January 1986, when the premises had clearly seen better days. The sign with the NBC corporate logo had originally displayed the London Country *Flying Polo*. Unlike the other garages that closed Swanley was destined to reopen eight months later on 16th August in order to house the buses used on LRT tendered route 51. Nick Agnew

western end 441 was extended from Staines to Heathrow. Developments in Watford saw Premier Albanian Coaches taking over part of route 319 but London Country provided a new 391 from London Colney and Bricket Wood to Watford and a W30 to serve Watford Business Park.

The existing Swanley and Dartford garages were closed after traffic on 18th January 1986 to be replaced by a new garage at Central Road, Dartford coded DT but only minor changes were made to the routes in the area. A Tesco superstore north of Gatwick Airport opened in February with diversions on 405 and 426 to double run and the provision of free routes T1–T6 to bring customers from as far afield as Merstham, Reigate, Dorking and East Grinstead. From 22nd March the Borehamwood local BW1 was replaced by B1 and B2 operated with MBMs from the Scratchwood outstation. Due to Mole Valley pulling out of stage work at short notice one MBM went to Addlestone to work a Surrey County Council contract route 264 between Hersham and Walton, replacing Mole Valley route 1. As a conse-

quence of the closure of London Transport's Loughton garage from 24th May 1986 route 201 was awarded by Essex County Council to West's Coaches with the London Country journeys also being acquired by West's. A new seasonal extension took place on 442 when it was extended to Thorpe Park via Runnymede.

The very last change on 31st August 1986 just one week before the split involved the acquisition from Luton & District, at short notice, of six HCC supported routes in the Letchworth area. The routes, which were worked by SNBs from Stevenage, had a hotchpotch of numbers with 78 being a Letchworth local, X78 Clothall Common – Hitchin, 91B Guilden Morden School – Hitchin and three schools workings 877/8/9. United Counties and Simmonds Coaches replaced other routes.

Fare revisions in the 1980s were not as frequent as they were in the days of raging inflation in the late 1970s. As previously stated 1981 saw a variation in increases according to the level of county council support. In March 1982 an increase of

broadly 10 percent applied but the opportunity was taken to raise the age limit for child fares from 14 to 16 years of age. Further increases of 7.5 percent applied in March of 1983 and 1984. In 1985 the increases were more fragmented as different levels of support varied across the counties and were spread over the year as different counties worked to different budget dates. The main revision on 24th March saw charges for dogs abolished after some 14 years. The revision of 23rd March 1986 featured the introduction of *Clippercards* in Crawley, Harlow, Hemel Hempstead and Stevenage. These represented a cheaper option than the corresponding weekly Travelwide ticket offering twelve journeys for the price of ten. One peculiarity of the successive fare increases involved the flat-fare fare box routes. When introduced the fares were comparatively low and could be met by the insertion of just one or two coins, but with subsequent increases more coins were required to meet the fare. Incredibly in October 1982 the Hemel Hempstead flat-fare was increased from a reasonably manageable 30p to 31p!

Above **Originally opened by Maidstone & District, Dartford garage passed to the newly formed London Passenger Transport Board on 1st July 1933. An awkward site with bays at right angles to the road most vehicles were kept in an adjacent yard it was closed together with Swanley to be replaced by new premises in Central Road.** Nick Agnew

Right **Watford Junction Interchange opened on 2nd February 1986 and replaced a hotch-potch of stopping places in the street and on British Rail property. LR 52 stops by one of the new shelters while working Watford local W4 which linked Abbots Langley and Maple Cross.** John Boylett

Bottom right **The Mercedes L608D minibuses were intended for Borehamwood routes B1, B2 and LRT tendered route 268 but with Mole Valley's abrupt departure from stage carriage work MBM 5 was transferred to Addlestone to work Surrey County Council contract route 264 which commenced on 1st April 1986. The route, which linked Hersham and Walton, replaced Mole Valley route 1 and ran on Mondays to Saturdays – MBM 5 is seen in the unfamiliar surroundings of Brighton one Sunday in connection with a bus rally.** Colin Brown

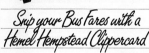

CLIPPER CARD

Snip your Bus Fares with a Hemel Hempstead Clippercard

★ 12 bus trips for the price of 10

★ Just £4.00 each (£2.00 child)

★ Sold at local Post Offices or the Bus Station

★ Saves fumbling for the exact fare at bus stops

★ No expiry date

★ Starts 23 March 1987

This new method of buying bus trips is so easy and simple to use. It not only saves money but also avoids the bother of finding change.

Clippercards were introduced as a cheaper alternative to *Travelwide* facilities in Crawley, Harlow, Hemel Hempstead and Stevenage from 23rd March 1986. They offered 12 trips for the price of 10 and had open-ended availability. The Hemel Hempstead facility cost £4.00 where as the weekly *Travelwide* cost £4.15 but was available for an unlimited number of journeys within the week.

Chapter 8

GREEN LINE DECLINE

THE GREEN LINE coach services were handed over by London Transport to London Country Bus Services Ltd in January 1970 along with the Country Bus services and, as previously described, the new company faced many difficulties. These difficulties extended to Green Line operations with constantly declining passenger traffic and some 60 per cent of the vehicle requirements being covered by 18 year old RFs.

There were several factors which contributed to this decline. During the period from 1959 to 1962 steam operation had been eliminated from the railways in Green Line territory mostly on the north side of London, resulting in fast diesel or electric trains running at frequent, regular intervals. This was a great change from the slow, irregular and often infrequent service offered by the steam trains during the slack hours and on Sundays, and it was now only in areas where the station was some distance from the town that Green Line had the advantage. They had had to contend with competition from

frequent electric train services in Kent and Surrey from their innovation in the 1930s, and had achieved this by charging single and return fares lower than those of the railway. But under the British Transport Commission an agreement had been reached whereby fares were standardised between LT and the railways. In 1960 the post-war Green Line network peaked when it carried some 36,000,000 passengers but by 1969 this figure had fallen substantially to 20,500,000.

When the New Towns in the Green Line area were in their infancy, much off-peak travel had been generated from the need to visit the nearby large towns or even London itself for shopping and entertainment. On Sundays there had been trips to relatives, and many relief coaches had been operated. By the middle sixties however, the main shopping and entertainment centres had opened up in the New Towns and many families now owned a car, leading to further drops in off-peak and Sunday loadings. The increasing number of cars and lorries fighting for road space started to play havoc

with the coach timetables resulting in many passengers finding alternative means of travel.

Turning to the vehicles operating the services at the time of takeover, 217 coaches were required on Monday to Friday, 215 on Saturdays, with 192 on Sundays to cover the timetabled operations of which one-man operated percentages were 61, 64 and 67 respectively. A fleet of 150 refurbished RFs covered 130 workings on Monday to Fridays with 136 on Saturday and Sunday on omo routes 701/2/6/8, 710/1/2/3/4/9, 720/4/5/7. Double deck requirements were met by 83 Monday to Friday, 77 Saturday and 62

When London Country was formed the most modern image of Green Line was represented by the RCL, the finest Routemaster sub class, then four and a half years old. RCL 2222 stands at Aldgate amid resurfacing work on busy route 721 which still saw up to five coaches per hour. Route 721 was a fast road and where circumstances permitted the full running potential of the RCLs could be experienced.
W.R. Legg

Sunday workings on routes 704/5/9, 715, 716/A, 718, 721/3 with RMC and RCL types which dated from 1962 and 1965 respectively. Officially one RT, one crew operated RF and two RCs made up the numbers in the allocation book. London Transport had realised in the early 1960s that the bulk of the Green Line fleet would soon have to be replaced, and back in 1964 had ordered a fleet of 14 AEC Reliance coaches fitted with 36ft Willowbrook bodies seating 49 passengers. These coaches were equipped with a luxurious type of seating, had panoramic windows, and were finished in a distinctive livery of silver and grey with a Lincoln green waist-band. Known as the RC type, they were placed in service on route 705 in 1965 but proved somewhat unsatisfactory to the rigurs of Green Line work and at the time of takeover only two were required for service, being rostered as spare coaches for route 727 (Crawley – Luton).

This then was the operating fleet on Green Line, and the tightness of the allocations with very few spare vehicles shows that, in spite of the age of most of the coaches, they were regarded as very reliable for their arduous duties. When spare vehicles were required RFs from the bus fleet were deployed, where circumstances permitted they were often taken from the batch of 25 refurbished RFs which had been demoted to bus use in 1968. Unlike the bus services Sunday remained a busy day for Green Line with vehicle requirements for that day representing nearly 90 per cent of the Monday to Friday figure. This was probably explained by the fact that many parallel bus routes had been reduced or withdrawn on that day and that railway travel was becoming increasingly unattractive on Sundays with excessively prolonged journey times caused by wholesale and often unco-ordinated closures of sections of line due to engineering works.

Nevertheless, with a view to extending one-man operation, the new Company quickly ordered a fleet of 90 AEC Reliance coaches, which took nearly two years to materialise as the RP class. London Country was preoccupied by many other matters in 1970 and did not turn its attention to the Green Line network until 1971 when some alterations occurred, comprising a few withdrawals of uneconomic sections of routes and some new ventures to tap new markets. Route 702 (Sunningdale – Gravesend) had been reduced on Mondays–Fridays to just a peak operation over the Sunningdale-Victoria section in 1968, while retaining its weekend through operation; this latter was still not well used and was withdrawn from 20th February 1971. The peak-hour western remnant was kept on but only until July 1973, a parallel Alder Valley coach service being able to cope with what few passengers there were. In south Essex, one coach per

Left **The practice of issuing a leaflet for each route or group of routes dated from Green Line's earliest days. The last LT issues, dated December 1969, explained the revised arrangements to apply from 1st January 1970 and London Country perpetuated the same design which incorporated their new logo.**

GREEN LINE COACH

714

LUTON AND DORKING
via
St. Albans Barnet
LONDON Oxford Circus
Kingston and Leatherhead

TIMETABLE AND FARES

DECEMBER 1969

LONDON TRANSPORT   55 Broadway SW1
Telephone 01-222 1234

Starting 1 January 1970, Green Line Coaches will
be taken over by a new company:-
LONDON COUNTRY BUS SERVICES LTD.
with head office at Bell Street, Reigate, Surrey.

GREEN LINE COACH

710·711

LONDON (Baker Street) AND AMERSHAM
via Ealing Uxbridge
and Gerrards Cross

REIGATE AND HIGH WYCOMBE
via Banstead Sutton Mitcham
LONDON, Oxford Circus
Ealing Uxbridge and Beaconsfield

TIMETABLE AND FARES

16 MAY 1970

LONDON COUNTRY BUS SERVICE LTD.
Bell Street, Reigate, Surrey

Below **The mainstay of the Green Line fleet in 1970 was the refurbished RF complete with the traditional route boards as typified here by RF32 at Rickmansworth. The route boards fell out of use by 1973. Route 724 was the first one man operated Green Line, being introduced in 1966 and providing an express service between Romford and High Wycombe which, due to the helpfulness and enthusiasm of the senior drivers who worked on the route, soon became popular. In June 1972 it was diverted at Rickmansworth to run to Heathrow and Staines and the express link between Watford and High Wycombe was lost. The Express nature of the route was gradually eroded over the years as far more intermediate stops were added.** Barry LeJeune

RMC 1470 is seen at Hammersmith while working on route 715 from Guildford to Hertford. The between decks LT bullseye has been removed, the new London Country logo has been applied and the gold Green Line fleet name retained. Route 715 was the first to receive RMCs in August 1962 and was the last Green Line route to retain them, finally being converted to RP operation on 29th April 1972.
Colin Brown

hour on 723 (Aldgate – Tilbury) was diverted further into the Belhus Estate in Aveley, being renumbered 723A. At the same date routes 712/713 (Dorking – Luton or Dunstable) lost their Luton service and were reduced to work between Dorking and St Albans with Dunstable only served in peak hours and on Sundays, the latter saving the operation of a bus service on that day. Busy route 727 gained a third airport to serve on 20th March 1971 when it was extended in

The hourly 710 service between Amersham and Baker Street lost the Uxbridge to London section in the February 1971 changes, lowering its status to a short express bus service. So short was the route considered by Green Line standards that it was provided with a lazy blind display. The remnant of the route lasted only until October 1972 and it is surprising that it lasted even that long. Amersham thus ceased to appear on the Green Line route map for

Luton from the Station to the Airport thus providing a unique direct link between all three of London's major airports. So much traffic was being generated by route 727 that relief coaches were often needed between Heathrow and St Albans, resulting in much drivers' overtime payments. Coincidentally for some time the passengers using the Watford to High Wycombe section of route 724 had been much less and from 3rd June 1972 the service was diverted to Heathrow and Staines to give two coaches per hour between St Albans and Heathrow.

the first time since 1933, and did not feature again for another five years.

Two interesting developments occurred in summer 1971. From 15th May alternate Saturday journeys on the 715 (Guildford – Hertford) were diverted through Kingston, instead of running via the Bypass, in an effort to tap some of the shopping traffic to this major centre. These journeys were renumbered 715A. On 4th July some summer Sunday journeys on routes 704 and 705 (Windsor – Tunbridge Wells / Sevenoaks) went to the new Windsor Safari Park, this extension being repeated in subsequent summers.

On the vehicle side, things at last started to happen in summer 1971. After refurbishing and repainting in standard Lincoln green livery, the RC class re-entered service on route 727 but reliability was poor and the 727 received the first of the new RP coaches on 18th December, the RCs moving to achieve the one-man conversion of route 723 from 1st January 1972. At this date all journeys ran via the former 723A variant in

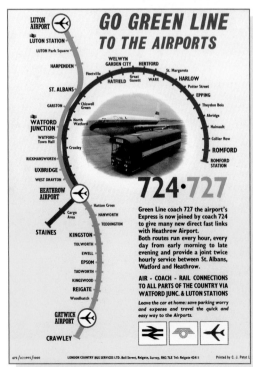

Upon the diversion of 724 to serve Heathrow Airport a magnificent multi-coloured poster advertised the *Airport Express* 724 and 727 routes, showing every single stopping point. The centre picture showed RP 3 alongside a Laker Airways Boeing 707 at Gatwick Airport. A combined leaflet featured another view of the same scene, but in black and white. From 1977 a series of posters was produced depicting the *Airport Network* of Green Line, together with other operators' services, which was frequently updated as new services were introduced.

The ill-fated RC class was shunted over to south Essex to replace Routemasters on the 723 from 1st January 1972. RC 5 is seen at the London end of the route in August 1973 by which time the London Country logo had been painted over. R.C. Riley

Belhus Estate, the coaches being numbered 723, and as the Tilbury Ferry terminus required a reversing manoeuvre this was abandoned in favour of Civic Square, but only until May 1973 when the route was cut back to Grays.

The subsequent batches of RPs were used from January to April 1972 to convert all the remaining crew-operated Green Line services to one-man operation, with one exception. The displaced Routemasters in turn replaced time-expired RTs on various trunk bus routes. Starting on 1st January routes 721 (Aldgate – Brentwood), 718 (Windsor – Harlow), 716/A (Chertsey – Hitchin / Woking – Stevenage) and 704/705 were converted, in that order, finishing with 715/A from 29th April, leaving just the peak-hour and Sunday route 709 (Godstone – Baker Street) with RCL operation, amazingly lasting another four years before one-man conversion. As previously stated London Country had a relatively high number of long serving staff particularly on Green Line. Under London Transport, coach drivers and double-deck coach conductors had received higher rates of pay than crew bus staff, so consequentially the senior staff at most garages tended to work on Green Line. These pay differentials had been discontinued in early London Country days with the employees being given a small personal allowance in recognition of their Green Line status. The omo conversions meant that many conductors who had worked continuously on Green Line since its resumption in 1946 were now displaced. According to circumstances at individual garages they reverted to the crew bus rota, in some cases filling vacancies rather than displacing junior staff, or were employed on alternative duties, or left the company through the voluntary severance arrangements.

Another new type of coach was received at this time when a fleet of 21 Alexander-bodied AEC Swifts intended for South Wales Transport were diverted to London Country. Classified SMA , they replaced RFs on route 725 (Gravesend – Windsor via Croydon).

The RP coaches replaced all RMCs and RCLs on Green Line (except route 709) between January and April 1972. Brand new RP 61 stands on Windsor garage forecourt in March 1972 prior to working on route 705 to Sevenoaks. Colin Brown

February 1973 saw the arrival of the first Leyland Nationals. Classified LNC type and painted in the NBC's dual-purpose green and white livery, their external appearance camouflaged the fact that they were merely buses within. Such rigid standardisation was imposed by the NBC and Leyland that constituent companies had to take or leave the standard product, hard upright pvc-covered seats and all. The first delivery was sent to Romford for route 721, and the passengers boarding them on the first day must have compared them most unfavourably with the RPs, and indeed the RCLs just over a year earlier, that they replaced. The unyielding decision that the Company was forced to take to use these vehicles on Green Line

routes must have had no little effect on the continuing decline. However at least some passengers benefited as the RPs moved on to replace RFs on busy routes 720 (Aldgate – Bishops Stortford) and 724 (Romford – Staines).

It took nearly three years for the remainder of the Green Line RF fleet to be replaced by Leyland Nationals, more LNCs and then some SNCs – shorter but still with bus seats. Partial relief was at hand from summer 1974 as SNCs then being delivered had more comfortable moquette-covered higher-backed seats, luggage racks and generally an improved appearance. This batch, delivered between June 1974 and March 1976, numbering 87 vehicles,

London Country adopted a lighter green livery early in 1972 and this was first applied to the SMA class; the pale green relief band traditional on Green Line coaches was retained. The result was very handsome, as can be seen on SMA 5 at Windsor on route 725. The forced ventilation and lack of opening windows were never a success on these vehicles and the only means of adjustable ventilation was by means of opening roof lights. BN 25 provides relief on the same service. Tony Wilson

replaced almost all the earlier Nationals which then moved on to bus work, in turn replacing many RTs and RFs. The very last three replaced the remaining RCLs on route 709 on 15th May 1976, bringing to an end scheduled crew operation on Green Line. Pressure from NBC Companies to produce the so-called local coach version of the National was obviously the spur to the manufacturer, but it still seems incredible that they had to be prompted. Even so, the characteristic noisy operation and the relative austerity compared with the RP, and even the RF which had to replace them whenever they broke down, served to alienate passengers from Green Line.

The first Rover Ticket to be available on Green Line was introduced on 16th August 1970 when the Golden Rover, priced at 15 shillings (75p) adult or 11 shillings (55p) child, appeared, available for unlimited travel on all coach routes, except initially 727, as well as green bus routes. At the fares revision of 3rd June 1973, a major alteration was made to the issue of day-return tickets. For some years a limited issue of this type of ticket had been in operation, but it was

replaced by a standard new system of day-return tickets available after 09.30 on Mondays–Fridays or any time at weekends. Return journeys could be made at any time of the day of issue, and at weekends a return ticket issued on a Saturday could be used for return on a Sunday. All single fares of 20p and over qualified for day-return facilities. The former 10- or 12-journey weekly tickets were replaced by a new type of weekly ticket available for seven days for an unlimited number of journeys during the week of issue. For the first time since 1942 monthly season tickets were offered, valid for a calendar month from any date, and for unlimited journeys between the points specified. Both weekly and monthly tickets were now issued for all fares of 15p and above, and have been a stimulus to commuter traffic ever since.

The only route alteration in 1974 was in May when the 720 was extended the short distance from Bishops Stortford to Stansted Airport. To save an additional vehicle being needed, the timetable was revised to include the extra running time. However this meant that a 67-minute frequency was scheduled instead of hourly and this must have lost

Below The LT influence was lost from the Green Line timetable leaflets in March 1971 when a revised style featuring a drawing of an RC, complete with route board, and incorporating a prominent green line in the design. Somewhat misleadingly the leaflets for the double deck routes featured a drawing of an RC. With the one-man conversions in 1972 RP 1 with blinds rendered unreadable featured on the leaflets for the appropriate routes. The 725 leaflets uniquely featured SMA 1 with a readable destination blind. From 1973 the NBC symbol was incorporated. Also in 1973 the RP operated route leaflets featured RP 44, the first of the class to appear in the new livery. With the gradual conversion of many routes to Leyland Nationals a view of LNC 45, complete with passengers, was used. The view was adapted from a photograph of the vehicle taken at Aldgate on route 721.

GREEN LINE **720**

STED AIRPORT
OPS
STORTFORD
LOW
NG
GHTON
STEAD
TFORD
END
DON
(ALDGATE)

mes & Fares: starting 4 May 1974

LONDON COUNTRY
Associated with the National Bus Company
Bell Street, Reigate, Surrey RH2 7LE Tel. Reigate 42411

Left **With the extension of route 720 to Stansted Airport the leaflet was given the 'airport treatment' being produced like the 724/727 publicity on glossy paper and featuring an aircraft. Whether an irregular service taking some two hours from end to end was quite what the prospective passenger expected when picking up the leaflet must remain a matter of conjecture.**

regular passengers along the main route. The extension actually lasted three years before the sight of empty coaches running to an equally empty passenger terminal ceased. Stansted was not, at the time, blessed with much air traffic but LCBS retained a licence for the service there, having borne in mind the eventual intention to develop the airport in the 1980s. A year later, on 31st May, routes 712 and 713 featured again in cutbacks when their Dunstable section was withdrawn in favour of local buses, except for the occasional summer extension to Whipsnade Zoo. Between London and Dorking they were superseded by new route 703, the split of cross London running being a foretaste of things to come on other routes.

Top **The SMAs were delivered in the 1972 lighter green livery, but later received the NBC corporate livery which they carried rather better than some classes. A busy West Croydon Bus Station shows Windsor bound SMA 19 loading up and an eastbound member of the class in original livery reveals the unusual position of the rear blind box below the rear windows.** Barry LeJeune

Above **The first Leyland Nationals to enter service on Green Line work did so on route 721 from February 1973. They looked smart externally but were fitted with plain bus seats within and must have been seen by passengers as a poor replacement for the RPs and earlier RCLs during a period of frequent and high fare increases. The original National coaches had PVC covered seats but from SNC 96–115 they acquired moquette covered bus seats, and from SNC 116–147 high back seats and luggage racks were fitted resulting in the so-called suburban coach.** Capital Transport

Above **Chartwell bound RF 154 takes on passengers at the Marble Arch coach stop in Park Lane in the summer of 1973. Route 706 was destined to be the last scheduled RF route with the Tring allocation receiving SNCs in October 1974 but, due to the need to lengthen the inspection pits at Chelsham their RFs soldiered on until SNCs could finally be used from 4th October 1975. The splendid E9 coach compulsory stop flag displays a full complement of E plates, most with destinations, prior to the withdrawal and renumbering of certain routes. With the withdrawal of route 716A on 15th**

May 1976 London Country replaced a number of coach stop flags, including this one, with DoT style flags. It was, however, subsequently decided that they should not be used within the Greater London area and the traditional LT flags quickly replaced them. John Bull

However the southern route was never a success, offering no late evening service, and was withdrawn in October 1976. A further

withdrawal came as something of a shock when route 701 (Gravesend – Ascot) ceased without replacement on 3rd October 1975. The cut was considered severe and the drivers involved the passengers in a campaign for its retention but to no avail. In May 1976 routes 716 and 716A were combined as 716 running from Hitchin to Woking, in this case removing Chertsey from the Green Line map for a few years.

The RCLs and RMCs may well have been swept aside in 1972 by the new coaches but for several years it was still common for double deckers to appear on Bank Holidays on popular routes. The 704 serving London and Windsor was a natural for *Green Line Reliefs* and recalling this once common operation is RML 2352 seen in the spring of 1976.
Peter Plummer

The drastic and somewhat arbitrary nature of some of the route changes made the Green Line network appear to be rather less than the comprehensive service that was provided across the whole area in London Transport days. By the end of 1976 the Monday to Friday vehicle requirement had fallen by over a quarter of the 1970 figure of 217 to just 158. This decline obviously could not continue if Green Line was to survive

and offer a comprehensive network of limited stop or express links, and clearly something had to be done quickly. The following chapters will explain how the fortunes of Green Line were reversed in the 1980s but not before the Monday to Friday requirement fell to 135 by the end of 1979 which represented just 62 per cent of the 1970 operations.

Above **In an era of vehicle substitution a noteworthy example occurred in 1976 when RT 3530 was based at Tring for a few months. It was so much more reliable than the Nationals that it was entrusted to a regular peak hour run to and from London each day, and an enthusiast made a special set of blinds especially for it. The bus is captured on 3rd August negotiating the traffic flow system around Marble Arch on its long run to Aylesbury.** Mike Harris

During 1974, 1975 and 1976 vehicle reliability was not good, to say the least, and many non-standard types had to be pressed into service. Often most unsuitable buses appeared, such as the BN, probably one of the most unsuitable for coach work. Here BN 44 is in Epsom on route 703, the southern section of the former 712/3. However relief was at hand and scenes such as this became increasingly rarer from 1977 onwards but this did not save the 703 which ran for the last on 1st October 1976.
J.G.S. Smith

Chapter 9

GREEN LINE DECLINE HALTED

BY LATE 1976 it seemed to the onlooker and the enthusiast that Green Line was on its last legs and that it was only a matter of time before it would fold up. After three years of Leyland Nationals on Green Line, it was obvious that they were not a success as far as the public was concerned. The plastic seats and austere interiors did not impress passengers and although the later SNCs made some amends, people were still deserting Green Line for other means of travel. Some of the traditional main-road routes out of London had been discarded in recent years but there were still several coach services that had outlived their usefulness or were dogged by traffic congestion and resultant unreliability.

The management set about improving the image, the vehicles and the network to bring it in line with modern requirements. A new fleet of AEC Reliance coaches was ordered, to be leased from the Kirkby Central Organisation, to be delivered in

Revitalisation of the network began on 29th January 1977 with the introduction of brand-new luxury coaches. First garage to receive them was St Albans whose SNC-operated 712 and 713 were seen off by new limited-stop 707 and 717. The familiar black on yellow destination blinds were retained, but their small size and position made them much more difficult to discern than those on the vehicles they replaced. The bold livery style was revolutionary at the time, but was subsequently copied by other operators in the NBC. Some 150 new coaches, classified RS (Plaxton) and RB (Duple) were delivered by 1980. RS 5 stands at Luton Airport shortly after its introduction. Mike Harris

batches of 30 per year for five years, and to be renewable after five years. Plaxton and Duple were to share the bodywork which would be of *proper* coach specification. A new livery was designed of white with a broad green relief band and bold white fleetname. No doubt some of the NBC's officials threw their hands up in horror at the deviation from their standard of all-white but there is no doubt that the striking and different livery made Green Line coaches stand out from the crowd and provided a good advertisement for the service. In the event deliveries were speeded up and all 150 of the new coaches, classified RS (Plaxton) and RB (Duple) were on the road by the first weeks of 1980. The 'S' represented Scarborough, and the 'B' Blackpool, the towns of the body manufacture. The Company expressed a rather rash opinion at the time, implying that within a few years passengers would never have to travel in old or unsuitable vehicles on Green Line. Six years later the Company had almost become the victim of its own success as with so many new services and improved frequencies, coupled with delays in new vehicle deliveries, many SNBs and RPs were having to be used. Further commitment to National Travel work caused a few more second-hand coaches, all AEC Reliances, to be acquired and P 8–12 and D 13–17 entered the fleet in 1978/79, their class letters referring to either Plaxton or Duple bodywork.

As far as the network was concerned, it had become obvious that the old system

whereby coaches ran from one terminal to another across central London was outdated. In many cases passenger movements consisted mainly of local journeys, and if there were any loadings left in London at all, it was not cross-town traffic but between the centre and the outer suburbs. Planners set about re-structuring the network and within 3½ years many routes were speeded up by limited-stop operation and by cutting out some little-used suburban stops. Several new links were created, some unconventional services appeared, and all cross-London routes were split. A number of garage closures in 1977, as well as more sensible timetables, helped to stem financial losses. In some cases revised Green Line routes replaced sections of bus services or vice versa.

The first alterations aimed at putting Green Line back on a sound footing came about on 29th January 1977 when the very first of the new coaches went into service at St Albans garage. The ailing 712 and 713 routes were finally withdrawn and route 714 was withdrawn between London and Luton. Luton garage was closed, much of its allocation having been withdrawn over recent years with various cutbacks. New services 707 and 717 worked between Victoria and Luton Airport, the former through Barnet and the latter through Borehamwood. Journey times were speeded up and the new services were immediately well patronised. They now had faster journeys to London and to several Underground stations, as well as

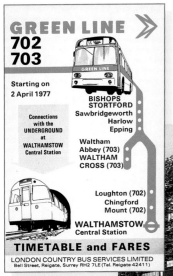

GREEN LINE »
702
703

Starting on
2 April 1977

Connections
with the
UNDERGROUND
at
WALTHAMSTOW
Central Station

BISHOPS
STORTFORD
Sawbridgeworth
Harlow
Epping

Waltham
Abbey (703)
WALTHAM
CROSS (703)

Loughton (702)
Chingford
Mount (702)

WALTHAMSTOW
Central Station

TIMETABLE and FARES

LONDON COUNTRY BUS SERVICES LIMITED
Bell Street, Reigate, Surrey RH2 7LE (Tel. Reigate 42411)

The timetable leaflet issued for the April 1977 changes when Bishop's Stortford and Harlow lost their Green Line link to central London especially emphasised the Underground connections available at Walthamstow Central. It also explained that the various local authorities involved had declined to support the old pattern of service.

From 2nd April 1977 a new 703 running from Bishops Stortford to Waltham Cross was introduced following a re-organisation of coach services in the area, only to be replaced by coach 712 and bus 329 on 20th May 1978. RP 39 is seen in Epping High Street bound for Waltham Cross shortly before the route's withdrawal. *Mike Harris*

Right **In 1977 the cover design for coach timetable leaflets was changed yet again, a peripheral green border running into a drawing of an RP. This style of leaflet was the last to include full faretables which, over the years, had gradually become more complex with bus fares applying over lengthy sections of some routes on Sundays.**

Far right **From 1st April 1978 a major new image for Green Line publicity appeared in a new 21cm by 10cm format, initially featuring RB 16. The covers had a drawing of a place of interest appropriate to the route concerned. The new leaflets listed a few fares for some of the more popular bookings.**

725·726
GRAVESEND
Dartford
Bromley
Croydon
Sutton
Kingston
Staines (725)
Heathrow
Airport (726)
WINDSOR

TIMES & FARES
From 21 May 1977

GREEN LINE »

LONDON COUNTRY BUS SERVICES LTD
Bell St., Reigate, Surrey RH2 7LE. Tel. Reigate 42411

GREEN LINE »
790
Amersham, High Wycombe,
Beaconsfield, Uxbridge,
Southall, London.
Including details of City of Oxford Service 290

gaining a direct facility on route 717 to Brent Cross Shopping Centre, recently opened and a major attraction. In April more of the new coaches converted prestige route 727 from RP to RS operation. Partner route 724 gained an extension from Staines to Windsor Castle via Runnymede but lost its Romford garage allocation in favour of one at Harlow. This left Romford with only route 721 and its unpopular and under-used LNCs; the garage was closed after 1st July 1977 and the 721 disappeared. At one time Romford had the largest coach allocation in the network.

A number of areas had their coaches altered from 2nd April 1977. The 718 was withdrawn between London and Harlow and the 720 from Aldgate to Stansted was withdrawn altogether; local buses between Epping, Harlow and Bishops Stortford were also much reduced. New coach services 702 and 703 – perhaps more accurately described as express bus services plied from Bishops Stortford, via Harlow and Epping, to Walthamstow Central Station (702) or Waltham Cross (703). The 702 direct connection with the Victoria Line saved much unproductive mileage and gave a much faster journey to central London. From 20th May 1978 route 703 was replaced by bus route 329 from Harlow to Waltham Cross and a new route 712 (Bishops Stortford – Romford) which also covered the 724 between Harlow and Romford, the latter being curtailed at Harlow. Withdrawal of the 706 (Chelsham – Aylesbury) was coupled with the closure of Tring garage and the long 708 was made even longer as it was extended to run from East Grinstead to Aylesbury via Hemel Hempstead Town Centre. This 66-mile run lasted only a year, after which more changes split the route. Routes 715/715A were also altered on 2nd April 1977, with all the service numbered 715 and running through Kingston, at last recognising the town for the major centre that it is. Interestingly, a diversion through Cobham village replaced LT route 215 which was cut back to Esher. Commuter needs from the Guildford area for a fast service to London continued with a limited-stop 710 with just a few journeys continuing to run along the Kingston By-pass.

With hindsight it seems somewhat surprising that no Green Line operations served the centre of Heathrow Airport until 727 in May 1967, joined by 724 in 1972. London Country finally awoke to more commercial opportunities from 21st May 1977 when routes 704 and 705 were diverted to double run from the Bath Road and alternate journeys on route 725 were diverted between Ashford and Windsor to run via Heathrow as 726. In the coming years the number of routes serving the airport was destined to increase considerably. RP 59, working a busy journey on route 704 *left* loads up at Heathrow Central in May 1978 with RB 26, bound for Windsor on the 726, in the background. Within a year the 704 would lose RPs, temporarily acquiring SNCs, before receiving RBs and then being curtailed south of London. SMA 11 is seen in Dartford on route 726 *below left* in 1978 while being completely devoid of any fleetname.
John Bull / Geoff Rixon

From 21st May 1977 a new service for the many tourists for Her Majesty the Queen's Silver Jubilee Year was the 700, running non-stop between London and Windsor along the M4 during the summer only. Traditional routes 704 and 705 to the town were diverted to double-run to Heathrow Central and alternate journeys on route 725 were renumbered 726 and diverted between Ashford and Windsor via Heathrow. It seems surprising that it was not until 1977 that the airport was served in this way in view of the amount of traffic it could generate – Heathrow was never overlooked again as we shall see. Also, another summer Sunday route was introduced in 1977, the 737 London to Whipsnade Zoo Motorway Express. Route 705 had certain journeys diverted during the summer in Westerham to double run to Chartwell in compensation for the loss of route 706.

High Wycombe garage closed after 30th

September 1977 and its coach route 711 was withdrawn, the section from London to Reigate not being replaced. However, two of the new RB coaches were allocated to a new route 790 between London and Amersham via High Wycombe. This brought Green Line back to Amersham once more but only because of the change to garage allocation. The publicity issued stressed the linked timetables between Green Line 790 and Oxford-South Midland's route 290. Although not a joint working, this was the first case of timetables between LCBS and another NBC operator being jointly compiled. It was a development that gave a hint of the greater co-operation to come. The southern section of the 711 was replaced by bus 422 between Sutton and Reigate. Unusually for a bus it ran limited stop by serving only the old 711 stops.

The popularity of Brent Cross was such that route 708 was diverted via the Centre

from 19th November 1977. Then from 14th January 1978 the split of the long 716 in London was made. The northern section was to be covered by limited stop routes 722 and 732, the latter being a variation to denote journeys via Brent Cross. On 1st April 1978 the 708 had its turn when it, too, was split in London. The section from Victoria to East Grinstead was surprisingly taken over by route 719, the old destination of Wrotham being covered minimally by a Monday to Friday peak-hour facility numbered 729 and starting at M&D's garage at Borough Green. M&D's route 919 served most of the old 719 stops from Tenterden and Maidstone to London which was altered to be similar to a Green Line route with local fares and pay-as-you-enter facilities rather than pre-booking. Brands Hatch was still served by Green Line though, with a 739 Express on event days from Victoria.

Reverting to the Windsor routes, on 20th May 1978 a semi-fast 701, running along the M4 between Hammersmith and Heathrow, took over part of the frequency from 704/705 and also the Safari Park extension. The cross London service was now just on 704, the 705 being withdrawn except on Sundays when the lack of buses between Bromley and Westerham ensured its retention, running from Windsor to Tunbridge Wells via Westerham. Final severance of the 704 came in on 28th April 1979 when the London to Tunbridge Wells section was renumbered 706 – the Sunday 705 stayed, but not west of London. A small extension in Tunbridge Wells from the Central to the West Station occurred with this latter change. Things were slowing down and October 1978 featured only a small diversion through Bexleyheath on the 725. From 2nd April 1979 a few journeys on route 712 were diverted through Chigwell as route 713. On 1st July 1979 a few Sunday journeys on the 716 were diverted at Addlestone to terminate at Staines in order to tap the leisure market for visitors to the new theme park at Thorpe Park, near Chertsey.

A new service in competition with the recently-introduced *Airlink* helicopter

In an attempt to improve Green Line image later SNCs were fitted with high-backed seats and luggage racks. On 1st April 1978 the Wrotham service was reduced to a peak hour journey on 729 and extended to Borough Green, while the 719 was diverted to run to East Grinstead when the 708 was curtailed at Victoria.

Right **SNC 199 is captured in Eltham High Street in April 1976 on route 719 which, at the time, linked Hemel Hempstead to Wrotham.** Mike Harris

Below right **SNC 182 on the replacement 729 stands at Eccleston Bridge.** John Bull

Bottom **Brands Hatch motor racing circuit events required duplication on route 719 but following its withdrawal from Wrotham in April 1978 a special service 739 from Victoria was used to serve the event. A smartly turned out RCL 2241 is seen in Eltham Road heading for Brands Hatch in July 1978.** Mike Harris

services between Heathrow and Gatwick Airports began on 28th April 1979 in time for the summer holiday air traffic. Marketed as *Jetlink 747*, it was non-stop, had a premium single fare £2.50 and was worked by coaches carrying a distinctive livery incorporating the yellow colours associated with Airports. Major international marketing including multi-lingual leaflets, entries in the ABC Airways Guide and overseas tourist publications, ensured good public awareness. Operation from Staines garage ensured an early departure time from Heathrow and a late arrival at night, the service running hourly every day. Within two years the frequency doubled and some night journeys were added.

A notable landmark was reached on 27th October 1979 when the last cross-London Green Line routes ran, after 48 years. The last coach routes connecting Croydon with central London also ceased with the 709 withdrawn and the 719 cut back to Victoria, running there from Hemel Hempstead via Kingsbury. An hourly express bus service covered the road from Croydon to East Grinstead, but not on Sundays. Route 715 was split at Oxford Circus, this number applying only to the Guildford end. A new 735 linked Hertford and Oxford Circus, but only hourly, the old half-hourly frequency being maintained between Hertford and Wood Green only with partner route 734. The orbital 734 provided a series of links across north-west suburbs that were most useful – if only people knew about them! The route served Brent Cross, Wembley, Ealing, Hounslow and Heathrow before terminating at Addlestone, and restored Green Line to many points long-lost from the coach map. Nearly a quarter-of-a-million leaflets were distributed to households, pages of advertising were taken in several north London local papers, but in spite of this the 734 failed to catch on. Little finance could be spared to promote it after the initial launch and traffic congestion caused great unreliability on such a long route. The arduousness of the 734 made it ideal for testing the experimental coaches delivered in 1980 – two Volvo (DV

Coaches to Swanley, Brands Hatch and Wrotham

Starting 1st April new route 729, replacing route 719, will run from London (Victoria) to Wrotham and Borough Green. Special service 739 will run to Brands Hatch on race days.

Please ask for a free leaflet.

LONDON COUNTRY GREEN LINE »

378/LC109(P)/100 (3ch) 200   Ripley

class) and two Leopard (DL class) – but lack of demand caused withdrawal of the Brent Cross to Addlestone section in April 1981, six months before the two-year trial period was completed.

In April 1980 Brent Cross gained a few more coaches when the 707 joined the 717 through the Centre; Hendon Central was also served by this diversion. Both points received more 732s when the 722 timings were transferred to it. However it was in Surrey that the main changes occurred, with 716 (Woking – Oxford Circus) being withdrawn. Between Hampton Court and Woking it was covered by the diversion of route 725, thus providing a useful link to Croydon without changing at Kingston. The old parts of the 725 to Windsor were covered by the diversion of the 718 via Ashford and the 724 via Egham. The Croydon – Gravesend section of the 725 and 726 had new timetables, effectively withdrawing the 725 from this section on Sundays. A totally new facility numbered 750 linked Gravesend and Crawley, via Bromley and Gatwick Airport, and was part of a scheme to provide connections from Kentish towns to Gatwick (M&D also introduced facilities to there from other towns). It also gave a good link from New Addington into Bromley but, in spite of a major promotion in 1981 it did not last beyond June of that year. Mid-July saw the inevitable transfer of Borough Green route 729 to Maidstone & District, becoming their 929 on the same timings. And then, on the last day of August 1980 a major upheaval of services in Surrey saw route 714 extended from Dorking to Horsham to cover the cutback of the long bus route 414, and restoring a pre-war facility. However the frequency between Kingston and London

Above **On 20th May 1978 route 712 from Bishops Stortford to Romford replaced part of 703 and part of 724. From 2nd April 1979 a peak hour variation of the 712 running via Chigwell station as 713 was provided but it lasted only until July 1981 following further revisions. RP 43 is seen at Abridge calling at one of the new style stops.** Capital Transport

Below **Jetlink** 747 was introduced between Heathrow and Gatwick on 28th April 1979 with coaches in a striking dedicated livery. While dedicated liveries are undoubtedly eye-catching and constitute very successful marketing measure a disadvantage is that circumstances sometimes dictate that a coach is operated on a different route as demonstrated by Staines' RB 65 in 747 *Jetlink* livery working on route 718 at Hampton Court. Geoff Rixon

A handy size plastic timetable card was produced for the prestigious route 747 which contained a service description on the reverse in five languages (English, German, French, Spanish and Italian).

Jetlink Gatwick ✈

Heathrow–Gatwick
Departures
05.30
06.30
07.30
08.30
09.30
10.30
11.30
12.30
13.30
14.30
15.30

Jetlink 747 is a luxury 49-seater coach service linking Heathrow and Gatwick – non-stop. The boarding points are outside the terminal at Gatwick, and in the Central Bus Station at Heathrow. The approximate journey time is 70 minutes, and the single fare is £2.50.

Jetlink 747 ist ein Luxus-Busservice für 49 Fahrgäste, der die Flughäfen Heathrow und Gatwick – non-stop – miteinander verbindet. Die Haltestellen für den Einstieg befinden sich vor dem Flughafen-Terminal in Gatwick und im Hauptbus bahnhof in Heathrow. Die ungefähre Fahrzeit beträgt 70 Minuten, und der einfache Fahrpreis £2.50.

Jetlink 747 est un service de cars de luxe avec 49 places assises, qui relie Heathrow à Gatwick non-stop. Les lieux de depart et à la gare routière centrale à Heathrow. La durée du voyage est d'environ 70 minutes, et l'aller coûte £2.50.

El "Jetlink 747" es un servicio de carruaje lujoso de 49 asientos que enlaza Heathrow y Gatwick – sin interrupción. Los puntos de abordaje están fuera del terminal en Gatwick, y en la Estación Central de Autobuses en Heathrow. El tiempo aproximado del viaje es de 70 minutos, y el precio de un viaje es £2.50.

Jetlink 747 e' un nuovo servizio di torpedone di lusso a 49 posti, che collega Heathrow e Gatwick – non-stop. I punti di partenza sono fuori dai terminal a Gatwick, e alla Stazione Centrale degli Autobus a Heathrow. La durata media del percorso e' di 70 minuti, e il biglietto di sola andata costa 2 sterline e 50 pence.

Conditions: Passengers are carried subject to the conditions and regulations of the company.

Operated by London Country Bus Services Ltd., Lesbourne Road, Reigate, Surrey, RH2 7LE, England. Telephone: Reigate 42411.

Some RPs eventually became equipped with blinds which featured the Green Line displays in the standard bus style of white on black. Hemel Hempstead's all over green liveried RP 54 shows the style which was also known to have been used at St Albans for routes 707, 717 and 727.
Geoff Rixon

was reduced considerably, the loss of the lengthy section through Richmond since March 1979 due to road subsidence at Petersham having not helped. The changes to 716, 725, 750, 729 and then 714/414 had much to do with the need to gain revenue support from Kent and Surrey County Councils and with lack of support within the GLC area.

However, two major developments in summer 1980 pointed to the nature of things to come. For this season route 737 travelled well outside the traditional area to serve Woburn Abbey. The 700 continued to be popular and a new tourist venture was the use of the coaches that had worked into London on commuter service from Guildford on the 710. On Tuesdays and Thursdays a 740 served Wisley Gardens and Guildford while on Mondays, Wednesdays and Fridays a 741 served Runnymede and Thorpe Park. The operation was not repeated in successive years but the points were served by other journeys on an improved frequency. Other than these tourist routes, the revision to routes from Oxford to London from 20th July brought Green Line coaches into that city working on routes 290 and 790 and introduced joint working with another operator, Oxford South Midland, for the first time. The 790 was routed to serve Heathrow Airport and both routes had fast runs along sections of the M40, in addition to when

working journeys to and from Amersham garage. The London terminus was Victoria Coach Station which meant that a regular Green Line service had returned to the latter place for the first time since 1934.

By late summer 1980 the route structure of Green Line had been changed all over the operating area. The 150 new coaches were in service on practically all scheduled workings and 135 vehicles were needed for the timetabled operations on Mondays–Fridays; fewer than were needed in 1970 but giving a more viable modern network. The system was leaner but the image had been restored as the Company had said it would be. The fleet and the image was in a good position to

capitalise on what was to come. As will be shown in the next chapters a lot of successful operation was based on speeding the service by using sections of motorway and enhanced trunk roads which, over recent years, had gradually been extended further towards central London.

By Green Line's Golden Jubilee in 1980 the network had turned the corner and the new route numbers, new destinations served and joint ventures with other operators were apparent in revised styles of leaflets.

On 27th October 1979 a grand new experiment came to north London – the 734 orbital service. The timetable leaflet listed places of entertainment and interest to be found along the route (also managing to get Golders Green and Hampstead out of sequence on the route diagram). Illustrations featured a exceedingly odd collection of passengers including a Viking. A vast door to door leaflet drop was made throughout the catchment area and, as promising the route may have appeared, very few, if any, Vikings used it or indeed anyone else, thus leading to the route's early demise.

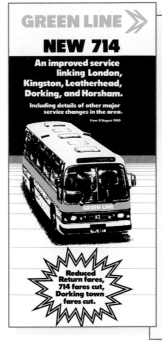

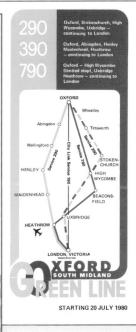

Chapter 10

THE GREEN LINE NETWORK EXPANDS

I T HAD BEEN made known that the Government's new Transport Act would become law in October 1980. This would, among other things, remove most of the restrictions from express service and excursion licensing and was hoped to introduce more competition. Green Line had some ideas of its own for expansion, but also quickly responded to the plans of other operators with similar or better services. Before long there were many commuter and shopping-type services, services to the coast and other places of interest and joint operation with other operators to many places well outside the traditional area. In this chapter the growth of regular services is traced over the remaining five years prior to the split of London Country as a single entity

Top **Following the passing of the 1980 Transport Act Green Line expansion really took off with many routes running far beyond the traditional operating area. From 16th May 1982 route 740 was extended from Guildford to Farnham and jointly worked with Alder Valley. RS 113 is seen at Hyde Park Corner in July 1982 working a popular journey to Farnham.**
Geoff Rixon

which is also the period immediately prior to De-regulation. During the remaining London Country years over 40 new regular Green Line routes were introduced to a variety of destinations, many outside the traditional operating area. A few failed to attract sufficient custom and were withdrawn but the vast majority prospered and represent a remarkable achievement on behalf of the Company and are due to the expertise of the staff concerned at all levels.

Pre-empting the Act and using the existing 740 tourist route's licence, three Monday–Friday express journeys numbered 740 connected Guildford and Victoria, running at commuter and shoppers' times. These began on 1st September, and eight weeks later the service was diverted through Merrow and extended around various Guildford estates, becoming quite popular. The route was considerably enhanced from 16th May 1982 when it was extended from Guildford to Farnham and jointly worked with Alder Valley. The existing Grange Park – Victoria section was retained and a jointly worked 741 linked with Whitehill and Victoria. Then the routes were further

revised from 29th October 1983 when 740 was withdrawn between Guildford and Farnham while the Grange Park journeys were extended to run to Tongham and more journeys were run as 741 between London and Witley. A Saturday only 742 provided one return trip from Cranleigh to London. A number of intermediate diversions and revisions to stops were also made and the routes continued to be jointly worked with Alder Valley who marketed their services as *Londonlink*. In May 1986 the joint operation ceased and the 741 was withdrawn while the commuter facility was enhanced by the extension of the 740 to Aldgate.

GREEN LINE ➤➤
ALDER VALLEY

740, 741
Two new coach links between Guildford, Farnham, Godalming, Whitehill and London

from 16 May 1982

Right **The first example of a joint route running well outside the traditional area started on 20th July 1980 when Green Line and Oxford South Midland jointly marketed routes 290, 390 and 790 on the London - Oxford corridor thus bringing Green Line to Oxford. RB 99 is in heavy traffic at Marble Arch on route 290 on the very first day of service.** Geoff Rixon

Below right **On 3rd December 1983 improvements were made to the London – Oxford corridor services with route 291 having more peak hour journeys, all Thame journeys extended to Haddenham and projections to Aldgate for City commuters. The first of the Plaxton bodied Tigers were allocated to Amersham for the enhanced services. TP 6 was one of 29 fitted with 53 seat bodies for stage work and is seen standing at Aldgate Bus Station prior to working a peak hour journey to Haddenham.** Mike Harris

The 740 development sets the scene for the 1980 to 1986 period showing that London Country was responsive to demand and changes in travel trends. Nothing was set in concrete, diversions and variations from route became widespread, sometimes attracting separate route numbers and sometimes not. It must also be remembered that during this period British Rail was imposing annual fare increases well above the rate of inflation while there was a marked decline in the standards of service provided thus many people turned to the coach services.

The London – Oxford corridor saw a new commuter route from Thame to London that had been started in September 1980 by Oxford-South Midland, numbered 291, and which Green Line took over one return journey in October. Once again the route went from strength to strength, gaining more journeys and a deviation through more villages in December and from January 1982 the route was extended to Haddenham. From 19th July 1982 a 291 duplicate journey from Amersham garage to London was run as 292 serving Holmer Green. The Oxford services underwent further revisions in June 1983 including the provision of a Green Line worked 293 from Askett to London. In December 1983 the 293 was withdrawn but other revisions to the group included the projection of 291 to Aldgate for City commuters and, except on Sundays, the withdrawal of most 790 journeys between Heathrow and London.

Luton had seen speeded up services in 1977 with 707 and 717 and from 1st November 1980 a 757 linked Luton Airport with Victoria, stopping only at Luton Bus Station then fast to central London via the M1. From January 1982 the new route was increased in frequency and was marketed as *Flightline*. In November 1982 the 707 and 717 were diverted in Luton to serve housing development at Wigmore Bottom and from 11th April 1983 a 756 (Luton Airport – Victoria) running via Wigmore Bottom, Kings Cross and Ludgate Circus was provided for commuters. The number 756 had previously been used for a joint operation with Maidstone & District from Tunbridge Wells in 1982 but Green Line

pulled out after five months. In September a commuter facility for Jersey Farm Estate in St Albans was added on routes 707 and 717, and 757 was increased to run every 30 minutes on Monday–Saturday. In January 1984 route 707 was diverted to serve Chiswell Green and Bricket Wood with a faster run to London via the M1 and from 1st April 1985 commuter journeys on 757 ran via Wigmore Bottom.

One of the interesting features of Green Line's renaissance was the very high quality publicity which appeared in a variety of styles to suit the particular service to be marketed. The introduction of the 757 express link between Luton Airport and Victoria on 1st November 1980 saw this A5 size leaflet with the theme *Fly up to London* with Green Line. The reverse contained the northbound service with the theme *Fly up to Luton*.

Fly up to London with

Green Line 757 EXPRESS

Green Line 757 is a new express coach service linking Luton Airport, Luton and London.

It's **fast, comfortable, regular,** and **CHEAP!**

Departure times from				Just look at these fares!
Luton Airport		Luton, Bus Station		fares between Luton and London
0705	1315	0713	1323	£1.50 single
0805	1415	0813	1423	£2.50 return (valid up to 3 months)
0905	1515	0913	1523	£1.85 OUTBACK cheap day return
1015	1615	1023	1623	£11.25 weekly season ticket
1115	1815	1123	1823	£42.00 monthly season ticket
1215	2000	1223	2008	£120.00 quarterly season ticket

fares between Luton Airport and London
£1.70 single
£3.00 return (valid up to 3 months)
£2.00 OUTBACK cheap day return

Journey time is approximately an hour from Luton and 70 minutes from the airport

Mondays to Saturdays only,
starting 1st November 1980

GREEN LINE ⟫ 757 EXPRESS – YOUR LUTON/LONDON LINK

operated by London Country Bus Services Ltd, Lesbourne Road, Reigate, Surrey RH2 7LE.
Passengers are carried subject to the conditions and regulations of the company

Left The revitalisation of the Green Line network did, in many cases, mean change, change and more change! Route 750 was introduced on 26th April 1980 linking Gravesend with Bromley New Addington and Gatwick as part of a Kent C.C. initiative to provide links to Gatwick. The route which skirted the major traffic objective of Croydon proved to be short-lived and, together with companion routes 760 and 761, it was replaced by 755 which sensibly linked Gravesend and Crawley via Croydon from 13th June 1981. SMA 1 is seen at Purley in February 1981 with the style of destination blind for Green Line that involved the use of overlapping displays, which began to appear in the late 1970s. Geoff Rixon

Centre left Airport services were seen by Green Line as a good traffic source and from 16th May 1981 route 777, marketed as *Flightline* and jointly worked with Southdown, was introduced from Crawley and Gatwick Airport to Victoria Coach Station. A good marketing tool was the provision of coaches in dedicated livery and unusually they carried both operators' fleetnames as displayed by RS 137 opposite Victoria Coach Station on the second day of service. Geoff Rixon

Bottom The 777 almost became a victim of its own success as not only was it used by air travellers but built up a large commuter clientele from Crawley and even gained a projection to Turners Hill. The service was increased and duplicates were run at busy times but, with the expansion of London Country's coaching activities, there were not enough new coaches to go round and buses had to be used causing season ticket holders to complain that they were paying for a prestigious coach not an SNB. Matters were eventually resolved as more new coaches came into the fleet. SNB 185 and RS 136 stand side by side at Crawley Bus Station.
Barry LeJeune

The *Airport Network* publicity first appeared in 1972 and was updated as new routes were introduced and also included other operators services. This version was produced to incorporate new routes 755 and 777 in summer 1981.

Not all new ventures were as successful as the Luton services. Routes 760 and 761 had been introduced on 31st January 1981 between Crawley estates and West Croydon only to be replaced together with the 750 on 13th June 1981 by a 755 running from Crawley (Broadfield) to Gravesend via Croydon. On 23rd July 1983 the 755 was revised to operate jointly with Southdown to run from Crawley to Victoria with a commuter journey from Broadfield to Croydon and a commuter projection from Victoria to Waterloo. In December 1983 the Waterloo journey was withdrawn but the entire service was projected from Victoria to Marble Arch while on Summer Sundays in 1984 a journey was extended to Sheffield Park for the Bluebell Railway. The London service ceased from 1st October 1984 when it became a Crawley to West Croydon commuter facility running for the last time on 14th February 1986. Crawley did not lose out however, as from 16th May 1981 a Victoria Coach Station – Gatwick Airport – Crawley service marketed as *777 Flightline* was jointly worked with Southdown. The service was popular with commuters in addition to air travellers and it was doubled to every 30 minutes within the first year of operation. In March 1983 a commuter journey was projected to Turners Hill and on the last day of 1984 a 778 conveyed commuters directly to Victoria and then on to Aldgate, avoiding Gatwick. Ever keen to attract new custom, by April 1986 Crawley to London season tickets had become valid, at no extra charge, within Crawley on connecting local buses at the Bus Station.

With the success of the Oxford routes the company's attention turned to Cambridge when two services running from Cambridge to Victoria Coach Station operated jointly with Eastern Counties from 25th April 1981. The 797 ran via Stevenage and Hatfield and the 798 via Puckeridge and Ware. At the same time half of the service on 732 was diverted at Hatfield to run to Watford via St Albans as 733 and the 734 was withdrawn between Addlestone and Brent Cross and reduced with additional journeys being provided on 735. The 734 was withdrawn completely after 29th October 1982 with the 735 being strengthened to cover the lost journeys. From 27th November the 732 was withdrawn except on Sunday between Brent Cross and Victoria and two days later a 796 commuter service linked Letchworth Jackmans Estate with Victoria. During the summer of 1983 certain 796 journeys were diverted to serve Knebworth Park. A major revision took place from 2nd July 1983 when 732 was withdrawn but replaced by a re-use of the number 734 running from Hitchin to Victoria through Welwyn Garden City and Hatfield (Potters Bar Sundays) then via the A1 to Apex Corner. The 733 was extended from Watford to Reading via Heathrow and jointly worked with Alder Valley and some summer 797 journeys also served

The style of the timetable leaflets had moved on considerably since the 1970s with high profile marketing of new services constantly using new designs. The company also ensured that the latest coaches were featured as depicted by TP 13 on the 777 leaflet.

The Leopards with Duple bodies were designated DL and had a slightly modified Green Line livery with a white waist-band just below the windows. From 25th April 1981 a joint venture with Eastern Counties saw Cambridge to London services provided with 797 running via Stevenage and 798 via Puckeridge. DL 1 is seen emerging from the British Airways Terminal which certain services were using due to shortage of capacity in Victoria Coach Station.
Mike Harris

Knebworth Park. From 29th June 1985 the Monday–Saturday service on 734 was replaced by 794 running from Stevenage to Victoria and in Stevenage Chells was provided with commuter facilities on both routers 794 and 797.

A small enhancement to the Windsor and Slough services took place on 18th May 1981 when a commuter 703 was provided from Windsor, Slough and Langley then via the M4 to Victoria. Just one year later 703 was diverted through Dedworth to seek more passengers. From 12th February 1983 the 704 was speeded up to run from Hammersmith to Brentford via the A4 rather than Chiswick High Road and, ever mindful of attracting traffic, the last 701 was back projected to start from Aldwych for theatregoers. A commuter 753 linked Hedgerley with Oxford Circus via Slough estates and a joint working with Alder Valley, the 754, ran

GREEN LINE
EASTERN COUNTIES

London/Cambridge 797 and 798

via Enfield, Hatfield, Ware, Stevenage Buntingford, Baldock and Royston.

(For full coach services between Stevenage and London see separate 732,733, 797 leaflet.)

From 1st November 1981

LETCHWORTH COMMUTERS

Don't forget coach 796 to London

Green Line 796 provides a fast convenient link to London at bargain rates. Look at our super savers!

Single **£2.35**
Day return **£2.85**
Weekly season **£12.85**
Monthly season **£51.30**
Three monthly season **£142.50**
Annual season **£513.00**

For further information please telephone Stevenage 54561

GREEN LINE ≫

29 June 1985

Left **Special publicity promoted new commuter facilities. This item advertised the fares which, no doubt, compared favourably with those of British Rail. Following the problems encountered with the success of the 777 small print on the reverse pointed out that the service generally operated with modern coaches but from time to time other vehicles may be substituted.**

from Marlow to Victoria with a last pick-up at Wooburn Green. The 754 was extended to Marlow Bottom in August 1984 and the service became Alder Valley X54 on 28th April 1985 when Green Line ceased to be a joint operator. On 19th May 1984 a major revision of these services took place when 701 was revised to run to Maidenhead jointly operated with Alder Valley marketed as *Londonlink*, replacing X12. Maidenhead had last seen a Green Line service in 1933! The 703 underwent minor re-routeings in Slough and Dedworth – the late Aldwych journey was provided on 704. The number 702 newly released from Harlow was used for a Victoria – Windsor (with projections to Safari Park) fast service from Hammersmith to Langley. At the end of the 1984 summer season the

Below **The 701 had been introduced on 20th May 1978 between Victoria and Windsor with a run via the M4 to Heathrow then via Colnbrook and Slough with seasonal projections to Windsor Safari Park. A new generation of coaches appeared in 1982 in the form of 42 Leyland Tigers with Eastern Coach Works bodies. The first 30 were 49-seaters with luggage pens for stage carriage work and the balance 53-seaters for coaching work all being fitted with tinted windows. TL 1–30 were allocated around the fleet to enable RBs and RSs to return off lease and are represented by a brand new TL 18 at Heathrow Bus Station on route 701. The provision of destination blinds inside the windscreen meant that passengers experienced difficulties in identifying the approaching coach.** Colin Brown

Bottom **From 16th January 1982 London Country and Alder Valley started a joint service, *Flightline 767*, from Victoria Coach Station to Heathrow on which Addlestone's DL 3 in dedicated livery is seen at the Coach Station.** Mike Harris

Below **This leaflet was produced in 1983 for the introduction of the 754 which provided a fast service to London from places outside the traditional operating area. Although the front cover makes no reference the service was jointly operated with Alder Valley. London Country usually produced the publicity for the services it operated jointly.**

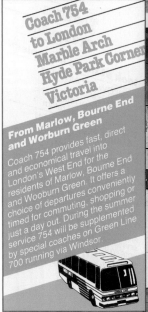

Coach 754 to London Marble Arch Hyde Park Corner Victoria

From Marlow, Bourne End and Worburn Green

Coach 754 provides fast, direct and economical travel into London's West End for the residents of Marlow, Bourne End and Wooburn Green. It offers a choice of departures conveniently timed for commuting, shopping or just a day out. During the summer service 754 will be supplemented by special coaches on Green Line 700 running via Windsor.

702 acquired journeys to Dedworth. The final alterations to the Windsor services under London Country auspices came on 12th April 1986 when 701 was diverted away from Maidenhead to serve Windsor and the Safari Park, the 702 was diverted in Slough to serve Chalvey, and the commuter 703 was diverted to serve Kensington. The slower 704 was withdrawn thus removing Green Line from the Great West Road in Greater London and with it the late Aldwych journey was also lost. Both 701 and 702 also provided a commuter and shoppers facility from the Cippenham area of Slough.

A Knaphill – Woking – Oxford Circus commuter and shoppers service 730 started on 16th May 1981 but despite a short-lived Saturday shopper service from Woking and a companion 731 from Chertsey the service did not develop and ran for the last time on 14th February 1986.

Turning to south Essex the long established 723 from Grays was extended from Aldgate to Victoria on 22nd August 1981. From 12th September 1983 a commuter and shoppers route 722 was provided from Corringham to Marble Arch being jointly worked with Eastern National while from 9th April 1984 a commuter service, 721, from Tilbury to Marble Arch was added but the 722 shoppers facility was withdrawn. From 29th June 1985 the 721 was extended to East Tilbury while the 723 was speeded up by running via the A13 between Poplar and Dagenham.

The Hemel Hempstead area was the next for improvements when from 26th September 1981 the 758 was introduced from Woodhall Farm Estate to Victoria which, after serving Grove Hill, Highfield, the Town Centre and Adeyfield ran via the M1. The service was a success and over the next two years enjoyed increased frequency, a projection to Redbourn and a Sunday service. It was joined from 18th October 1982 by a 759 from Two Waters garage serving the Chaulden, Stoneycroft and Gadebridge areas of the town. Within a year this service had acquired off peak journeys, a Saturday service and from 1st October 1984 was projected to Bovingdon. From 8th August 1983 a commuter 748 linked Northchurch and Victoria via the M1, Kings Cross and Ludgate Circus and from 1st July 1985 the route was extended to Tring. On 30th April 1984 a new commuter route 769 from Two Waters garage to

Victoria served the Bennetts Gate area and from 25th February 1985 a commuter route 749 ran from Kings Langley via Abbots Langley and North Watford to Victoria. At the end of June 1985 the traditional service 708 was speeded, up away from the Edgware Road, to run from Bushey Arches via Aldenham Road, the M1 and Finchley Road.

Another successful operation was the 720, which started on 2nd November 1981 linking Gravesend estates with Victoria via the A2. The route gained an evening service in 1983 and was diverted to serve Coldharbour Estate in August 1986. Curiously a companion 721 from Dartford Fleet Estate was not a success and proved to be very short-lived.

Airports were seen as good traffic objec-

The extension of route 711 from Redbridge to Victoria produced more publicity aimed at commuters once again emphasising season ticket rates. Although 711 was not an example one or two such ventures were to be short lived – purchase of annual season tickets being no guarantee of routes lasting the year!

Good news for Harlow Commuters!

711 711 711 711

Starting Monday 28th March the 0659 coach from Old Harlow will run beyond Redbridge direct to London providing a convenient through journey to the City.
In the evening the coach returns from Victoria *Buckingham Palace Road* at 1656 providing an alternative facility to the 1725 departure on service 799. The existing service from Redbridge will continue to run.

Economy Tickets!
A single fare of 90p is charged to Redbridge or £1.85 to London and our economical season ticket rates will help you save even more.

	To Redbridge	To London
Weekly	£5.70	£10.15
Monthly	£22.00	£40.50
3 Monthly	£62.00	£112.50
Annual	£220.00	£405.00

For season ticket sales and further information please call in at the Bus Station Enquiry Office (telephone Harlow 26349 or 21971).
GREEN LINE »

New London service introduced from 28 March!

Above **Commuter and Stansted Airport traffic on routes 711 and 799 continued to expand and the Company was obliged to operate double deck buses to meet demand. At least in the case of LR 68 it was one of the newest buses being from a batch of 15 LRs delivered in 1985 which, due to the closure of Roe, had ECW bodies. The ECW bodies had the offside traffic indicator light positioned to the rear of the front wheel arch whereas on the Roe bodies it was higher and further forward. Relief was for the 799 at hand with two of the 1986 intake of LRCs being drafted for such duties.** Mike Harris

GREEN LINE UNITED COUNTIES »

A new frequent coach link

760
Northampton, Milton Keynes, Bletchley, Dunstable, Hemel Hempstead, Kings Langley, Uxbridge, Heathrow Airport

Left **The new joint route 760 timetable prominently featured both operators and a coach without a registration number. Quite whether six journeys a day (two on Sundays) constituted a frequent link remains a matter of conjecture.**

tives and from 16th January 1982 a 767 *Flightline* service ran from Victoria Coach Station to Heathrow Airport being jointly worked with Alder Valley. The latter operator pulled out in April 1985 leaving Green Line to work the entire service. From 26th October 1985 the 747 *Jetlink* which had been established in 1979 between Gatwick and Heathrow was projected northwards by two routes, one to Watford Junction, Hemel Hempstead, Luton and Luton Airport and the other fast to Luton then on to Luton Airport and Stevenage. In 1984 the drivers regularly working on the prestigious airport routes 747, 757, 767 and 777 were provided with new airline style uniforms which included dark green jackets, shirts with epaulettes and name badges.

On 16th January 1982 a commuter and shoppers' service was introduced from

109

The vast expansion of Green Line operations often meant that there were not enough coaches to go around. A brand new LR 62 performs a duty on route 733. The destination blind box has not been fitted with masking thus two destinations are displayed. John Boylett

In June 1984, RB 86 is seen at Southend Bus Station on route 795. It was an ambitious joint venture with Southdown, Southend Transport and Eastern National, linking Southend with Crawley and Brighton via Dartford Tunnel, from 1st April 1984. During the following year all remaining members of the RB and RS classes were returned off lease. Mike Harris

795 Your new coach link
Southend Basildon Gatwick Brighton
From 1 April 1984

Victoria Park, Aylesbury to Victoria via Amersham and the Chalfonts. The route was extended to Bedgrove in October 1982; two years later peak journeys were projected to Blackfriars and from 25th April 1986 were further projected to Aldgate. A companion 789 from Chesham was, after a short time, worked as a feeder into a 788 journey at Amersham and was withdrawn from 2nd October 1982. The distinction of being the last Green Line route to be introduced by London Country proper falls to a later version of the 789 which was a commuter service from Widmer End to Aldgate

SPEEDLINE 750

Hemel Hempstead,
Luton, Luton Airport,
Hitchin, Stevenage,
Hertford, Ware

from 26 October 1985

Now serves Hitchin

SEALINE 773

The coach for all reasons

**HOVE – BRIGHTON
HURSTPIERPOINT
CRAWLEY
GATWICK AIRPORT**

including *Jetlink 747*
connections to or from
HEATHROW AIRPORT

FROM 22nd JANUARY 1984

GREEN LINE »   SOUTHDOWN »

Hertfordshire County Council's utopian desire for a cross county Green Line resulted in Speedlink but this branding was not carried on the coaches. The route was allowed to wander out of the county to serve Luton and the airport and eventually fizzled out at Ware, Fanham Common – hardly a Green Line traffic objective.

Striking and varied publicity was produced for the new ventures to the south coast with the 773 timetable prominently advertising the connections with route 747 to Heathrow for which through bookings were available.

between Heathrow and Northampton via Hemel Hempstead, Dunstable, Bletchley and Milton Keynes. One journey each way also served various towns and villages including Wolverton and Roade. This route ran for the last time on 28th September 1984.

From 15th May 1982 a jointly worked hourly route with Southdown, 773 marketed as *Sealine* was introduced between Gatwick Airport and Hove via Crawley, Hickstead and Hassocks. Passengers could book through to Heathrow by changing on to 747 at Gatwick. A joint operation with both Southdown and Alder Valley commenced on 22nd January 1983, numbered 762 it formed a Reading – Aldershot – Guildford – Gatwick – Crawley – Brighton link. The route ran for the last time on 13th April 1985 but Alder Valley maintained a Reading – Brighton one trip route and Southdown continued a Brighton – Gatwick commuter journey as 762 and the 773 was extended hourly from Gatwick to Guildford to cover part of the route.

The next joint venture stemmed from Hertfordshire County Council's desire to have a cross county link to complement the 733. On 22nd October 1983 route 750 marketed as *Speedline* and jointly worked with United Counties linked Hemel Hempstead and Waltham Cross via Luton, Luton Airport, Stevenage, and Hertford. From December 1984 Green Line became the sole operator and from 29th June 1985 the route was extended to Uxbridge and Heathrow but curtailed in the east at Ware. Presumably County Council parochialism prevented the eastern end continuing across the county border to the obvious traffic objective of Harlow? On 26th October 1985 the projection of the 747 to serve Hemel Hempstead and the curtailment of 733 from Reading to start from Heathrow saw the 750 diverted intermediately to serve Hitchin and terminate at Hemel Hempstead.

Two new routes started on 1st April 1984. A Green Line operated 765 linked Stevenage and Brighton via Hertford, Harlow, Romford, Dartford, Sevenoaks, Gatwick Airport and Crawley. Two of the four journeys terminated at Crawley with a connection to and from route 795. This route linked Southend and Brighton via Basildon, Grays, Swanley, Orpington, Gatwick and Crawley and was jointly worked with Southdown, Southend Transport and Eastern National. Southdown involvement ceased from 26th January 1985. From 29th June 1985 the 765 was extended to Luton via the Airport but unlike the previous winter the route was suspended at the end of the summer season. Green Line workings were also suspended on the 795 for the winter and, in the event,

route 765 did not reappear for the 1986 season. Green Line resumed on a revised 795 from 27th April when the route was diverted at Dartford to run via Bexley, Orpington and Sevenoaks as a part replacement for the 765. Brighton was a popular destination and a new 737 started on 27th April 1986 running from Slough via Windsor, Heathrow, Gatwick, Crawley to Brighton. This was a joint operation with Brighton & Hove.

The more mundane Green Line operations were the recognisable remainder of the traditional network as inherited in 1970. The days of these long established routes running in to central London were clearly numbered. Other than total withdrawal, the solutions offering were the speeding up of the services, such as happened with the St Albans and Luton services in 1977, or the curtailment of all or most journeys short of central London. From 21st April, 1981 route 706 was considerably reduced over the Bromley to Victoria section, the entire service was run via Weald and certain journeys also served Halstead while others

By the Company's last years some very attractive styles of leaflet had been developed with depictions of the newest coaches. The 1978 feature of showing a drawing of a place of interest served was revived and as other parts of the National Bus Company were re-organised new names became featured on the publicity for the jointly worked services.

commencing on 1st September 1986, just six days prior to the split. The service had previously been a commuters' club private hire operation.

Returning to 1980, commuter route 711 was introduced on 10th November linking Old Harlow and Harlow with Redbridge Station via the M11. Redbridge was, at the time, the southern end of the motorway and passengers for central London could change to the Underground. The route was joined on 13th June 1982 by a third route from Cambridge to Victoria Coach Station the 799 which ran via Saffron Walden, Bishops Stortford, Harlow and Redbridge and was jointly worked with Eastern Counties. In March 1983 the 711 was extended to Victoria and most 799 journeys were diverted to serve Stansted Airport and on Sundays some journeys ran via Duxford, replacing Eastern Counties 112 on that day. On 29th October 1984 an Eastern National 712 route linked Bishops Stortford estates with Victoria. In May 1986 additional 799 journeys were provided for Stansted Airport and one morning journey on 711 was back projected to start from the airport.

Having re-established a network of viable routes to and from central London the Company began to consider ambitious, daily, cross country routes to more distant towns. On 27th March 1982 a 760 jointly worked with United Counties was introduced

The expansion of Green Line's new ventures, coupled with older coaches being returned off-lease, meant that the 706 and other such routes which were effectively acting as buses over lengthy sections often saw SNBs, with some actually being scheduled. Dunton Green's SNB 117 with its reduced area blind box and grubby worn blinds is hardly in keeping with the prestigious image of the service that the company wished to promote. The bus is passing a London Transport style coach request stop near Green Street Green in March 1983. By the summer of 1986 the situation had improved as illustrated by TP 62 at Green Street Green on route 706 – a vast improvement on an SNB. Geoff Rixon/Barry LeJeune

were tailored for school requirements. Bus 402 was entirely withdrawn and the 454 was considerably reduced. The Sunday only 705 was also diverted via Weald. In later years the 402 was destined to return as the main service between Bromley and Tonbridge.

From 25th July 1981 route 712 Bishops Stortford to Romford was diverted between Epping and Collier Row, away from Chigwell Row, to run via the withdrawn LT 247 route through Ivy Chimneys and Passingford Bridge. Lewington's route 6 provided a partial replacement through Chigwell Row but the companion Green Line 713 via

Chigwell Station was withdrawn. From 24th April 1982 the 702 Bishops Stortford to Walthamstow was diverted away from Whitehall Road to serve Woodford Green and from 4th December 1982 702 was curtailed at Harlow leaving the 712 to provide the service to Bishops Stortford. These routes were performing the function of express buses and the position was ratified from 12th May 1984 when together with buses 329 and 339 they were replaced by express buses numbered 500 to 503.

Attentions were turned to the 725 which was split at Croydon from 16th May 1982

British Rail's atrocious industrial relations record meant that from the mid-1970s disruptions and even total strikes were by no means isolated occurrences. London Country cashed in by running double deckers and duplicates on Green Line services.

Left **ColorBus AN 5** is seen at Cobham on the evening of 29th June 1982 with homeward bound commuters on route 715. Geoff Rixon

Below **LR 7 approaches Eccleston Bridge to help clear the crowds on 7th July 1982.** Mike Harris

with the Gravesend to West Croydon section retaining the number and the East Croydon to Woking (Monday–Saturday) and Staines (Sunday) section reusing the number 716. From 29th October 1984 route 725 was curtailed at Dartford, diverted via Thamesmead, and reduced to five return journeys on Monday to Saturday. The 726 was reinstated daily to Gravesend and acquired additional journeys between West Croydon and Dartford to cover those lost on 725. The Gravesend reinstatement was reduced to peak hours and garage runs from 27th July 1985 and from 12th April 1986 the route

was withdrawn between Gravesend and Dartford. On the same date the route was diverted at Hampton Court, away from Sunbury and Ashford, to run via Hanworth and Hatton Cross in order to serve Terminal 4 at Heathrow. At this time routes 727, 733, 747 and 767 were also diverted to serve or extended to Terminal 4.

The number 713, redundant from Harlow was used again from 30th June 1984 when some of the 715 Guildford – Kingston short journeys were diverted to run via Merrow, Clandon and Effingham Junction replacing the Leatherhead to Guildford section of bus

416. From 27th July 1985 the 713 was diverted at Esher to serve Lower Green. The popular cross-country 724 route from Harlow to Windsor ran for the last time on 25th October 1985, although it was destined to reappear after the demise of London Country. It was replaced by an express bus 524 between Harlow and Watford with re-routeings in Welwyn Garden City which enabled bus 334 to be withdrawn and 324 to be considerably reduced. Additional journeys were provided at the western end of the route on buses 436 and 441 to overcome the effects of the withdrawal.

Chapter 11

NEW DEVELOPMENTS FOR GREEN LINE

A S STATED IN the previous chapter the Transport Act of 1980 removed licensing restrictions and gave the Company a good opportunity to expand its coaching activities. Freedom to operate excursions was an important feature of the Act and plenty of medium-distance ones were advertised, running on certain days and periods of the year only, with bargain day-return fares and pay-as-you-board facilities. Several of these eventually blossomed into regular Green Line routes. Excursion traffic had been developed only in a modest way before now, the acquisition of some Southdown excursion licences in the Redhill and Crawley areas in 1972, followed by those of M&D at Gravesend in 1977/78, providing a base. M&D had also passed to London Country responsibility for some weekend workings on National Express routes in 1978 and these, with more operations since, continued. The increase in services caused the Company to negotiate another 30 coaches on lease from Kirkby Central, this time Leyland Leopards, as the Reliance was no longer in production. All arrived in 1981 and were much needed. Between August 1980 and August 1982 the service requirements leapt from 135 to 167 coaches.

The Act became law at the wrong time of the year to offer coastal excursions but the development of off high street shopping complexes was seen as a market to be tapped. In November 1980 the following routes were introduced: 736 Welwyn Garden City – Milton Keynes, 738 Watford – Milton Keynes, 742 Harlow – Victoria and 743 Bishops Stortford / Harlow – Brent Cross. In May 1982 the 736 was revised to provide a service from Borehamwood but a new 766 linked Potters Bar and Welwyn Garden City with Milton Keynes. The Harlow routes were less successful and 743 lost its Bishops Stortford projection in 1981 and ran for the last time in September 1983. The 742 finished in June 1982 but a 744 linked Harlow with Milton Keynes from 28th July 1981. A 743 was revived for the Christmas shopping and January sales period of 1983/4 and '84/5 running from Harlow to Victoria for the first season and to Kensington High Street the following year. Milton Keynes gained two further routes, 746 from Windsor on 5th December 1981 and 761 from Hemel Hempstead on 30th September 1984 following the withdrawal of regular service 760. From 10th October 1983 a 764 service was provided from Hatfield to Oxford Circus; it lasted until May 1985.

Coastal excursions began on 11th April

1981 with a 709 from West Croydon to Brighton and a 773 from Westcott and Dorking estates to Brighton. The latter route was renumbered 776 on 15th May 1982 when the original number was required for *Sealine* and was replaced from January 1983 when it was covered by regular route 762. A third service to Brighton, 774, started from Merstham on 11th July 1981 and it was joined by 775 from Banstead in December 1981, which was extended to Sutton from April 1983. The 709 started from Thornton Heath in May 1984 when it also gained a projection to Worthing. Such was the success of some routes that double-deck vehicles were often provided.

The summer season of 1982 saw additional routes from Caterham to Eastbourne (779) and Hastings (778). In 1983 they were revised to start from West Croydon and from 1984 Thornton Heath. A 745 from Harlow to Southend also started in June 1982. The following year saw the market tested with a number of new routes. The 772 ran from Westcott to Eastbourne (operated that season only), Gravesend had a 781 to East-

bourne, 782 to Rye, and 783 to Worthing while Thamesmead saw a 784 to Eastbourne and 785 to Worthing. In 1984 a 786 from Thamesmead to Rye and 789 from Greenhithe to Eastbourne joined them while the existing Gravesend routes started from Perry Street. Also new in 1984 were 729 Harlow to Clacton, 768 Kingston to Brighton, 793 Swanley to Folkestone and 794 Catford to Eastbourne.

A vast expansion to the seasonal excursion traffic took place in May 1985 with the provision of some sixteen new routes. New destinations included Alton Towers, Margate and Ramsgate but the existing Rye services were curtailed at Hastings. With this number of new routes spare numbers in the 700 Green Line series were at a premium and a logical step was taken to renumber the existing shopper and excursion routes into the 900 series. This was a straight exercise whereby the numbers were simply increased by 200 with the exception of route 709 which became 977. This meant that the routes remaining in the 700-series could be instantly recognised as regular Green Line

SPECIAL SATURDAY SHOPPING EXCURSIONS TO MILTON KEYNES

Central Milton Keynes contains the most modern and comprehensive range of shops and services ever assembled under one roof, offering comfortable, convenient shopping in a spectacular setting.

Now, **GREEN LINE 738** will take you there in comfort.

Our special shopping coaches will depart every Saturday from the following points:

		Day Return Fare
Watford, Exchange Road	1115	£1.60
Kings Langley, High Street	1128	£1.60
Hemel Hempstead Bus Station	1140	£1.40
Adeyfield, Great Road	1145	£1.40
Milton Keynes Shopping Centre	1220	

Departing from Milton Keynes Shopping Centre at 1645 for the return journey.

738 also picks up in Watford at Hemel Hempstead Road/Langley Road and in Hemel Hempstead at Two Waters, Bus Garage.

Forget parking worries, relax and enjoy yourself.

GREEN LINE >> 738
Takes you shopping in comfort

Passengers are carried subject to the conditions and regulations of the company.

services. Only three of the 1985 new routes failed to appear the following year but a further 15 new routes were added which included new destinations of Portsmouth, Chichester, Littlehampton and Bognor. The provision of a 905 from Victoria to the Garden Festival at Stoke on Trent proved rather too adventurous and the route was

Take a trip to the seaside!

Green Line 745 to Southend-on-Sea

Southend-on-Sea boasts the longest pier in the world, plus a unique atmosphere for day trips. There are plenty of shops and amusements to cater for all tastes.

Green Line 745 will take you direct to Southend-on-Sea from most residential areas of Harlow as well as North Weald and Ongar.
Alternatively, stop off at Basildon for shopping or visiting friends and relatives.

Such a reasonable fare, too! A cheap day return ticket from any part of Harlow to Southend-on-Sea costs only £2.50. With value like that you can afford to spend a fantastic day by the sea with Green Line.

GREEN LINE

Every Friday from 18 June 1982

Below **Following the 1980 Transport Act London Country built up considerable excursion traffic offering facilities to the coast, shopping centres and other places of interest. In 1983 the new development of Thamesmead was tapped with a Tuesday 784 to Eastbourne and a Thursday 785 to Worthing which proved so successful that further destinations were offered in** subsequent years. Northfleet's TD 2, a 53-seater for private hire work fitted with public address equipment, is seen taking on passengers in Thamesmead in August 1983. The coach was new in April and was one of the first to appear in the revised two tone green livery following the rather uninteresting livery carried by the previous year's TLs. Mike Harris

In May 1985 the Green Line excursion and shopper services were renumbered from the 700 series into a new 900 series. TP27 is seen at Waltham Cross on a 930 working from Sele Farm Estate, Hertford to Southend. John Boylett

withdrawn after just three weeks due to lack of passengers. Probably due to an error the number 966 allocated to the existing Potters Bar – Milton Keynes shoppers service was also used for a Walton to Portsmouth and Southsea service. At the time of the London Country split it was operating over 50 of these excursion and shoppers services to a variety of destinations whereas just six years earlier there were no such London Country services.

A number of other routes were introduced or extended seasonally to places of interest for visitors and tourists. The summer 700 non-stop service between Victoria and Windsor had been established in 1978 and in the 1981 season acquired an extension to Windsor Safari Park. From the following winter it was not entirely withdrawn and provided a few positioning journeys for other routes working the London – Windsor services. In the 1982 season it was extended from Windsor to Addlestone via Runnymede, Thorpe Park and Chertsey. A new 770 linked Victoria and Thorpe Park from the 1983 season and the 700 was once again extended to the Safari Park and, for this year only, also had one journey to Marlow. For the 1984 and 1985 summers the 700 reverted to its original Victoria – Windsor Castle role but was again extended to the Safari Park in 1986. The latter place was also served by summer extensions of other services on the London – Windsor corridor.

The Summer Sunday 737 between Victoria and Whipsnade had started in 1977 and from the 1980 season was extended from Whipsnade to Woburn Abbey where from 1981 it provided an optional tour of the Wild Life Kingdom at an additional fare if required. In 1983 it was diverted to serve London Colney and St Albans when it replaced the Sunday extensions on buses 84 and 342 to Whipsnade. There seems to have been some indecision as to the exact status of the route as it retained the 737 number for the 1985 season but was renumbered 937 the following year.

Chartwell, the Westerham home of the late Sir Winston Churchill, had opened to the public in 1966 and was seasonally served by coaches on route 706. Following the withdrawal of the 706 some route 705 journeys were diverted to double run via Chartwell for the 1977 season. From the next summer the 705 ran on Sundays only with certain journeys double running which set the pattern for subsequent years. The service was enhanced for the summers of 1985 and 1986 when a non-stop Victoria to Chartwell service on 705 was also provided on Wednesdays, Thursdays and Saturdays.

The publicity for new routes to places of interest featured the appropriate theme for the particular venue and was well produced on glossy paper. These emphasised that pre-booking was not required and offered reasonable return fares for the day out.

Two further routes started in May 1982, a 728 Victoria to Penshurst Place and Hever Castle and 729 Victoria to Sheffield Park for the Bluebell Railway. From 20th June 1982 the Sunday journey on 729 was back projected to start from High Wycombe via Amersham. The 728 did not return in 1983 but 729 was revised to operate from Amersham via High Wycombe but did not reappear in 1984. Sheffield Park was subsequently served by projections on route 755 and later 777. A new 728 ran in 1984 and 1985 between Victoria and Hampton Court.

London Country had first worked on National Express on 21st May 1978 when it acquired five summer Saturday services which had previously been worked by Maidstone & District. To work the services five Plaxton bodied Reliances were acquired from National Express South East. The routes ran from the Gravesend and Dartford area to Hastings, Bognor Regis, Hayling Island, Southsea and Walton-on-the-Naze. The 1979 summer saw the use of P, D and RB coaches, additional services two of which ran daily, and the West Country was now reached with a journey to Paignton. Further increases took place during the next two summer seasons, and from November 1981 with a new National Express venture of *Aircoach* services which took London Country vehicles to Cardiff, the company now worked on the services daily throughout the year.

The year 1984 saw a major expansion in workings with coaches reaching Wolverhampton and Colne and, during the height

Green Line 728
to Penshurst Place and Hever Castle.

Penshurst Place in Kent is a 14th Century Manor house and is one of the outstanding stately homes in Britain. Its core is the breathtaking Great Hall, completed in 1341 and still perfectly preserved. The State Rooms contain a fine collection of early portraits, tapestries and splendid furniture. The Toy Museum and Venture Playground are much loved by children.

Alternatively, stay on the coach a little longer and visit the magnificent Hever Castle and Gardens. The castle dates mainly from the late 13th and 15th centuries and was the home of Henry VIII's second wife, Anne Boleyn. The extensive gardens and pleasure grounds laid out in 1905 include a formal Italian Garden, containing topiary, fountains and a unique collection of classical statuary and sculpture.

"The next coach from Amersham is the 729 to Sheffield Park calling at High Wycombe, Central London, Croydon and East Grinstead"

This summer we're running a special coach, **each Sunday** to Sheffield Park allowing six hours for a visit to the famous Bluebell Railway and nearby Gardens. The **Bluebell Railway** was the first preserved standard gauge passenger railway in Britain and readily captures the atmosphere of an old country branch line. It is a living museum for steam trains with a magnificent collection of veteran locomotives, carriages and wagons. So a ride on a vintage steam train rattling through the beautiful Sussex countryside to Horsted Keynes is a must.
Sheffield Park Gardens extend over 142 acres and offer superb displays of rhododendrons, azaleas, maples and ornamental conifers. The gardens include 62 acres of woods, parkland and five lakes on different levels – ideal for a family picnic.

No pre-booking required! Just turn up at the stop and pay as you board. And the fares are reasonable too – a day return from High Wycombe and London is as little as £2.95 (£1.48 child).

NOTE: Extra coaches running during the Summer from Croydon, Godstone and East Grinstead to Sheffield Park on Green Line 709/778/779 and 776. Please see coach stop timetables or separate leaflets.

Passengers from London, Victoria can buy a combined ticket which includes coach and train travel from the Green Line enquiry office at Ecclestion Bridge.

GREEN LINE >>

Tel: Reigate (STD 07372) 42411

Whipsnade Zoo by GREEN LINE >> 737

The 'country zoo' comprising 500 acres on the Dunstable Downs. Its purpose being as a park in which wild animals have more space than in London Zoo. The animals are not caged but roam free in large enclosures. You can tour this wonderful zoo by steam train on the authentic Whipsnade and Umfolozi Railway. Travel there by Green Line 737 any Sunday or Public Holiday until 24th September 1978. Coaches depart at the following times:

London (Victoria)	1113	Whipsnade Zoo	1750
Golders Green Stn.	1141	Golders Green Stn.	1838
Whipsnade Zoo	Arr. 1229	London (Victoria) Arr.	1906

Return Fare: Adults £1.55   Children 78p

Above **Existing Plaxton coaches used for private hire work were re-painted in this new colour scheme in 1977, and were also classified for the first time, as the P class. From 1978 National Express participation became an important part of Green Line work, particularly from the South East Area. Carrying the Green Line fleetname well outside the area is (P) 5, parked at Cardiff Bus Station.** J.G.S. Smith

Below **Due to an increased involvement in National Express operations London Country acquired five Duple bodied Reliances of 1973–4 vintage from National Travel London in 1979. Becoming D 13–17 (being numbered on from the P class), they were given very deep green bands with Green Line fleetnames. Northfleet-based D 16 rests at Ventnor, Isle of Wight on National Express 077 from Gravesend in 1982.** Nick Agnew

of the season, Tralee in Eire. The company also worked on a *Skyrider* service for National Holiday passengers from Southend Airport to Bradford, Liverpool and Swansea and for *Insight International* passengers a service linked London hotels with Heathrow, Gatwick and Dover Docks. For Wardair, Capitol Airways and Air National passengers, non-stop duplicates were run on route 799 between Victoria and Stansted. Other ventures included National Holiday tours, while some of the National Express Saturday services were marketed as Green Line Seaside Specials, later to become Green Line Holiday Specials, retaining their existing service numbers and pre-booking facilities.

The 1985 season saw London Country participating in services that reached such far-flung places as Penzance, Aberdeen and Llandudno in addition to the provision of two new services with coaches in dedicated liveries. From 1st March a Hoverspeed service commenced from Victoria Coach Station to Dover Hoverport worked by BTLs based at Northfleet. This was followed on 7th October 1985 by *Speedlink*, a prestigious

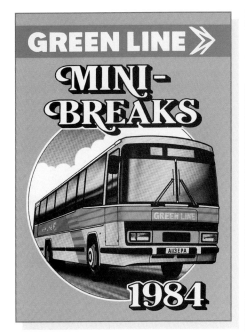

This leaflet offers some 11 different mini-breaks involving two or three nights away to both U.K. and overseas destinations. Among the latter Amsterdam, Paris and the Dutch Bulbfields are included while the U.K. venues include North Devon, Scarborough and the Lake District. Passengers were expected to be early risers as the earliest pick up is at 05.30 in Chertsey!

service replacing the Gatwick – Heathrow helicopter, which provided special departure lounges at each airport and attracted a premium fare. It was worked by Staines and Crawley garages with BTLs and was known to have run some contract journeys for airline staff on Christmas Day 1985 which is believed to be the only occasion under London Country auspices when any service was run on that day.

To meet the requirements of the rapidly expanding Green Line network, the increasing participation in National Express workings and the expansion into new ventures, coupled with the impending expiry of the RS/RB leases, a considerable number

SPEEDLINK

THE LUXURY
INTER-AIRPORT
SERVICE

The luxurious *Speedlink* service featured 43 daily departures from both Heathrow and Gatwick and offered a choice of reclining or table seats, an on-board toilet, and driver contact with the terminals by cellular telephone. Check-in desks and departure lounges were located in Heathrow Terminals 1, 3 and 4 and at Gatwick and the cost for this 'unashamed luxury' was £9 single.

BETWEEN HEATHROW & GATWICK

of new coaches were acquired in the remaining years of London Country. Thirty Leyland Leopards, 15 bodied by Duple (DL) and 15 bodied by Plaxton (PL) were ordered for 1981 under a leasing agreement. The decision to order Leylands rather than Volvos followed the trial of the two types on route 734. The views of drivers and engineering staff were sought and the drivers preferred the Leylands as their larger engines permitted faster acceleration on stage work while the engineers found that the Leylands offered greater accessibility to the major mechanical units. The Volvo was quieter and preferred for private hire work and the fuel consumption between the two types proved to be similar. DL 3-8 were intended for private hire work and the balance for the 747 and delivery commenced with DL 15 in April. The Plaxtons (PL 18-32) also began to arrive in April and went to SV, CY, and DS for Green Line stage work. As delivered all had 49 seats but four DLs

Top **In 1980 two each of Volvo and Leyland Leopard coaches came into the fleet for evaluation. Volvo DV 1 was painted in Green Line Golden Jubilee livery during 1980 and is seen standing outside its home garage, Hertford, from which it worked in this condition for over a year.** Mike Harris

Above **The Leopard was ordered for quantity delivery and 30 came into the fleet during 1981. Dorking garage was one of the recipients of the Plaxton bodied version and their PL25 is passing through Surbiton in August 1981. The bodywork style was similar to the 1979 delivery of RSs.** Geoff Rixon

were upseated to 53. Five of the P coaches were withdrawn in 1981 but with the completion of the DL and PL deliveries the company now had 184 omo equipped luxury coaches.

A new type of vehicle was ordered for 1982 – the Leyland Tiger having Eastern Coach Works bodies with some 42 coaches being leased directly from Leyland and delivered between June and November. TL 1–30 were 49-seaters for Green Line work and the balance were 53-seaters for coaching duties and all coaches were fitted with tinted windows. Their distribution

around the fleet was dependent upon the allocation of the 1977 batches of RBs and RSs which had to be extensively refurbished prior to return upon the expiry of the leases. During the year RS 1–15 and RB 16–30 were duly returned to Kirkby-Kingsforth. In 1983 a further 70 Leyland Tigers were delivered, TD 1–45 having a mixture of 53, 49 and 46-seat Duple bodies and TP 1–25 with 53-seat Plaxton bodies which represented the start of the 1984 order. The practice of numbering the class on with one series of numbers irrespective of different bodies, as the RS/RB and DL/PL classes, was discontinued. The 46 seaters were TD 29–38 for 747 and brought reclining seats to Green Line for the first time while TD 25–28 were in National Express livery and carried the Green Line rather than the London Country fleetname. Some coaches carried a revised Green Line livery which seemed to set the scene for future years with new batches incorporating various differences. TD 7 was the first to enter service in April 1983 with the TPs in December. The allocation of new coaches now caused a chain of reallocations around the fleet as RS/RB and older types were withdrawn with the new vehicles often going on to the more prestigious routes and the higher capacity coaches to busy commuter workings. In addition coaches destined for private hire work often saw spells on stage services. Some 62 coach or dual-purpose vehicles were withdrawn in 1983 comprising 19 RS/RB, 34 RP, 7 P and 2 SMA.

Further interesting developments in the coaching fleet continued with TP 26–40 following in 1984 from the first 25 which had been delivered in the previous year. A further batch of twenty 12-metre coaches, designated TPL, were numbered on from the TPs and were delivered by the end of March. TPL 41–50 were 51-seat private hire coaches, TPL 51–57 had 57 seats for busy

Top left **London Country first participated in National Express operations in 1978 and its involvement in such work expanded in the 1980s reaching some far-flung destinations including Penzance and Aberdeen. Northfleet's TL 31, a 53-seater for private hire duties, is seen at Bournemouth on National Express working 055 to Dartford. In 1986 a start was made in re-painting the TLs into the two tone green livery which represented an improvement in their appearance.** Capital Transport

Centre left **London Country returned to Plaxton and Duple bodies from the 1983 order of Leyland Tigers with the latter using the Duple Dominant IV bodies with the destination blinds being easily read. The livery of the TLs seemed a little bland and a new style of livery incorporating two shades of green was devised but *Jetlink* coaches TD 29–38 had a bold yellow substituted for the light green to produce a very striking livery. The batch had 46 reclining seats and is represented by TD 36 at Gatwick.** Barry LeJuene

Left **In 1985 the *Jetlink* TD 29–38 were displaced by new BTLs and, with the exception of TD 37 which was repainted in National Express livery, were repainted in National Holidays livery. When not required for such duties the coaches were deployed on other work as illustrated by TD 33 at Hammersmith, Butterwick on Green Line route 715.** Colin Brown

Right **Twenty 12-metre Leyland Tigers with, after a gap of three years, Duple bodies were delivered in March and April 1986. The class was designated TDL but numbered on from the 1983 TD class thus becoming TDL 46–65 and all appeared in what was regarded as standard Green Line livery, complete with green roof, for 1986. Most of the class went on to Green Line stage work as shown by Slough's TDL 57 on route 702 at Hyde Park Corner. The 702 was introduced on 19th May 1984 to provide a motorway run between Hammersmith and Langley on the Slough/Windsor services.** Colin Brown

Bottom **In 1984 regular double deck operation returned to Green Line in the form of five Leyland Olympians with luxuriously appointed Eastern Coach Works 72-seater bodies similar to those used by Alder Valley and Maidstone & District on London services. They all went to Northfleet for route 720 as illustrated by a very striking brand new LRC 2 in Parliament Square.** Mike Harris

commuter services 720, and 758/9 while TPL 58–60 were 57-seaters for National Express use. A DAF/Berkhof was hired from Ensignbus of Purfleet to access the market for a very prestigious luxury coach. It was in yet another revised version of the Green Line livery, was 12-metres in length and had reclining seats which could be arranged to seat 53 passengers but this could be reduced by the provision of a toilet and tables. Its registration number was A832 NTW and it carried no fleet number, garage stencil holder or destination equipment and was initially allocated to Dunton Green.

Regular double deck operation returned to Green Line with the acquisition of five Leyland Olympians with Eastern Coach Works bodies which, unlike previous coaches, the company purchased outright. They were numbered LRC 1–5 and were similar to those vehicles used on Alder Valley

BTL 26 was one of a batch of eight delivered in August 1985 for the prestigious *Speedlink* service which commenced in October running between Heathrow and Gatwick. They seated 37 passengers and offered tables with lamps and some seats facing rearwards. John Boylett

and Maidstone & District London commuter services. They went into service at Northfleet on 14th May on commuter route 720, where they proved popular with passengers, and also appeared on Seaside Specials and National Express services. A further 30 RB/RS types were returned off lease and D 13–17 were disposed of and further inroads made into the RP class leaving only RP 25 remaining available for passenger service at WY with a farewell tour taking place on 18th February. Three RPs were also in use as trainers with RP 87, also at WY, lasting into early 1985.

The 1985 order included 12-metre Leyland Tigers with Berkhof bodies, designated BTL; 17 were delivered and licensed in 1984 with the balance following in the new year. Some were to be allocated to the Airport services where there was competition and the company was keen to use its best coaches. Five were to be placed in service on what eventually became the

Speedlink service but at the time of their delivery was known as *Groundlink* – thus these coaches became referred to as the Groundlink type. The class appeared in Green Line, National Express, Jetlink, Gatwick Flightline, Town & Country and Insight International liveries, the last two being contract operations. The five *Groundlink* coaches BTL 1, BTL 12, BTL 14, BTL 16 and BTL 18 were repainted into *Hoverspeed* livery and allocated to Northfleet for a contract service between Victoria Coach Station and Dover Western Docks which commenced on 3rd March 1985.

Coaching operations were again becoming a victim of their own success and during the year the last 70 RB/RS coaches were returned off lease. The company had previously held some coaches beyond their return dates and incurred financial penalties as a result. There was a shortage of coaches and as a result route 716 was operated with SNBs which also had some scheduled

workings on routes 706, 713, 714, 715, 723 and 733 and LR buses were being used on 799.

Two 1982 12-metre Leyland Tigers with Plaxton bodies were transferred to London Country from National London for National Express work and were designated NTL 1 and NTL 2. In January a further batch of fifteen TP coaches (61–75) was delivered for stage work and these were followed by TPL 76–95 which were allocated to Private Hire, National Holidays and National Express duties. The position was eased when an order for Leyland Tigers with high floor Plaxton Paramount 3500 bodies was brought forward with twelve coaches being taken into stock in July and August. History repeated itself as they were classified as the STL class, the S standing for Scarborough, the town in which they were manufactured. STL 1–6 were in Green Line livery while STL 7–12 were delivered in white pending a decision on their use. In the event STL 7–10

In July 1985 a Volvo B10M with a Berkhof Esprite 53 seat body was hired from Ensign Bus. The coach arrived in the yellow and blue livery of the previous operator, Southend Transport, but carried the Green Line fleet name. It went to Hemel Hempstead for private hire work and was subsequently numbered VB 1 in the London Country fleet and was returned to Ensign in June 1986. John Boylett

The 1985 order for new coaches included 25 of the 12 metre version of the Leyland Tiger with high floor Berkhof bodies the first of which appeared in October 1984. A further batch was ordered for 1986 which included BTL 36-41 which were delivered in February carrying a revised livery for 767 *Heathrow Flightline* as displayed by BTL 37 in Grosvenor Place. The Company was always keen on using the newest coaches on the prestigious airport services. They were fitted with dot matrix destination equipment at the bottom of the upper windscreen on earlier coaches but following complaints from passengers that their forward view was obstructed the fitting was repositioned to the top of the windscreen as this view shows. Commencing with the 1985 orders all types of coaches were no longer fitted with the traditional garage and running number holders but carried the running number on the near side dashboard with the garage code appeared in one of the licence disc holders. Capital Transport

were put into Green Line livery and the remaining two into 747 *Jetlink* livery. The remaining BTLs, 26–33 were delivered in August and were the *Groundlink* type for use on the *Speedlink* service which finally started in October. They were in a special livery and seated 37 and provided tables with lamps with some seats facing the rear. A further five LRCs (6–10) went into service in March at St Albans for 757 in *Luton Flightline* livery and seated 69 instead of 72 provided by the original batch, the space released being used for luggage accommodation. Tragedy struck in April when LRC 7 came into contact with a low bridge at Luton Station and had to be rebuilt at the Central Repair Works re-entering service in August.

Leyland Leopard withdrawals due to lease expiry had commenced in December 1985 and continued into 1986 with the last examples being DL 17 at WY on 18th February and PL 27/8 at DS on 6th March. A batch of 20 BTLs entered service between

February and March with 34/5 in *Speedlink* livery, 36–41 in 767 *Flightline* livery, 42–46 for National Holidays, 47/8 for *Jetlink*, and 49–53 appearing in a pale yellow and dark blue livery for Insight International. A batch of twenty 12-metre Leyland Tigers in Green Line livery was delivered between March and May. After a gap of three years there had been a return to Duple bodies, thus the new coaches became TDL 46–65. The last new vehicles to be acquired prior to the split of the company were a batch of five LRCs (10–15) with LRC 15 being delivered on 11th June. They all received a distinctive livery and went into service fairly immediately with three going to St Albans for 757 *Flightline* and two to Harlow for the 711 commuter route.

Over the period of London Country's existence the fortunes of the coaching operations were completely turned around. In 1970 the Monday to Friday coach requirement had been 217 which, by 1980, had

fallen to 135 but by August 1986 the figure had risen to 215 including all contract and National Express requirements. It is to the great credit of the company's managers and staff that through the use of modern coaches and innovative marketing coupled with the inherited famous Green Line name that the company had become one of the leading coach operators.

Five further LRCs went onto route 757 in 1985 and had yellow relief instead of the light green as they were in the *Airport* livery branded *Luton Flightline* losing three seats to the provision of additional luggage accommodation. Five more (LRC 11–15) entered service in 1986 – the last vehicles to be acquired by the company appearing in June. Two went to Harlow and the balance to St Albans for Flightline duties with a revised livery where the white of the 1985 batch was substituted by light green. A splendid looking LRC 13 is passing Hyde Park Corner on 12th June 1986. Mike Harris

Chapter 12

TOWARDS PRIVATISATION

BY THE mid-1980s road transport was once again becoming a political pawn with the Conservative Government's policy of privatising many nationally owned organisations coupled with their manifesto commitment to abolish the Metropolitan county councils which included the Greater London Council. Prior to abolition the GLC was obliged to relinquish its powers over the London Transport Executive from 29th June 1984. Three days earlier London Regional Transport had been established under the

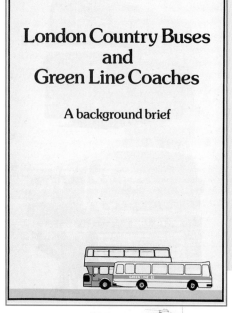

terms of the London Regional Transport Act, 1984. The GLC appointed Executive members were sacked and the new LRT board was obliged to set up subsidiary companies to operate both buses and the Underground as separate activities from April 1985. The bulk of London Regional Transport's funding was from Central Government and financial targets were set together with a view expressed that private capital would become involved with both businesses. Inevitably there was much protestation over the revised arrangements which included strike action and the resignation of Dr David Quarmby the Managing Director of London Buses.

As a means of showing that the monopoly of London Buses would be eliminated and of down-sizing that organisation with a view to privatisation a process of tendering bus services in London was established with London Regional Transport effectively acting as a licensing authority. The tendering process purported to maintain controls over quality, safety and maintenance and would allow London Buses and other operators to compete for contracts to run the routes concerned. In order to maintain the integrated network fares would be standardised and travelcards and elderly and handicapped permits would be accepted. The first routes to be offered for competitive tendering were 81, 84A, 146, 152, 193, 215, 228, 258, 313, 493 (an LCBS route operating

within Greater London), H2, P4 and W9. Operators were required to register an interest in November 1984 with a view to the first services being contracted out by mid-1985. Somewhat surprisingly London

Left **London Country produced this 16-page booklet in 1982 following the Greater London Council's *Fares Fair* debacle in the light of the strained relationship between the council and Central Government. The booklet explained the functions and activities of London Country, its relationship with local authorities and its finances. The crux of the matter was that the Company was concerned about the future of transport in the Greater London area in which it claimed it operated some 20 per cent of its mileage. Rumours were rife that a Passenger Transport Authority might be established and London Country's wish was that it would cover the entire South-East commuter region rather than just the Greater London Area.**

Below **A number of London Regional Transport routes were offered for tender to both London Buses and other operators in late 1984 and the first route to be awarded to London Country was 313, running from Chingford station to Potters Bar, being transferred on 13th July 1985. Traditionally 313 was a London Country route running from St Albans to Enfield but the section east of Potters Bar had been passed to London Transport with the 24th April 1982 reorganisation. The route was operated by Hatfield with buses interworking onto the 300/303 at Potters Bar. Roe-bodied Leyland Olympian LR 39 was new in 1983 being one of a batch of 15 all allocated to Hatfield. The bus is seen in Enfield Town and, as a contractual condition, should be displaying an LRT service board on the front but this lack of attention to detail was not untypical of the standards adhered to at the time – a situation which LRT manifestly countenanced.** *Nick Agnew*

Below **London Regional Transport continued to issue the publicity for their tendered routes, producing the timetable leaflets according to the then current style. In the case of 313 it was made clear that London Country operated the service but passengers, comments should be addressed to 55 Broadway.**

Local News
from London Regional Transport

A brand new look for Bus 313

STARTING 13th JULY

From Saturday 13th July, Bus 313 will be operated by London Country Bus Services on behalf of London Regional Transport.

A new look
You'll find buses on Route 313 will look different too—they'll still be double-deckers but in the familiar green and white livery of the new operator.

Potters Bar Station served
There are improvements to the service as well—the route will continue to run on Mondays to Saturdays from Chingford to Potters Bar but will terminate at Potters Bar Station, reaching there via Mutton Lane with some journeys extended to Cranborne Road.

The 313 will still provide the same handy links with Enfield Town's shops and market as well as with Chase Farm Hospital from the Chingford, Ponders End and Potters Bar areas. In Enfield Town, buses towards Chase Farm and Potters Bar will call at point 5 in Cecil Road instead of point V in Sydney Road.

More buses
On Saturdays the service between Chase Farm and Chingford will be improved to run every 20 minutes for most of the day. Outside peak hours on Mondays to Fridays, a half-hourly service will run between Chingford and Chase Farm Hospital with an hourly service between there and Potters Bar (the new timetables in this leaflet give full details).

The fares are unchanged
Fares on the 313 between Chingford and The Ridgeway, New Cottage Farm are just 30p for adults (or 25p for 'Short Hop' rides of up to about a mile) and 15p for under 16s to 10pm. For journeys to and from Potters Bar, higher fares apply and there's an off-peak maximum of 65p and a maximum of 30p for under 16s to 10pm. (14 and 15 year olds must have a Child Photocard)

Bus Passes, Travelcards, Capitalcards, Elderly and Handicapped Persons' Passes and all other similar tickets will continue to be accepted.

Operated by **LONDON COUNTRY** »
for London Regional Transport

Above right **A batch of eleven second-hand Park Royal bodied Atlanteans acquired from Northern General Transport of Gateshead started to enter service from July 1986, with all but one being allocated to Chelsham. AN 355 is seen working on route 127.**
John Boylett

Right **The most interesting development in tendered routes concerned the 268 running from Golders Green to Finchley Road station which was the only London Country tendered operation to use brand new buses in the form of Mercedes-Benz Minibuses complete with brand naming and a special livery. A very attractive MBM 9 is seen at Swiss Cottage Station shortly after introduction on 31st May and was no doubt highly suitable for negotiating the narrow streets of Hampstead. The buses were out-stationed at Scratchwood (now London Gateway) Services on the M1 motorway, sharing the base with other members of the class in *Borehamwood Bustler* dedicated livery.** Mike Harris

Country opined that it 'remained to be convinced that tendering for individual routes will serve the passenger best' but it did, however, make bids for routes that it felt it could operate conveniently from its existing garages.

London Country was awarded the tender to operate route 313 (Chingford Station – Potters Bar) from 13th July 1985 which was worked by Hatfield Garage using LRs. This route had traditionally been a London Country route but the Potters Bar to Enfield section was passed to London Transport in 1982. A condition of the contract was that buses should carry boards on the front to the effect that it was a *London Regional Transport Service*. To facilitate vehicle

positioning and for driver requirements the route was initially interworked with LC routes 300 and 303 and, indicative of the standards of the time, the simple task to display the board when working on the 313 proved to be difficult, if not impossible, to achieve. This resulted in buses on the 313 appearing without boards while buses in far off Hitchin were purporting routes 300/3 to be London Regional Transport services! Little wonder that the travelling public was often confused by the effects of the tendering process. Although the concept of duplicated route numbers within London Country had become established by this time the High Wycombe local 313 was renumbered 364 from 7th July.

The second route to be acquired, on 3rd August, was P4 (Lewisham Bus Station – Brixton Station) which was worked from the National London premises at Catford. National London had apparently been ceded to London Country in 1984. The travelling public must have been further confused by this operation as previously stated, four SNBs eventually carried National London fleetnames while a fifth vehicle was in a white livery. Initially, on Saturdays additional SNBs, in standard London Country livery, were borrowed from Chelsham.

Further LRT routes were offered for tender and prior to the split of London Country a number of routes were acquired. Monday to Saturday route 127 (Tooting

Broadway – Sanderstead Church) and its Sunday counterpart 127A (Streatham Hill Station – Sanderstead Church with projections to Selsdon) went to London Country on 22nd March 1986 worked by ex Southdown ANs from Chelsham. The only tendered route to be worked by brand new London Country buses commenced on 31st May with 268 (Golders Green Station – Finchley Road Station) using MBMs in dedicated *Hampstead Hoppa* livery based at the Scratchwood outstation.

On 21st June London Country lost the 84 to London Buses but in a highly expedient stratagem was awarded the 142 (Watford Junction – Brent Cross) which was worked from Watford garage. The loss of the 84 at St Albans was equalised by transferring a part allocation of route 321 from Watford. The 142 was worked with a mix of LRs and genuine London Country single door ANs

Below **London Country won route 142 (Watford Junction to Brent Cross) from 21st June using a mix of LRs and single door ANs. The LRT produced publicity announced that green buses would be running on the route. No account was taken of *ColorBus* AN 169 advertising National Travelworld which also carries both LRT and *Watfordwide* branding – no wonder that passengers were confused by the tendering process! The bus is seen in Edgware High Street.** Mike Harris

Right **As the number of tendered routes slowly increased the design of the leaflets was changed slightly to give prominence to the colour of the buses that were to be found on the particular route, probably in response to public confusion. At this period, after the removal of GLC control, the full title *London Regional Transport* was the standard but *London Transport* eventually returned to common usage.**

Local Bus News
from London Regional Transport

Green buses for Route 142
FROM 21st JUNE

Route 142 will be operated by London Country under contract to London Regional Transport, in conjunction Hertfordshire County Council, using green pay-as-you-enter double-deck buses.

No change to number of buses
Buses will generally run at the same intervals as now, although on Saturdays, during shopping hours, they will run to an easy-to-remember 10 minute timetable instead of every 9 to 12 minutes as they do now.

Changes to the 142 and 258 in Watford
To serve recent office developments in Watford, the 142 (and also red Bus 258) will run in both directions along Clarendon Road instead of running in one direction via Station Road, St Albans Road and the Town Hall.

No change to Passes
Bus Passes, Travelcards, Capitalcards, Elderly and Handicapped Persons' Permits and all similar tickets valid on London Buses will continue to be accepted on Bus 142.

Bus 142 your useful local link
Bus 142 gives a handy local bus link between Watford Junction Bus Station and Brent Cross Shopping Centre on Mondays to Saturdays. It passes Watford Town Centre, Bushey, Bushey Heath, Stanmore, Edgware, Burnt Oak, Colindale and West Hendon on the way. On Sundays, buses run between Watford Junction and Edgware Station.

Operated by **LONDON COUNTRY** »
on behalf of London Regional Transport

with the acquired ex-Strathclyde ANs working on 321, 347 and 348. Also awarded to London Country was route 298 (South Mimms, Clare Hall Hospital – Turnpike Lane Station) which was worked from Hatfield with ex Strathclyde ANs.

A further batch of ex Strathclyde ANs went south to Dorking to work route 293 (Epsom – Hackbridge) from 19th July. On 9th August London Country was awarded the revised 197 group in Croydon. Route 197 ran on Monday to Saturday between Norwood Junction and Katharine Street with ANs from Chelsham and 197A ran from West Croydon to Caterham using LRs from Godstone. On Sunday a 197B using LRs from Godstone linked the two routes running through from Norwood Junction to Caterham.

Left **The Company's success in the tendering process meant that additional buses were required amongst which some Alexander 'AL' single door bodied Atlanteans ex Strathclyde PTE were acquired with 31 arriving prior to the London Country split. The Strathclyde ANs had a distinctive appearance but at nearly 12 years old were really life expired and they proved underpowered, unreliable and leaked when it rained – hardly the quality that the tendering process promised. Some went to Hatfield for route 298 (Clare Hall Hospital – Turnpike Lane Station) which was also transferred on 21st June. AN 323 is seen in Mutton Lane, Potters Bar on 6th September, the very last day of London Country's existence, but already carries the new *London Country North East* fleetname, which first appeared on some buses in August.** David Ruddom

On 9th August 1986 London Country retained the working of route 403 which had been through the tendering process as, despite being a traditional London Country route with origins back to August 1921, most of the route was in the Greater London area. It continued to be worked by Chelsham but had to be exclusively double-deck worked.

On 16th August services in Orpington were completely revised using Orpington Buses Limited as a low-cost subsidiary of London Buses with mini-buses based in an industrial unit and marketed as *Roundabout*. The new operation replaced London Country routes 431 and 471 and even reached Sevenoaks. The 493 retained its Ramsden Estate section and continued to be worked by London Country, but as a tendered route. Also part of the Orpington scene was route 51 running to Woolwich which was awarded to London Country who were obliged to reopen Swanley garage, albeit as an outstation of Dartford, to house the ex Strathclyde ANs.

The concept of route tendering was to cause new difficulties and problems for the bus industry, the staff and the passengers. At the time that a company submitted its tender it could hardly be expected to have the necessary additional buses and staff in place and when the results of the tenders were announced such additional resources could not be obtained overnight. The lead-time was often insufficient to order new vehicles, thus such second-hand buses as were available had to be acquired. The various Atlanteans that the company acquired were all older than the 12-year NBC target – so much for the protestations about the aged (but reliable) fleet in 1970. The age of these vehicles had not gone un-noticed by the Passenger's Committee who duly expressed their concern. The ex-Strathclyde vehicles in particular proved to be unreliable and also leaked when it rained, public complaint quickly causing the buses on the 51 to be replaced by standard ANs acquired from around the fleet. In some instances the company had failed to recruit the required numbers of additional drivers but it had to be seen to perform on the tendered services at the expense of their traditional routes, which became the victims of cuts due to the lack of adequate resources.

The process of monitoring tendered routes quickly turned out to be about quantity not quality. The main measurement of performance was the purported mileage run compared with that scheduled, but the more important criterion of headways achieved was seemingly not taken into account. It was deemed preferable to operate non-aimworthy mileage with, say, three buses running together rather than to lose mileage by turning one of them short of its

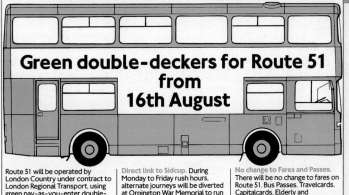

Above From 16th August a major LRT revision took place in the Orpington area with tendered route 51 (Orpington – Woolwich) passing to London Country which necessitated the re-opening of Swanley garage albeit as an outstation of the new DT. The route received ex-Strathclyde ANs as illustrated by AN313 negotiating the Orpington Station turning circle. The poor condition of these Atlanteans did not escape the notice of the Passenger's Committee and following numerous complaints newer vehicles were drafted in. *Mike Harris*

Green double-deckers for Route 51 from 16th August

Route 51 will be operated by London Country under contract to London Regional Transport, using green pay-as-you-enter double-deck buses.
Much as before. Bus 51 will continue to provide the main service between Orpington and Woolwich via Sidcup, Welling and Plumstead Common. Frequencies will not change.

Direct link to Sidcup. During Monday to Friday rush hours, alternate journeys will be diverted at Orpington War Memorial to run to Green Street Green rather than Orpington Station. This will provide a direct link to Sidcup for passengers wishing to avoid the detour via St Pauls Cray Estate on new Roundabout Route R1.

No change to Fares and Passes. There will be no change to fares on Route 51. Bus Passes, Travelcards, Capitalcards, Elderly and Handicapped Persons' Permits and all similar tickets valid on London Buses will continue to be accepted.

By the time of the Orpington changes a bold new style of leaflet, in addition to depicting the colour of the buses, also showed the type of bus but the London Country title and logo no longer featured. The 493 had now become a London Regional Transport service with London Country being awarded the tender. The 51 leaflet illustrated a modern double-decker rather than a life-expired ex-Strathclyde Atlantean

Roundabout services bring changes to Route 493 from 16th August

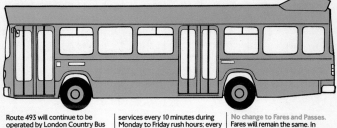

Route 493 will continue to be operated by London Country Bus Services but now on behalf of London Regional Transport.
Shortened route for Bus 493. Bus 493 will continue to run between Ramsden Estate, Orpington High Street (Walnuts Centre) and Railway Station. A new timetable will give

services every 10 minutes during Monday to Friday rush hours; every 15 minutes between the peaks and on Saturdays; and hourly in the evenings and on Sundays. The rest of Route 493 to Green Street Green via Chelsfield Station will be replaced by new Roundabout service R3.

No change to Fares and Passes. Fares will remain the same. In addition, Bus Passes, Travelcards, Capitalcards, Elderly and Handicapped Persons' Permits and all similar tickets valid on London Buses will continue to be accepted on Route 493, and also on all Roundabout services in the Orpington area.

terminal in order to fill a gap in the other direction. Other quality points and conditions of the tender such as the provision of buses with 100 percent no-smoking accom-modation, the displaying of the LRT board and correct blinds and route numbers displayed on the rear and side often fell by the wayside. Whether or not the standard of the service provided under tendering arrangements was an improvement on that which had formerly been provided by London Buses was often a matter of conjecture.

More far-reaching than competitive tendering in Greater London was the Government's proposals to privatise the road transport industry. A White Paper entitled *Buses* was published on 12th July 1984 which set out the following criteria. Road service licensing was to be abolished and so-called quality licensing (operator's licences) established to both protect safety standards and to enable free competition. Local authorities could continue to subsidise unprofitable but socially necessary services once competitive tenders had been obtained. Blanket subsidies for a whole network would not be allowed – routes were to be costed individually. The National Bus Company was to be reorganised into smaller units and privatised. Other provisions enabled the Government to make financial grants during the transitional period, protected concessionary fares schemes and relaxed restrictions on taxis and hire cars to allow them to operate as alternatives to bus services.

Predictably much opposition and criticism from within the bus industry and local government (as far as political allegiances would permit) was voiced. Lord Shepherd, the Chairman of the NBC who was due to retire, was one of the few professional busmen to attack the proposals stating that the Government's 'less than thoughtful approach' to the regulation and financing of the industry would lead to 'collapse and disintegration'. Lord Shepherd felt that the removal of cross-subsidy would mean a loss of £180 million of internally generated support overnight. Later in the year the Government announced that privatisation plans for the NBC would go ahead before proposed deregulation of local bus services in 1986 with the group being split into units of between 200 to 300 vehicles. The Transport Secretary rejected the NBC's own proposals for a four way split of their group. Upon retirement in 1985 Lord Shepherd further attacked the Government's proposal to split the NBC as 'quite inexplicable'. The new Chairman of the NBC was Robert Brook who had been Chief Executive since 1977 and a life-long busman. He was faced with the unenviable task of planning the demise of his company. In the event Mr Brook retired after only 15 months in the role when Ministry appointee Robert Lund – who was widely seen within the industry as a hatchet man – became NBC Chairman in April 1986.

The Transport Bill was made public on 31st January 1985 and it was not a surprise to see that the advice of the transport professionals had not been heeded and there was little change from the White Paper. The NBC constituent companies were required to plan their local operations to compete fairly

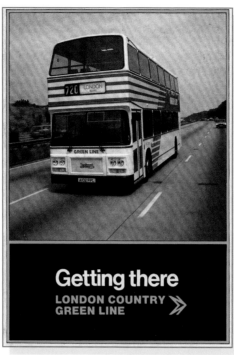

Getting there
LONDON COUNTRY »
GREEN LINE

Left **Following the publication of the Buses white paper the Company produced this booklet setting out its achievements in the 'comparatively short period of time' of its existence. The last section was headed 'The Bus Bill: A Challenge and A Gamble' in which concern was expressed that cross subsidy between profitable and unprofitable routes would disappear as competition would force down fares. Not only did it forecast a reduction of loss-making rural routes but also suggested that early morning, late evening and weekend journeys would be at risk on other routes. In conclusion London Country felt that it was strong enough to live in the new regime but, at the time of this publication, the proposal that it should be split into smaller units was yet to be announced.**

within the scope of deregulation and to transfer them to the private sector within three years. Deregulation day was set as 26th October 1986 and Road Service Licensing was to be replaced by the registration of commercially viable services with the Traffic Commissioners. Existing Road Service Licences that were valid on 30th October 1985 were automatically extended to deregulation day. Operators were required to register the services that they proposed to run from deregulation day by 28th February 1986. The NBC accepted that further protestation would be to no avail and preparations for deregulation progressed. London Regional Transport was temporarily excluded from deregulation as, in the words of the Transport Minister it needed 'a period of convalescence' to recover from the 'debilitating effects of GLC stewardship'.

The Minister felt that London Country, together with Ribble and Crosville, were too big to be privatised as single entities. In the words of the Minister, Mr Nicholas Ridley, if London Country had remained as a single unit it would have 'undermined the development of competition in large areas of the country and deny many bus passengers the benefits that deregulation is designed to bring'. Thus London Country was split into four area companies, largely as per the 1978 reorganisation as described in Chapter 1, plus Gatwick Engineering Ltd and Green Line Travel Ltd. The initial proposal was that the split would take place on 1st September, but for NBC internal reasons the change was subsequently deferred to 7th September.

London Country (South East) was established with headquarters at Dartford with Mr W.M.L. Gunning, the former LCBS Traffic Manager as Managing Director. It

took 171 PSVs into stock from London Country, three other buses – RF 202, AN 3, and LNB 48 plus, from National London six SNBs for route P4, four sightseeing tour ANs and 55 coaches. It worked from Dartford, Northfleet, Dunton Green, and Catford (National London) garages surrendering Chelsham to the South West company and, quite logically, Grays to the North East.

London Country (South West) was by far the largest of the four companies both in terms of garages and vehicles and, appropriately, the former LCBS Managing Director, Mr C.E. Clubb took up the same role with the new, Reigate-based company. Garages comprised Chelsham, Godstone, Crawley, Reigate, Dorking, Leatherhead, Guildford, Addlestone and Staines, the latter formerly being in the North West Area. Some 374 PSVs were taken into stock from London Country plus, RMC 4, AN 2/6, LN 1/7 and LNB 50.

London Country (North West) was based at Watford with Mr D. Ord, formerly Fleet Engineer with Luton & District, as Managing Director. Garages were at Slough, Amersham, Hemel Hempstead and Watford plus the Scratchwood outstation and 299 PSVs ex-LCBS plus AN 1/8/14, RP 87, BL 6 and LN 13 were acquired.

The larger of the two companies in the north was London Country (North East), based at Hertford with Mr A.B. Jones, the former LCBS Chief Engineer, as Managing Director. It had garages at St Albans, Hatfield, Stevenage, Hertford, Harlow and Grays with 347 ex-London Country PSVs plus AN 4/7/9, LNB 64 and BL 3 being taken into stock.

Following the split, buses appeared with the new fleet names which were easily amended by applying the appropriate geographical description under the existing London Country fleetname. Few route alterations took place until deregulation day, 26th October, when massive changes including renumberings and in some cases transfer of operators took place. The four companies were now able to operate wherever they wished outside Greater London but others were able to move into their operating areas. In the event most competition, such as it was, came from large neighbouring operators. London Buses commenced 306

Kingston – Epsom and 310A Hertford – Enfield with Eastern National competing with 333 Bishops Stortford – Loughton. The only other competition came from Epsom Coaches route 5 and Tillingbourne 22 and an independent operator in Gravesend who lasted only a few weeks – perhaps hardly what Mr Ridley's proposals had envisaged! Within deregulation, any services not registered could be tendered by county councils, and this process could be extended to individual journeys. It led to different operators running over the same routes. Furthermore, the failure to register some routes paved the way for small operators to gain a foothold. In several cases, some routes and operators continue to thrive 15 years later. It is true that under the 17 years existence of London Country there had been many changes of routes, vehicles, operating methods and the closure of nine of the original 28 garages, although three new ones had opened. No doubt many thought that this had represented a lot of change. However, all this had been properly structured in its implementation. With deregulation and the following privatisation it was to be very much a case of 'You ain't seen nothing yet'!

London Country achieved a great deal in its existence from its establishment in 1970, at the whim of politicians, when it was heavily dependent upon London Transport

AN 76 stands at Harlow Town station showing the London Country North East fleet name some days before the official split of London Country Bus Services on 7th September 1986. *Nick Agnew*

INTRODUCING LONDON COUNTRY BUS (NORTH EAST) LTD.

From September 7th 1986, your local bus and Greenline coach services have been provided by a brand new company–London Country Bus (North East) Ltd. With our headquarters in Hertford and six garages in Hertfordshire and Essex (see overleaf), we are well placed to provide a first class service in central and east Hertfordshire and west Essex.

From October 26th 1986, local bus services are deregulated following the Government's 1985 Transport Act.

This means that we have identified our commercially viable services. However, some services will not survive unless

subsidised–these services have been put out to tender by County Councils so that overall service levels should not go down.

We will supply you with full details as matters progress. Most important of all don't worry, we're still here to answer all your queries!

providing many ancillary services. The fleet at the time was very traditional with high proportions of both elderly vehicles and crew operation with unique operating agreements and high rates of pay compared with other NBC companies. The Company's efforts to modernise the fleet were retarded by the problems encountered with the reliability of the new generation of vehicles and the acute shortage of engineering spares during the mid-1970s. The older ex-London Transport vehicles were retained much longer than originally envisaged in order to cover shortages of available newer vehicles. The fortunes of Green Line which seemed to be in terminal decline in the mid-1970s were largely saved by the 1980 legislation and the enhancement of the motorway and trunk road network within the London Country area. The route network was much altered but most places still saw London Country buses, perhaps not so many as had been customary in the past. The 1980s saw London Country emerge from its difficulties to become a model NBC subsidiary.

In 1970 London Country employed approximately 5,600 staff but this figure fell progressively – mostly due to the elimination of conductors and general service reductions – to a low of 3,677 in 1982 and by the split had risen to 4,137. London Transport passed 1,267 buses to London Country and at the end of 1980 the fleet consisted of 1,073 PSVs while at the split the LC fleet comprised 1,191 PSVs plus a further 65 ex-National London. Accounting methods no doubt changed over the years of London Country's existence thus financial information must be analysed with some caution. In 1970 the turnover was £11.8 million which, by 1980, had risen to £39.8 million and in 1985 was £64.9 million. The company made a loss

before taxation prior to 1978 but its fortunes were reversed from that year. In 1980 a pre-taxation and interest payable operating profit of £567,000 was reported and in 1985, the last complete year, this figure was £1.7 million. As might be expected the number of passenger journeys per year fell progressively over the company's first decade and then remained reasonably constant. In 1969, the last year of London Transport control, some 198 million passenger journeys were made on Country buses and Green Line coaches, this figure being 113 million in 1980 and 107 million in 1985.

The four 'London Country' operating companies were duly privatised, North East being the last in 1988. There followed a succession of ownership changes, plus a combination and splitting of operations. Later consolidation of the large transport groups has seen further change.

Looked at with hindsight the London Country years saw much change but nevertheless represented a buffer when the green country bus that had been created by London Transport was still a recognisable entity.

The time-traveller from the 1970s would not see familiar buses, or colours, but could still pick out a few routes such as 310, 321, 370, 406, 409 and 480 which would still be familiar thirty years later. At the time of preparing the second edition of this book it would appear that in the vast majority of the former London Country area, deregulation and privatisation has ultimately served only to turn a vast public monopoly into a vast private monopoly.

Appendix 1. Summary of London Country vehicles

Taken over from London Transport at 1st January 1970 (Total 1,267)

Class	Total	Type	Year new	Last used*
Double-deck buses				
RT	484	AEC Regent III	1948–54	1978
RLH	17	AEC Regent III (low-bridge type)	1952	1970
RMC	69	AEC Routemaster (mostly Green Line coaches)	1957/62	1980
RCL	43	AEC Routemaster (Green Line coaches)	1965	1979
RML	97	AEC Routemaster	1965–66	1980
XA	3	Leyland Atlantean	1966	1973
XF	8	Daimler Fleetline	1965	1981
Single-deck buses and dual-purpose vehicles				
RF	413	AEC Regal IV (150 were Green Line coaches)	1951–53	1979
GS	10	Guy Special (small 26-seat buses)	1953	1972
RC	14	AEC Reliance (Green Line coaches)	1965	1977
XMB	1	AEC Merlin	1966	1973
MB	33	AEC Merlin	1968	1980
MBS	75	AEC Merlin	1968	1980

Secondhand vehicles acquired by London Country

Class	Total	Nos.	Type (and previous operator)	Acquired	Last used*
SMW	15	1–15	AEC Swift s/d bus (South Wales)	1971	1981
MS	3	5–7	Metro-Scania s/d bus (Hants & Dorset)	1973	1978
MBS	1	4	AEC Merlin s/d bus (LTE)	1973	1979
T	4	1–4	AEC Reliance coach (M&D) (Used as training vehicles)	1974	1978
LS	3	1–3	Leyland PD3 d/d bus (Southdown)	1975	1976
LR	20	1–20	Leyland PD3 d/d bus (Ribble) (Used as training vehicles)	1975/6	1980
RN	10	1–10	AEC Reliance s/d bus (Barton)	1977	
P	7	6–12	AEC Reliance coach (National Travel)	1976/8	1983
D	5	13–17	AEC Reliance coach (National Travel)	1979	1983
P	5	18–22	AEC Reliance coach (National Travel)	1980	1983
DMS	7	630/1/3, 640/1/3, 654	Daimler Fleetline d/d bus (LTE) (Used as training vehicles)	1980	1983
NTL	2	1, 2	Leyland Tiger (National London)	1985	
AN	12	294–305	Leyland Atlantean (Southdown)	1985–86	
AN	31	306–336	Leyland Atlantean (Strathclyde)	1986	
AN	11	346–356	Leyland Atlantean (Northern General)	1986	

New vehicles delivered to London Country

Class	Total	Fleet Nos.	Type	Year delivered	Last used*
Double-deck buses					
AF	11	1–11	Daimler Fleetline	1972	1983
AN	293	1–293	Leyland Atlantean	1972–81	
BT	15	1–15	Bristol VRT	1977	1981
LR	75	1–75	Leyland Olympian	1982–5	
Single-deck buses and dual-purpose vehicles					
SM	138	101–148 449–538	AEC Swift	1970–71	1981
RP	90	1–90	AEC Reliance	1971–72	1985
MS	4	1–4	Metro-Scania	1971–72	1978
SMA	21	1–21	AEC Swift	1972	1981
LN	23	1–23	Leyland National	1972–73	1983
LNB, LNC	47	24–70	Leyland National	1973	1985
SNB, SNC	473	71–543	Leyland National	1973–79	
BL	23	1–23	Bristol LHS	1973	1980
BN	44	24–67	Bristol LHS	1974/77	
FT	5	1–5	Ford Transit	1974	1977
MBM	12	1–12	Mercedes	1986	
Coaches					
P	5	1–5	AEC Reliance	1973	
RS	60	1–15, 31–45, 106–120, 136–150	AEC Reliance	1977–79	1985
RB	90	16–30, 46–105, 121–135	AEC Reliance	1977–79	1985
DV	2	1,2	Volvo B58	1980	
DL	17	1–17	Leyland Leopard	1980–81	
PL	15	18–32	Leyland Leopard	1981	1986
TL	42	1–42	Leyland Tiger	1982	
TD	45	1–45	Leyland Tiger	1983	
TP	55	1–40, 61–75	Leyland Tiger	1983–85	
TPL	40	41–60, 76–95	Leyland Tiger	1984–85	
LRC	15	1–15	Leyland Olympian	1984–86	
BTL	53	1–53	Leyland Tiger (high floor)	1984–86	
STL	12	1–12	Leyland Tiger (high floor)	1985	
TDL	20	46–65	Leyland Tiger (high floor)	1986	

* With the exception of classes acquired solely for training duties this column indicates the last year in which members of the class were used as PSVs by LCBS. In some cases examples were retained for non-PSV duties. Where no year is shown the class passed to successor operators.

Appendix 2. One-man operation

The Conversion to 100 per cent Scheduled One-man operation

Garage	Code	Final crew	Principal routes	Type displaced	Remarks
Amersham	MA	19.2.71	353, 362/A	RT	
Romford (London Road)	RE	30.12.71	721	RCL	
Dunton Green	DG	24.3.72	704, 705	RCL	Last day of RT bus operation 7.1.72
Addlestone	WY	16.6.72	420, Works journeys	RT, RMC	
Guildford	GF	16.6.72	408/A	RT	
Luton	LS	3.12.76	360	—	SNB/AN replaced RTs 4.9.76
Tring	TG	1.4.77	312	RML	Garage closure
East Grinstead	EG	8.7.77	409	RML	
Harlow	HA	15.7.77	339	RML	
Dartford	DT	22.7.77	499	RMC	
Dorking	DS	30.9.77	414	RCL	
High Wycombe	HE	30.9.77	326, 363	RML	Garage closure
Staines	ST	30.9.77	441/C	RML	
Stevenage	SV	30.9.77	303/C	—	RPs replaced RTs 15.5.76
Hatfield	HF	18.11.77	341	RMC	
Hertford	HG	18.11.77	341, 395	RMC	
St Albans	SA	18.11.77	330	RMC	
Crawley	CY	30.6.78	405B	—	ANs replaced RCLs 12.4.78
Garston	GR	1.9.78	347/A	RML	
Hemel Hempstead	HH	1.9.78	347/A	RML	
Godstone	GD	27.10.78	411	RML	
Leatherhead	LH	27.10.78	406	RMC	
Reigate	RG	27.10.78	406, 411	RMC, RML	
Grays	GY	5.1.79	Journeys 323, 328, 371	RCL	Crew operation continued on school contracts.
Northfleet	NF	25.4.80	480	—	ANs progressively replaced RMLs by December 1979
Windsor	WR	30.5.80	407/A	—	ANs replaced RMLs 16.2.80
Chelsham	CM	30.8.80	403, 453	—	ANs replaced RCLs 16.2.80
Swanley	SJ	13.3.81	477	—	ANs progressively replaced RMCs by March 1980

The following points should be noted:

a) In some cases replacement vehicles were worked with a crew prior to the change date.

b) With certain conversions, due to inadequate numbers of new vehicles, RM types continued to be used for a short period.

c) Where conductors were available after the conversion odd RM types were sometimes employed to cover shortages of more modern types.

LONDON COUNTRY ≫ GREEN

COUNTRY ≫ GREEN LINE ≫

GREEN LINE ≫ LONDON C

INE ≫ LONDON COUNTRY ≫

LONDON COUNTRY ≫ GREEN

COUNTRY ≫ GREEN LINE ≫

GREEN LINE ≫ LONDON C

INE ≫ LONDON COUNTRY ≫

GREEN LINE ≫ LONDON C